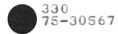

BEYOND ECONOMIC MAN

BEYOND ECONOMIC MAN

A New Foundation for Microeconomics

Harvey Leibenstein

HARVARD UNIVERSITY PRESS

Cambridge, Massachusetts, and London, England   1976

Library of Congress Cataloging in Publication Data

Leibenstein, Harvey.
  Beyond economic man.

  Includes bibliographical references and index.
  1. Microeconomics.   I.   Title.
HB171.L613   330   75-30567
ISBN 0-674-06891-2

To Marge

Preface

Several days after I presented a lecture on X-Efficiency at Cambridge University, a young English economist brought me a quotation from Tolstoy's *War and Peace*. The passage, abridged for convenience, is as follows:

> military science assumes the strength of an army to be identical with its numbers. Military science says that the more troops the greater the strength. *Les gros battaillons ont toujours raison* (Large battalions are always victorious) . . .
>
> In military affairs the strength of an army is the product of its mass and some unknown x . . .
>
> That unknown quantity is the spirit of the army, . . .
>
> The spirit of an army is the factor which multiplied by the mass gives the resulting force. To define and express the significance of this unknown factor—the spirit of an army—is a problem for science.
>
> This problem is only solvable if we cease arbitrarily to substitute for the unknown x itself the conditions under which that force becomes apparent—such as the commands of the general, the equipment employed, and so on—mistaking these for the real significance of the factor, and if we recognize this unknown quantity in its entirety as being the greater or lesser desire to fight and to face danger.*

Without straining his meaning too much, Tolstoy's argument is similar to one of the central theses of this volume, despite the fact that his concern is the art of war, and mine economics, one of the arts of peace. To shift to the common language of economics, what Tolstoy is saying is that merely knowing the observable *inputs* (the number of guns, men, the commands of the generals, and so on) does not tell you the outcome, contrary to the claims of the "military scientists." Something else is in-

---

* Leo Tolstoy, *War and Peace* (New York, Simon and Schuster, 1942), pp. 1148–1149.

volved, an X-factor that Tolstoy equates with "spirit." Similarly, in Chapter 3 and in most of Part Two of this volume I argue that knowing the allocation of inputs and the state of the arts of production is not enough, there is also something else involved—what I have called the X-efficiency element. In this book the counterpart to Tolstoy's "spirit" is the concept of "effort," not only in a physical sense but in terms of its broadest psychological dimensions. A commonplace to anyone who observes the creation of goods is that it takes effort, yet effort is not a key notion of contemporary economic analysis.

The central notions of this volume arose out of a dissatisfaction with contemporary microeconomics as a tool of analysis for at least some important problem areas. I arrived at these views in part as a result of personal experience in business firms and in part as a consequence of my attempts to understand the processes of the economic development of developing countries. In many cases observed practices seemed to go counter to what conventional theory suggested should happen. There were some elements missing in conventional theory—and at the very least they were worth looking for.

In writing this book, and in trying to explain some aspects of it in lectures and seminars, a problem that often arose was the difficulty I and others had in accommodating two modes of thought simultaneously: optimizing behavior and the alternative type of behavior central to this volume. Frequently listeners would attempt to translate and force my ideas into the conventional optimization mold, when part of my argument, at least implicitly, was that the presumption of maximizing or optimizing behavior may be inappropriate for the understanding of the problem at hand. It was as though an individual was having difficulty listening to a particular piece of music because the score he or she was following was for a different work. I hope that economists in particular, as they peruse the pages that follow, will keep this last in mind.

In writing a book of this sort, one the author likes to think contains some novel aspects, I am aware of a general intellectual indebtedness to others as well as specific instances of indebtedness. It is rather difficult to determine the nature of the general indebtedness I owe. There is a family resemblance between the ideas developed by Herbert A. Simon and his colleagues at Carnegie-Mellon University and those presented in this volume. I have certainly gained from reading some of their writings, but despite the overlap, in general the notions in this book differ from theirs.

Instances of specific indebtedness are much easier to spot and acknowledge. It is a pleasure to be able to thank a number of scholars who took the trouble to read this book in part or in entirety. Among these are my colleagues Marc Roberts, A. Michael Spence, and James Duesenberry, and T. Y. Shen of the University of California. I am especially indebted to Professor Walter L. Nonnenan, University of Antwerp, who read the complete manuscript and made detailed comments. Similarly, Ralph Biggadike of the University of Virginia, read the manuscript from the point of view of a student and faculty member of a school of business, and I am grateful for his help.

The chapter on "selective rationality," which involves psychological issues, presented special problems. I am indebted to Dr. Gregory Rocklin, M.D., a noted psychiatrist, and to Professor Chris Argyris for their cogent and helpful comments.

Many individuals read portions of the manuscript or presentations of some of the ideas in other formats, and I found their criticism especially helpful. I wish to express my gratitude to Oliver E. Williamson, Julius Margolis, and Richard R. Nelson, who made detailed comments on a paper presented at a conference on the Economics of Internal Organization at the University of Pennsylvania. Some of the ideas in the paper form part of the material in this volume. Others who commented on papers, parts of which found their way into this volume, are Michael Crew, Anthony Atkinson, Göran Ohlin, Maurice Scott, Wilfred Beckerman, Paul Streeten, and Aubrey Silberston; it is a pleasure to note my appreciation. I am grateful for research assistance to Samuel S. Lieberman, Lee E. Edlefsen, and Paul Albanese. Needless to say, none of these individuals are in any way responsible for deficiencies or errors which may remain in the text.

Three of the chapters in Part One are based on articles previously published in professional journals. I thank the *American Economic Review, Kyklos,* and the *Quarterly Journal of Economics* for permission to borrow freely from my earlier publications. Katherine Howard typed most of the manuscript and helped with its preparation for the press. Some of this was done under rushed and sometimes difficult circumstances, and I am happy to acknowledge her help and cheerfulness in carrying out these tasks. I am also grateful to Ann Louise McLaughlin for the skillful and sensitive manner in which she edited the manuscript.

The National Science Foundation provided a research grant several years back which gave me sufficient free time to develop some of the basic ideas found in this volume, and it is a pleasure to acknowledge this assistance. A month's stay at the Villa Serbelloni enabled me to put some of the chapters into their final form. I feel especially grateful to the Rocke-feller Foundation, and to Bill and Betsy Olson, for helping to make the stay at the Villa especially pleasant and fruitful.

Cambridge, Massachusetts   *H.L.*
October 1975

Contents

PART ONE

The X-Efficiency Problem
and the Interdependent Consumer

1   Atomistic versus Molecular Economics

Meaning and Motivation

To employ a gastronomic metaphor, my aim in this chapter is to provide an appetizer and a glimpse of the menu. The more substantial fare comes later. One way to indicate the nature of the contents of this book is to start with its former title, "Atomistic Microeconomics." "Atomistic" is to be contrasted with "molecular." Although the term "atomistic competition" is sometimes used in conventional microtheory, the essential nature of the theory, in my view, is not atomistic at all. The units of conventional theory, the *household* and the *firm,* normally are visualized as the *basic* decision-making entities or actors. However, there is an important sense in which this is not the case, and in which conventional microtheory is not consistent —except in the very special case in which households and firms are composed of one person only. The view to be taken here would appear to most noneconomists as almost self-evident. It is simply that only individuals make decisions, and not the socially or legally constituted entities we call firms and households, although individuals may make some decisions in the name of such entities. Thus, the conventional units, the household and the firm, are probably more appropriately viewed as molecular units. They are basic social and legal units in the economy, but they are not *the* basic units.

The view to be taken in what follows does not deny the importance of the firm and the household, but emphasizes that we can only understand the behavior of such molecular units through the study of the organization and structure of their atomic constituents. To depart from the physics metaphor for a moment, we shall try to understand household behavior by examining how individuals make decisions within households, and attempt to infer possible generalizations about households on the basis of the behavior of individual constituents. Initially, households as such will not be presumed to pursue objectives. Rather, it is only household members who can have objectives. Whether or not it is meaningful or useful as a shorthand to speak of household objectives depends on the analysis of individual objectives.

In a similar sense, and perhaps more strikingly, we assume that individuals rather than firms have objectives. Thus, initially firms are not presumed to maximize profits, or to maximize or optimize anything else for that matter. (This contrasts sharply with almost all existing microeconomic models.) Only individual members of firms have motives, and the meaningfulness and nature of firm motives depend on the study of individual motives. In other words, whether or not it is proper, meaningful, or useful to view firms as profit maximizers becomes a problem to be subjected to analysis and solution and is not something about which we simply make assumptions at the outset. It will all depend on the analysis of individual behavior, of the interaction of individuals within groups, and of the behavior of the groups that constitute the firm which will determine the answer.

Of course, there is no scientific imperative that we look at the problem in this way. There is nothing to stop anyone from viewing households and firms as profit- and utility-maximizing entities. Implicitly or explicitly this is more or less the way the problem has been handled for over a century. But it is probably time that we consider reversing the procedure—to start with individual behavior and to see how multiperson group behavior emerges as a result.

Some scholars have studied entities smaller than households and firms. For the most part this has been the domain of sociologists, psychologists, and anthropologists. Among economists those who have been concerned with the nature of organizations have looked into this question. Most prominent among these are the followers of Herbert Simon (a political scientist) and what has come to be known as the Carnegie school. But for the most part, this has not resulted in the revamping of economic theory. Somehow there has been a gap or a lack of connection between the work of these investigators and those who have simultaneously been at the forefront of refining and rewriting conventional microtheory. We shall consider at various points of this book the difference between my own viewpoint and that of the Carnegie school.

The Silent Logical Leap and the Possible Logical Flaw

There has been a silent logical leap in the gradual and refined construction of textbook microtheory. The nature of the leap is easy to expound. We shall want to examine briefly whether there is a sense in which a logical flaw may be also involved.

Suppose a world in which all households and firms are made up of single individuals. We are only concerned with logic, not with realism, and hence need not worry about the artificial nature of such a world. In their capacity as consumers (that is, households), individuals maximize utility, and in their capacity as firms they maximize profits. Since firms are single individuals no labor as such is bought and sold. As a consequence, the evaluation of labor's productivity within the firm does not enter explicitly as a problem. Now suppose we try to generalize the results and shift to multiperson households and firms, and we *assume* that they behave the same way, in terms of basic motivations and responses to motivations, they would behave if they were individuals. We then proceed to develop the implication of such a theory. It seems to me that one can speak of a logical leap in this area in the sense that we do not examine in detail whether such a shift from single-person to multiperson units can be made without involving possible internal contradictions, and under what circumstances this transition can be carried out. By and large this question has not been examined; it has been silently passed over, as it were. While it may be appropriate to argue that a relatively silent logical leap has occurred, is a logical flaw involved?

Once we shift to multiperson firms it is necessary to introduce a labor market and to make some implicit assumptions about the nature of labor contracts. We shall see later that a very narrow *implicit* construction of labor contracts has created a special set of difficulties. But for the moment we are concerned only with whether a logical flaw exists. Workers are produced by households. They receive a wage equal to the value of their marginal product. Implicitly a close connection between performance valuation and payment is presumed to exist.

The critical question is to ask whether there are any implications for the behavior of individuals as utility maximizers in their role as consumers, broadly interpreted, that permits their role in production units to be such that it does not conflict with the assumption of profit maximization for such production units? There are two possible answers to this question. In part this stems from semantic difficulties, and in part from an incomplete specification of the assumptions of microtheory. We normally think of individuals who become members of firms as being "employed" by them, and whose efforts are completely controlled, perfectly agreed upon, and/or controlled or manipulated by the firm. But this is too narrow an interpretation. Similarly, the concept of consumption is narrowly construed as occurring only within the household. Yet there is no reason why the work experience within a firm cannot also be viewed as a form of consumption. Many individuals quite readily attribute satisfaction (utility) to the work experience. A good, after all, is anything that yields satisfaction to the consumer, and is scarce in some sense. There is no reason why individuals should not behave in such a way that attempts to increase their utility (as consumers of their work experience) conflicts with the presumed profit maximization ideals of the firm to which they belong. Furthermore, utility maximization for some individuals may conflict with attempts of utility maximization by others. The compromises achieved may not maximize the utility of either individual or even of both as a group. This is not the place to set out the exact nature of this argument. My point is only to indicate enough of the problem and general line of discussion to suggest that a possible logical flaw may in fact exist.

Another way of looking at the matter is to consider the implications for microtheory of the distinction between principals and agents. Conventional microtheory may be viewed as a theory of behavior of principals. If principals engage in trade it makes sense for them if both parties gain by the transaction. Trade does not take place if one of the principals expects to lose. Now consider a world of agents in which principals have imperfect control over their agents. Will agents engage in transactions in such a way so that the transactions are always in the interest of their principals? Not necessarily. Agents have their own interests and it may "pay" them to avoid transactions that would be in the interest of their principals, just as it may pay for agents to engage in some transactions under which one or both sets of principals lose. In modern firms over a certain small size most transactions are carried out by agents. Even many household transactions are carried out by agents in behalf of households. It is unlikely that a world characterized mostly by agent-agent trade (and under which agent-principal contracts are vague and incomplete) will yield the same results as a world in which transactions are only between principals. More on this later. It suffices for present purposes to suggest the possibility of a flaw in the argument when economists shift from single-person firms to firms of any size in which agents must carry out transactions in behalf of principals and proceed as if the essential nature of the behavior does not change.

On the other hand, it is quite likely that one could develop a model in which the behavior of individuals within households and firms are sufficiently circumscribed so that no logical flaw results. In other words, it is possible to make up assumptions so that the leap from the behavior of single individual units to multi-individual units involves an accurate logical transition. But we have to consider that there is something wrong with a theory that allows for interpretations so that inconsistencies of the type considered can occur. It is not at all clear that inventing assumptions which circumscribe individual behavioral options so that we get the "right" answer for the behavior of households and firms is the right way of going about it. There are good reasons to reexamine household and firm behavior from the point of view of the results of interactions of individual behavior.

A related matter borders on the semantic difficulties already alluded to. Some writers have retreated from the position of the profit-maximizing firm to that of the utility-maximizing firm. But firms do not have feelings and cannot maximize utility. Only firm members can be presumed to enjoy satisfaction or dissatisfaction connected with firm behavior. This perforce requires that we analyze intra-firm relations in terms of the utility derived from the work experience. We cannot choose, as part of the assumptions or options open to us, that if firms do not maximize some accounting magnitude (profits, growth of output, and so on), they can maximize utility in which these accounting magnitudes enter as arguments.

The Effort Decision

Among the insufficiently considered aspects of microtheory is the analysis of effort. This probably arises as a consequence of the symmetrical treatment of all inputs (and effort is simply another input which is purchased) and the simultaneous lack of consideration of intra-firm behavior—that is, the lack of the study of real atomistic decisions and events. A major element in the scheme of analysis to be developed in this book is the treatment of effort, and the effort decision, as a central element of the theory. This approach need not ignore the reward aspects involved in effort decisions, but it will not presume that monetary rewards are the only elements that determine effort decisions.

There is a sense in which three separate elements have to be considered in examining intra-firm behavior: the effort decision; the reward arrangements in a broad sense; and the degree to which a reward-effort nexus exists. In other words, it will be argued that the atomistic treatment of the firm, as well as the household, puts effort decisions and the relationship between effort decisions by different individuals, as well as the various motivational aspects involved, at the center of the analytical scheme.

Psychological Assumptions

The atomistic analysis suggested in the previous pages can be carried out on the basis of some of the psychological assumptions in conventional microtheory—that is, either on the basis of utility maximization for individuals, or income maximization in some areas of behavior, or a combination of the two. However, the existing assumptions, while valid in a sense, seem to be to assume an unnecessarily constrained vision of rationality.

Once again, the problem may be partially semantic. A lot depends on how we interpret the word utility. One can interpret utility in such a way so that *all* behavior is subsumed under some version of utility maximization. But this would rob the concepts of utility and maximization of real meaning. If we are presumed to do something which has some degree of specificity, then there must be something else for which it can be said we are not filling the criteria of the first type of action. In other words, the idea of utility maximization must contain the possibility of choice under which utility is not maximized. As my research progressed, it appeared to me that in order to offer a fairly deep analysis of the problem of the effort decision it was desirable to loosen the psychological assumptions behind normal economic behavior in such a way so that rationality did not necessarily imply maximizing utility, as that concept is normally used. Although utility maximization is consistent with rational behavior, it is not a necessary ingredient of it.

A Theory for X-Inefficiency

Some of the motivations for the writing of this book have already been suggested implicitly. Simply as an intellectual exercise or game it is of interest to see what happens to the nature and structure of microtheory if we try to work it out on a basis different from that within the conventions which have dominated microtheory for over a century. I have indicated two of the nonconventional approaches to be tried: the first is to start with individuals as the basic unit and to see to what extent the behavior of the conventional units such as households or firms turns out to be similar or different from the existing theory. The second is to try to insert, as a basis for individual behavior, variations in the psychological assumptions which are presumed to be the determinants of behavior.

Although playing intellectual games seems reason enough for the research which resulted in Part Two of this book, more serious reasons also had a significant role. For two decades I have felt a general disquiet and ambivalence about textbook microtheory. On the one hand some real problems do lend themselves admirably to the type of analysis that can be carried out on the basis of existing theory, and such analyses do lead to useful results. But for a great many other problems analysis based on current theory is either not very useful or the essential points are actually obscured or masked by the conventional mode of thought. For example, many short-run pricing and rationing problems where a great many producers are involved are handled reasonably well on the basis of the existing theory as long as price elements and allocational elements are the essentials of the problem. However, once productivity aspects enter the picture—or other aspects that influence the supply function, especially in the long run, or situations in which the market is composed of relatively few producers or of a mixture of a few very large and many very small producers—then the application of the existing apparatus can lead to serious errors. Thus, there is a wide range of problems for which a broader based theory (in terms of behavioral assumptions) is called for as a basis of analysis and diagnosis.

Perhaps the most important impetus toward the writing of this book is to find a theoretical solution to what might be called "the X-inefficiency problem." In an article written in 1966 (see Chapter 3) I attempted to establish the point that in a great many interesting instances, what is termed allocative inefficiency accounts for a very small welfare loss, whereas there is a non-allocative component, which for want of a better term I designated as "X-inefficiency," and which turns out to account for a much greater welfare loss. The essence of the message is that if microeconomists are interested in efficiency, then in most cases their talents would be more fruitfully employed if they studied the determinants of X-efficiency rather than allocative efficiency. Understandably there is considerable resistance to this viewpoint. A century of practice is not readily abandoned.

One of the good arguments put forth against my view is that we need more than simply a definition of X-efficiency. What is needed is a theory as to why X-inefficiency should ever exist in the first place, and one that suggests or enables us to analyze the circumstances under which greater or lesser degrees of X-inefficiency is likely to exist. In several articles I attempted to answer this question to some degree. This book represents an attempt to provide a more adequate answer than permitted by the space constraints of the article form. In addition, the theory to be presented provides implications for an application to not only the theory of the firm and industry but also to the theory of the household. Both demand and supply are covered by the underlying structure suggested in the pages that follow.

"The Menu"

The next three chapters set the stage for the theory proper outlined in Part Two. Chapter 2, concerned with methodological issues, presents my preconceptions and represents my methodological standpoint. To some degree it differs from the one that appears to be dominant among economists in the United States, at least in emphasis and degree. I am not primarily concerned with methodological debate since this is an endless and unresolvable process. Matters of taste, as well as of background and train-ing, seem to be involved in subtle ways. The chapter indicates enough of my preconceptions to clarify the nature and motivations contained in the rest of the book. Because the book as such does not depend on my methodological preconceptions, readers who do not have a taste for such discussions can omit this chapter or leave it until the end to be read as though it were an appendix. However, to me it seemed natural to put it at the outset since I am saying in a sense, "here are my methodological preconceptions, accept them or not as you will, but let us proceed with the other business as though these views are valid." The hope of such a procedure is that it may minimize less essential and less likely to be resolved arguments.

Chapter 3 sets the stage. It indicates why we might expect X-inefficiency to be more significant than allocative inefficiency.

Chapter 4 is a revised version of an early article of mine on household interdependencies in the theory of consumers' demand. Such interdepen-dencies enter in a critical way in the revision of the theory of consumers' demand developed in Chapter 11. It seemed useful to present the basic analysis of the treatment of household interdependencies (but not the treatment of *intra*household behavior) prior to the presentation of the atomistic theory of the household. Even for the theory of the industry the approach developed in Chapter 4 is helpful since some interdependencies between firms can be handled in a parallel manner: as there is emulation between households we can visualize emulation between firms.

Part Two presents the theory proper. Chapter 5 discusses the expanded psychological theory which forms the motivational basis for individual behavior in the subsequent chapters. Chapter 6 discusses the behavior of the individual, and Chapter 7 extends these behavioral patterns in the context of group behavior.

Chapters 8 and 9 consider interpersonal economic relations from two different viewpoints in order to show why many of these relations end up in less than optimal arrangements. Chapter 10 combines several of the pre-ceding ideas and adds some new ones to present an X-inefficiency theory of firm behavior. Chapter 11 uses some of the concepts developed in earlier chapters in order to reconsider the theory of household behavior as well as the theory of demand.

In Chapter 12 the basic ideas already developed for the theory of the firm are applied to competitive industry. Chapter 13 examines the possibil-ity of applying all of these ideas in order to understand at least some aspects of duopoly and oligopoly behavior. In all of Part Two, the nature and essence of X-inefficiency emerges to different degrees and in various guises as a behavioral element that *results* from the initial assumptions.

Part Three deals, only to some degree, in the payoff to the entire exercise. Are there interesting implications and applications that result from the theory and differ from what we would expect on the basis of conventional microtheory? The chapters in this part of the book suggest that this is indeed the case.

2 Romance and Realism
in the Theory of Theories

A prejudice against methodological work is part of the tradition in English-speaking countries. As a consequence many economists do not write on the subject or examine their own methodological preconceptions in a careful fashion. Nevertheless, there is some discussion of these matters on an informal basis. Certain views have been developed that, to the extent one can judge, seem to have a fairly high degree of acceptance. I believe that these views, many of which have developed informally and some of which have developed as a consequence of Professor Friedman's famous essay,[1] represent what might be called a "romantic" approach to economic theory. To be specific, we might look upon the following assertions as part of the romantic view: (1) an economic theory should be testable; (2) it should lead to prediction of at least a conditional character; (3) it should be conceivably falsifiable by events in the outside world if it is to be considered a meaningful theory; (4) if it is true, then it should not have been falsified by events; and (5) it should pass the same tests in principle, and possibly in practice, as theories in laboratory sciences.

The Romantic View of Theory and the Predictability Test

The essence of the romantic view is that prediction is the only criterion of really meaningful "scientific" knowledge. Why should there be so much concern about prediction? The virtue of prediction as a test of a theory is that it can be a *sharp* test, a test less subject to argument than other tests. This is especially true of laboratory prediction. If A claims that his theory produces a certain result and states the nature of his experiment to prove it, then B can replicate the experiment and determine whether or not the claim is justified. But as a sharp test, prediction functions most effectively as a rejection rule. That is to say, if the prediction does not work out, then the theory should be rejected. It shows that, within its sphere, the theory does not have universal predictive capacity. We cannot have a prediction test that is also an acceptance test, since there is always the possibility that the next prediction will fail. Acceptance is always tentative.

The importance of prediction as a scientific test is open to debate. It is not a matter that scholars will necessarily agree about, since it depends neither on logic nor on empirical matters. Although it may be true that the majority view in economics is that the purpose and test of scientific propositions is prediction, this is simply a matter of faith or of taste. It is just as reasonable to argue (indeed I believe it to be more reasonable) that the purpose of scientific theories is to obtain coherent explanations of phenomena and events. And it so happens that increased predictive power is often a by-product of having a coherent explanation.*

Predictive capacity without explanatory capacity is worthless. Mere clairvoyance, irrespective of its sharpness, does not itself have scientific standing. Only predictive capacity that arises out of having coherent and communicable explanations has scientific standing. The power to predict is subsidiary to the power to explain. Explanation without prediction is sufficient, *but prediction without explanation is of no consequence from a scientific standpoint.*

The prediction test is frequently restricted to "conditional prediction": the theory is supposed to work only under some specified set of conditions, and in some sciences these conditions can be established artificially in a laboratory. Where the specified conditions cannot be established artificially, or where the effects of changing conditions cannot be calculated exactly, then the prediction test ceases to be a sharp test. Aggregative economic theories fall into a category where conditional prediction cannot, strictly speaking, be applied. Microtheory especially faces difficulties in this area.

Since we cannot stop one segment of the world while another segment of the same world is allowed to change, conditional prediction cannot readily be applied as a sharp test that yields true or false answers to the questions of validity. The experience that such theories attempt to analyze is imbedded in an essential way in the matrix of general history. It is usually impossible to separate clearly from the total historical experience only

---

* Science creates bridges between facts. We integrate these bridges and facts with other experience. It is this awareness of "bridges" and their integration that enables us to understand relationships. These "bridges" are frequently facts arranged in precisely describable patterns—sometimes expressed in equations. These patterns or sets of patterns sometimes have a time dimension, hence they make prediction possible. But prediction is a frequent, although not a necessary consequence of explanation.

those elements that we arbitrarily choose to study. Although a conditional prediction test may be possible for some individual hypotheses, if a prediction test is to apply generally, it must predict actual events.

The Prediction Engine and the Separability Hypothesis

Theories are more than just prediction engines. Even when they fail as prediction engines they may have many useful properties. This, in part, accounts for the fact that theories may be retained even after they have clearly failed as predictive devices. What other properties can we look for in a theory?

Some minimal expectations from a theory are, first, a consistent vocabulary—a set of concepts that enables us to reduce the multiplicity of detailed observations into a small enough bundle of general concepts that they may be discussed efficiently—and, second, some notions about the relations between the various components of economic behavior to enable a partial understanding of how they operate simultaneously. But we probably want something more. Let us pause and see what we cannot expect from an economic theory. We cannot expect a theory that will tell us how history unfolds indefinitely, given certain data to begin with. Although economic theories are often written so that they appear to do this, they in fact cannot. For example, some theories of the business cycle appear to suggest that if only we could determine the parameters underlying the difference or differential equations in which such theories are couched, we would be able to predict how the cycle will unfold, given certain initial data. Of course, we are usually not surprised when it does not work out quite that way. But we should not blame our failures on our lack of ingenuity in measuring parameters. Rather, the difficulty lies in some intrinsic qualities of social phenomena that often make it impossible to succeed at such efforts, qualities frequently forgotten because we seek theories analogous to theories in physics.

By the very nature of things our theories must be partial—they cannot take into account all human and social phenomena. But the unfolding of economic history is a consequence of the totality of the interactions of all human and social relations. This in itself would not be crucial if the set of phenomena that economists choose to study were separable from other phenomena; that is, if economic events were determined only by the economic relationships considered within our theories and not influenced by anything else. Since they are influenced by other matters, and since these are matters that cannot be accounted for on the basis of existing knowledge, we cannot determine the unfolding of economic history simply on the basis of economic theory.

Another way of looking at the matter is to distinguish between two types of parameters and to recognize that some parameters are likely to change, irrespective of our ingenuity in measurement. We may distinguish between environmental parameters and the internal parameters of the system. By internal parameters we have in mind the values of the constants of the equations that describe the relations of the system. By the environmental parameters we have in mind the values of those elements that describe the environment under which the system operates. When economists elaborate their theories they assume the environment to remain constant but they do not specify the nature of the environment in detail. It is obvious that the environmental parameters change constantly and that the operation of the system is not empirically independent of the values of these parameters. Hence, a correct system in the predictive sense—a system that will predict what will actually happen—is, in principle, impossible. Even if we knew all the necessary initial data, as the system unfolds the environmental parameters would change; they would influence some of the variables within the system and the results would not be in accordance with what we would have predicted at the outset.* This is precisely the sort of thing the laboratory scientist is able to get away from by creating in the laboratory an artificial environment whose state he is able to control. Until the economist can obtain laboratory-controlled economic conditions, he will not be able to test many of his theories in the same sense that the laboratory scientist is often able to do. This suggests not that the labora-

---

* The French mathematician and physicist Henri Poincaré developed this idea from a somewhat different viewpoint: "I imagine a world in which the various parts can conduct heat so perfectly that they maintain a constant equilibrium of temperature. . . . Now let us imagine that this world cools slowly through radiation; the temperature will remain uniform, but will diminish with time. I imagine also that one of the inhabitants falls into a state of lethargy and awakens after a few centuries. Let us grant, since we have already assumed so many things, that he is able to live in a cooler world and that he can remember previous experiences. He will notice that his descendants still write treatises on physics, that they still make no mention of thermometry, but that the laws which they teach are very different from those which he knew. For example, he had been told that water boils at a pressure of 10 millimeters of mercury, and the new physicists observe that in order for water to boil the pressure must be decreased to 5 millimeters. A body which he had known in the liquid state will now be found only in the solid state, and so forth. The mutual relations among the various parts of the universe all depend on temperature, and as soon as the temperature changes, everything is upset." *Mathematics and Science: Last Essays* (New York, Dover, 1912), p. 11.

tory scientist never runs into situations similar to those facing the economist, but that the economist cannot create the situation for his work that the laboratory scientist is *often* able to create.

The problem of predicting economic history is deeper than that. If a partial theory were correct it would still not be possible to predict changes in the environmental parameters because this involves a knowledge of the total system that the economist does not even attempt to know. The problem is more difficult because it is impossible to know in principle, as well as in fact, whether the partial system is correct or not.

The system the economist is interested in is part of a larger system of relations that is unknown in its totality. Thus he is interested in part of a total system. Can we know the part without knowing the system as a whole? Consider the simplified case in which the system as a whole is a three-variable system and the part a two-variable system. Let X, Y, and Z be the variables in the larger system; the relations between them will form a surface in three-dimensional space. Now suppose that we could only observe X and Y without taking into account the relations between X and Z, and Y and Z. Suppose our theory assumes that X is a certain function of Y. We may, in fact, observe historical values of X and historical values of Y and attempt to draw a regression line from these two sets of values. However, an infinite number of such lines can occur because the value of X that happens depends not only on the value of Y that occurs but also on the value of Z that occurs simultaneously. Hence, the regression line so obtained is not really a reflection of the relation between X and Y but may be much more a reflection of the way in which Z happens to change historically. Similarly, any set of relations of the partial system obtained while ignoring the rest of the system, are really pseudo-relationships that depend to some extent on historical circumstances.

This problem would not arise if the partial system could be separated entirely from the total system. Suppose that all but one of the equations of the partial system did not involve any variables of the total system. And suppose further that the one equation involving such a variable connecting the partial system to the total system could for some reason be predicted in each instance on other grounds. In that case the degree of separability of the two systems would be virtually complete and it would make sense to consider the partial system as a system in its own right. But it is unlikely that this is the case for many aspects of economic behavior. The consequence of this condition is that if we work with the partial system and try to estimate its parameters on the basis of historical data, the estimates will have no relation to the parameters of the total system, even in those equations that are the same in the two systems. These parameters are, in principle, of a type that will appear to change from time to time, even if the parameters of the total system are stable and fixed. Of course, we do not know whether the parameters of the total system are in some sense or other given for all time.* Even if they were, the subsystem that we work with would still be one that would appear to be changing all the time. On the basis of these considerations we could not expect our economic subsystem to be a theory that predicts the unfolding of economic history if the theory is really a partial system rather than a complete system.

Analytical Frameworks, Theories, and Models

Not all theoretical work ends in the creation of theories in the narrow sense. There is no standardized vocabulary in this area. But it may be useful to distinguish three types of theoretical work.

1. We want especially to distinguish an analytical framework from a theory proper. By a theory we have in mind a set of relations that are sufficiently specified so that some conceivably falsifiable conclusions can be reached. At least some of the conclusions resulting from the theory are, in principle, in a form that makes it possible for facts not in conformity with the theory to occur. Such a theory says something about the world of facts. Usually this requires that the parameters of some of the equations describing the relationships be sufficiently specified that the variables of the system can take on only some values and not *all* values. In sum, theories enable us to make assertions about the world of events. Under controlled conditions in laboratory situations these would often enable us to make predictions.

2. By an analytical framework I have in mind a set of relationships that do not lead to specific conclusions about the world of events. In an analytical framework the parameters are not sufficiently specified to lead to conceivable falsifiable conclusions. An example should illustrate the distinction between an analytical framework and a theory. Consider the relations usually employed in price theory, the simple demand and supply functions. If we say merely that price is determined by these two relations—the quantity demanded as a function of price, and the quantity

* F. S. C. Northrop emphasizes the importance of the law of conservation in classical physics and the lack of a counterpart postulate in economics. His essential point seems to be that the specific properties of economic relations are not based on parameters that are fixed over time. In fact, he argues that relations in economics are specified only in terms of their generic properties whereas, in the physical sciences, both the generic and the specific properties are specified. See his "The Methodology and Limited Predictive Power of Classical Economic Science," in *The Logic of the Sciences and Humanities* (Meridian ed.; Cleveland, World Publishing, 1962), pp. 235–254.

supplied as a function of price—then we have an analytical framework. As long as the parameters are not specified, specific events cannot possibly contradict the confluence of these two relationships. However, once we say that the relationships are of a certain specific type so that we can draw a conclusion as to what would happen in the event that there is, say, an increase in demand, then we have a theory rather than an analytical framework. The analytical framework may be looked upon as the mold out of which the specific types of theories are made. The sort of predictions that the theory has to yield in principle for it to be a theory need not be a specific numerical character. It may be sufficient that it predicts a specific direction of change and no more. If this direction could be falsified by the facts, we have a theory that explains changes in direction.

Very often it may not be possible to tell when we have a theory and when an analytical framework. The distinction may be subtle. For example, price theory may be written in such a way, so many forms of the basic relations may be considered on the basis of shifts in some of the basic relationships. Textbooks in economics from this point of view usually provide analytical frameworks rather than theories. They may be looked upon as toolboxes from which we can fashion theories to explain events, but they are not themselves such theories.

3. Another distinction often made is between a theory and a model. Here especially there is no standardized and well-recognized usage. Sometimes the words are used interchangeably while at others they are meant to refer to different types of abstract entities. Sometimes models appear to be used in the sense of what we have described as an analytical framework. However, I wish to use the term in a somewhat different way. Roughly speaking, by a model I will have in mind a less rich form of a theory. For instance, let us assume that Keynesian theory should have, say, fourteen equations and fourteen unknowns. Now a theoretical construct that gives some of the same results as the Keynesian theory with fewer equations and fewer unknowns may be looked upon as a model of the Keynesian theory. Obviously the model allows for a smaller range of possibilities and considers a narrower range of phenomena than the theory, but it reaches some of the same *qualitative* conclusions. As a consequence, models are especially useful for didactic and illustrative purposes. Another variant of a model would be to have the same set of relationships as the theory, but with the parameters restricted to a much greater degree to bring out some of the conclusions more clearly. Thus a theory may be said to have a large variety of models that are consistent with it. For example, if in the theory of price we assume that the demand relation is negatively inclined, then a model of the theory may assume that the demand relation is not only

negatively inclined but that it is also linear. It would be easy to think of many models of this kind. Very often we have exceedingly broad and to some extent unstated conceptions of our theories, and to elucidate their nature we are forced to use models. It is easier to understand a model than a theory since it is either simpler or, by assuming simple specific relations, more sharply drawn.

What We Can Expect from Economic Theories

The viewpoint I wish to propound is that knowledge is incomplete and that the known and unknown aspects of social and economic phenomena are usually not completely separable but are organically intertwined as part of entities larger than the entity being studied. Clearly, the idea of something being "known" is different than it is in areas where knowledge is separable.

In considering the preceding argument about the difficulty of prediction in economics, a sharp distinction must be made between predictions that involve the operation of an economy as a whole and those that involve only propositions about the operation of *some* economic entities under controlled conditions. For example, some economic propositions may turn out to be testable for the behavior of individuals or firms under controlled conditions. There is nothing in principle to eliminate this possibility, but there is nothing to guarantee it either. An industry in which a firm finds itself may be more unstable than an economy. Obviously it will all depend on specific circumstances.

If we cannot count on the predictive test, then what conditions should we expect our theories to fulfill? Some conditions can be stated, but ultimately they depend on a belief in the nature of the empirical world that is warranted by experience. Let me suggest three major conditions that a theory should fulfill: logical consistency; *sound behavior assumptions;* and consistency with *some* past experience. The meaning of these conditions is far from obvious, although that of logical consistency is probably the easiest to agree upon.

Consider the second condition. Theories usually have two types of assumptions: those that indicate the area under which the theory is supposed to work, and those that indicate how the various elements or entities in the theory are assumed to behave. For example, in the theory of price an assumption about the nature of the market falls into the former category, while the assumption of profit maximization falls into the latter. Assumptions about the area encompassed by the theory are in a sense arbitrary, but assumptions about behavior are not. The entities either do or do not behave as the theory says, and I suggest that these behavior assumptions should usually be consistent with experience where comparisons with experience can be made.

The third criterion is the most difficult to interpret. Experience is determined by a larger system than the one under study. Hence, what can we mean by consistency with past experience? We mean that there may be events that so definitely are not suppressed or distorted by changes in the environmental parameters that we can suppose them to be determined largely by the economic system. In that case, theory should be consistent with the *possibility* of such events. Of course, whether or not the events are of the kind indicated may be a matter of dispute. Nevertheless, this does form a desirable condition, for the theory should have some contact with the world of experience and there are at least some experiences for which such contact exists.

If we cannot expect theories to tell us the detailed sequence of events that will occur, what degree of consistency between theory and fact can we expect? At the very least we should expect theory to throw light on the events that are not submerged by changes in the value of the environmental parameters. We may inquire how the theory can tell us anything if in principle we cannot obtain the correct values for the parameters of a model because it is part of a larger and unknown model. The situation, however, may at times be one in which the parameters obtained are for periods in which the other variables do not play too great a role in determining events. As a consequence, the subsystem that we used may for the time being give some degree of reasonable consistency with the events that occur. That is, the model has temporary predictive value.

Note that prediction in the strict sense is still out of the question. We cannot know whether in the future the environmental parameters will or will not be relatively stable. We may, however, be able to use the system for an assessment of events in the past. For with respect to the past events we may be able to determine whether the general situation was one of tranquillity or not, and whether the environmental parameters changed greatly or little. Even though we may not know this with respect to small changes, we may believe that there has been considerable stability so that the environment had little influence in determining large changes, that is, we may reasonably expect the theory to help explain large changes.

Now, a theory and the estimates of equation parameters should in many situations be able to at least explain some general trends. Accordingly, one thing we might expect of a theory is the explanation of trends of some sort that are not submerged by environmental influences. For example, a theory of price in some market should not lead us to expect a long-run decline in price when in fact persistent increases are observed.

A more difficult matter arises with respect to turning points. Since a turning point is likely to be the consequence of opposing influences that to some extent balance each other out, and since close to the turning point such opposing influences are near to being balanced, we would expect the difference between them to be sufficiently small so that they will be submerged by the environmental influences. However, if significant turning points actually are observed, our theory must at the very least permit them to occur in principle. In addition, there should be states on either side of the turning point where the theory would suggest that prior to the turning point the trend direction is one way, and after it another.

Explanation, Diagnosis, and Policy

It should be stressed that from the point of view taken here a theory should be judged on whether, as far as possible: it provides and presents a coherent structure of pertinent facts and relations including known behavioral patterns; it possesses the capacity to enhance our understanding of the behavioral area covered by the theory; and it facilitates the formulation of connected and logical explanations of those events which come within the purview of the theory's area of application. All of this implies that a significant consideration is the *relative* degree to which the selected behavioral assumptions agree with an accurate perception of reality. The theory cannot be faulted if the perception of reality is faulty. None of this denies the essential principle of abstraction involved in theoretical work. Comprehensibility requires simplification which in turn frequently necessitates that we leave out of our theories many details of a complex reality. However, the previous suggestions conflict with the view that the nature of the assumptions chosen are impervious to criticism. Thus, great importance is attached to the realism of assumptions from a relative standpoint. In other words, theory A is superior to theory B if theory A's assumptions are more realistic than B's, other things equal.

Although a sharp test for a theory may not exist, a theory may be judged by general effectiveness in the work it is expected to do. Such judgments would not lead to definitive conclusions. Many scientific matters cannot be settled beyond any shadow of doubt and there is no reason to expect definitive judgments. Therefore, a theory's effectiveness can form the basis for some degree of judgment about its "validity," given the evidence about its effectiveness.

The area in which a theory could prove its effectiveness needs to be clarified. The view taken here is that the two main jobs of a theory are: as an engine of analysis, and as an instrument for policy determination. These elements are closely related. My basic assumption is that explanatory power is a basis for diagnosis, and that diagnosis should precede prescription. Policies cannot be determined once and for all in such a way as to set the system right forever after. As a consequence, there is a need for continuous diagnosis. Therefore, a theory that *in some way* (and to some degree) provides an organized set of diagnostic tools is desirable.

I have spoken of analytical frameworks. The job of the theorist is in part to provide the frameworks that function as a mold for different kinds of models. This is one of the things we might expect from theoretical efforts in the social sciences. Now the models that result from such frameworks should be seen to contain sample propositions. These propositions are essentially relationships that in themselves are not necessarily true. They are samples in the sense that they suggest the form that the theory should take. After investigation, the actual relationships decided upon may be different from the initial samples. Yet obviously it is desirable to have samples at the outset.

Ideally, some of the sample relations should involve propositions that in this initial form or in some modified form are likely to work frequently. It is useful in this context to conceive a theory to be constructed from an integrated and organized system of sample relations, at least some of which are presumed to work "frequently."

Although sharp prediction employed as a rejection rule is an inappropriate criterion, I have by no means eliminated some degree of prediction as a quality of some aspects of a theory. An example from medicine might clarify this idea. We may know, for example, that a given quantity of aspirin will frequently cure a headache. This type of knowledge contains some of the qualities we might expect in a good economic behavior theory. (1) It is a useful bit of information. (2) It is knowledge that does not pass the prediction test employed as a rejection rule. There are some headaches that aspirin does not cure; nevertheless, we do not throw out information because of this discovery. (3) It is the sort of knowledge that lacks precision but is nonetheless highly useful. The word "headache" is not clearly defined, nor for that matter is "frequently." Yet if this were all we knew about the relation between aspirins and headaches, it would certainly be useful. Also we can look upon it as a sample relation. We may, if we wish, get a more precise relation for some specific individual. We can take a sample and study its effectiveness with specific individuals and thereby improve upon the precision of the relation in this context. For some we may find that a given dosage cures headaches all the time. For others it may work but with certain undesirable side effects. And for some individuals it may not work at all. Nevertheless, it is quite obvious that as a sample relation it was useful and further that it contained some degree of predictability.

Previously I mentioned the prediction of trends. Trends may be predicted because some well understood elements that change in a given direction are seen to change with sufficient magnitude in that direction that we believe this direction of change will continue into the foreseeable future. Again, some degree of predictability is involved. There is also a relation between the magnitude of the independent variable and our feelings about the degree of predictability. In the previous example we may believe that very small dosages of aspirin are unlikely to cure the headaches, but that if we increase the dosage the likelihood of cure might increase accordingly, at least up to some point. Similarly, in driving an automobile it is unnecessary to know the exact relation between the pressure on the accelerator and the speed that will be achieved. All we need know is that under given road conditions an increase in pressure will yield an increase in speed. Indeed, knowing this much about any automobile operates as a useful sample relation despite the fact that the actual relation will differ in degree for different types of automobiles. Similarly, an economic theory may contain relations of a monotonic nature between increase in capital and increases in output. This relation may be a useful sample relation despite the fact that it lacks precision. As with the aspirin example it would be useful even if it did not work all the time but it did work frequently.

Frequency is a matter of degree. However, we cannot say on a priori grounds what degree of frequency is adequate. On a *ceteris paribus* assumption a theory whose relations work more frequently is superior to one that works less frequently. But the *ceteris paribus* assumption may not hold in different instances. In addition, some degrees of frequency may be so low as to make the theory uninteresting from an applied viewpoint. But the concept "interesting" is admittedly a subjective notion. This means in essence that judgments on these matters cannot be mechanized.

However, we want theories that enable us to predict broad, stable equilibrium paths for some time period with a reasonable degree of frequency, where "reasonable" is a subjective, undefined term. The sample relations of the theory should suggest real relations so that prediction within some bounds may follow. The bounds will deal with time if the prediction is only of a directional character, and with the value of the variables that are predicted if the predictions are numerical. In other words, on the basis of some initial condition there should be a time period such that within that time period we predict the values to fall within a certain broad path. This is illustrated in Figure 1. Time is shown on the X-axis and the predicted variable on the Y-axis. The area *I* is the area in

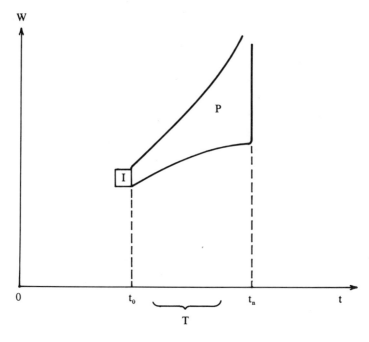

Figure 1

which the initial conditions fall, and the area P is the area in which the predicted path should fall. At each time point the predicted path has a width W and the time dimension of the path is T.

Normally we would expect that the frequency with which the prediction holds would depend on the variable width vector W and the time T. Thus we would have a function relation:

$$F = g(W,T).$$

To say that a theory works, in the sense I have used the term, means that F is greater than zero for some values of W and T. Of course, to be interesting, the value of F would have to be greater than some minimum for a value of W less than some maximum, and a value of T greater than some minimum. Although this introduces matters of judgment into what I mean by working, the concept is meaningful, even if some subjective judgment elements are involved.

How are these ideas related to the notion of theory as an engine of analysis? The sample relations suggest the areas we should investigate in an actual economy in order to see the extent to which any of them have worked frequently. The analytical framework would suggest additional sample relations and would operate as a means of organizing disparate relationships. To the extent that a number of the relations seem to have worked frequently we may, after study, come to understand some components of the economy for at least some periods. This is a stage where some prescriptions could be attempted. There is a possible long-run process which contains a continuous interaction between theory refinement, the analysis of a particular economy or parts thereof, and prescription.

Return now to the basic notion that although detailed prediction is out of the question in many cases, it may be possible to predict the direction of events. Even that may not be possible in all cases because the environmental parameters or variables may be more important at times than the forces considered in the theory. However, some policy instruments may be of such a kind that they can be used in various sizes or to various degrees, and for some sizes or degrees their impact will be larger than that of the environmental parameters. Under such circumstances it may be possible to determine the direction of change by using the policy instrument to a sufficient degree. Where this is done successfully it would surely prove the usefulness of a theory (even if it would not prove its "correctness").

Consider a Keynesian type theory in a situation of underemployment. The theory may suggest that an increase in the rate of investment is necessary to increase the level of employment. It may not be possible, however, to determine the exact relation between a given increase in investment and a given increase in employment. The environmental parameters make such a determination impossible. We would expect, if the theory is a good one, that an increase in investment would increase employment. Perhaps a small increase in investment would not do so. In that case we would increase the investment rate still further and see what happens. If the theory about the direction of change is correct, then we would expect that under normal circumstances a sufficiently large increase in investment would overcome any environmental forces operating in the opposite direction. Thus each increase in investment would result in a change that would tell us whether we have gone in the right direction. If not, we could correct the situation by increasing the dose. In such a way we should eventually be able to approach a full employment state. A theory that would lend itself to procedures of this sort would clearly be more persuasive than one that would not. It is similar to a capacity to drive a car on unknown and unmarked roads in order to reach a certain destination with the aid only of a compass, and with a knowledge only of the initial point and the end point. We cannot determine the optimum way of getting to the destination, nor can we always be sure that we will get onto a road that will go in the right direction. The compass enables us, every so often, to check our progress with respect to direction, to correct errors, and eventually to reach the destination. Obviously, some predictive power is necessary in such cases. But it need not be a power that is universally correct and the quality of the prediction is of a much lower order than that required by the strict prediction-rejection test.

Briefly put, we should expect a conceptual framework that would facilitate the creation of theories or models that contain manipulable variables whose dosages can be raised sufficiently to swamp the environmental effects and sufficiently to obtain accurate directional predictions for a limited period of time.

Summary and Conclusions

The validity of a set of methodological ideas does not determine the value of a price of substantive analysis. However, this chapter may help the reader to see somewhat more clearly some of the things I am driving at. Although many of its points are well known, the viewpoint I end up with differs from that which is frequently accepted. I have dealt with both negative and positive aspects of the problem. On the negative side I have argued against the prediction test as a rejection rule. On the positive side I have put forth a view of theory as a set of sample relations that are helpful in the discovery of specific relations in specific contexts and that we hope will work frequently.

What is the job of the theorist? It is twofold: to create analytical frameworks, and to create sample theories consistent with the analytical framework. In the absence of specific studies, or in the absence of specific policy situations, the sample theories are not to be looked upon as working theories but simply as illustrations of the kinds of working models that could be created.

This view of the matter also means that our sample hypotheses or relations need to be based on fact. The view that looked upon theories as entities to be subjected to a rejection rule did not need to concern itself with the manner in which the hypotheses were arrived at. All that mattered was whether they passed the prediction test time after time. If, however, we no longer expect our theories to work in a precise predictive sense, but view them only as samples, then it is important that our sample hypotheses have some degree of credibility. And credibility would depend in part on experience. We would expect hypotheses that consistently flout experience to be poorer samples than those that frequently agree with experience.

Some recent work suggests that existing economic theory (as well as other types of theories) possess both a *hard core* and a *protective belt*.[2] This felicitous terminology has interesting suggestive overtones irrespective of the exact meaning attributed to them by the originators. The protective belt of a theory allows for a range of reinterpretation of what I have termed "sample relations" in the face of criticism so that the criticism is disarmed; but certain critical elements of the theory—the hard core— remain. A major example from microtheory comes to mind. If counter examples are discovered which point to the conclusion that firms do not maximize profits, the theory is restated so that firms are now presumed to maximize a utility function in which profits enter as one of the arguments in the objective function.

The prediction test approach has frequently been used as a part of the protective belt of existing microtheory. If assumptions are immune from criticism, then one broad area of possible counter examples—those that deal with behavioral hypothesis—are ruled out of court so to speak and therefore cannot be brought to bear in the critical evaluation of the theory. The prediction test also seems to encourage rationalization when the implied consequences of the theory differ from known observations. If the prediction does not work, the theory itself can be reworked so that the faulty prediction no longer emerges. An example may indicate what is involved. If a worker who is paid by the day does not show up for work, the theorist might conclude that the worker is trading leisure for income. Thus income maximization is dropped and the maximization of the utility of *income plus leisure* is substituted. In fact, the individual involved may have had an accident which prevented him from coming to work. The prediction of the theory is saved but the explanation is obviously incorrect. Of course this is all a matter of degree and judgment. Beyond a certain point some economists will interpret a frequent need for such rationalizations or reinterpretations as a basic weakness of the theory.

In the process of disputes about the validity of a theory a consideration that frequently comes to the fore is the degree to which the burden of proof rests with any particular contending party. Although at times this element may be made explicit, it is frequently left implicit and utilized in a subtle fashion by one or both of the contenders. The game in this case is to put as much of the burden of proof (and to maximize the rigor of the proof required) on the opposing party. The view taken in this book is that the proper attitude is one of strict neutrality. Precedence in terms of time or in terms of what is traditionally accepted in no way requires that the burden of proof be borne to any greater degree by one party as against the other. If someone criticizes conventional microeconomic theory there is no reason why any special burden of proof be borne by the critic. A new theory need be no more well-founded (in terms of agreement with reality) but no less so than the existing theory. This should be taken for granted irrespective of the length of time during which the existing theory has held sway.

To sum up much of what has been said, prediction as a rejection test for theories is limited and unnecessarily severe. Useful knowledge frequently does not fall into this mold. Also, the prediction test does not follow from the view that science provides coherent explanations of experience. Thus it may not be meaningful to say that a given theory is correct or incorrect in a strict sense. Where the phenomena that a theory covers are inseparable from a large system in which it is imbedded, it may be impossible in principle to discover the true relations between variables. Although no single simple test may exist for a class of theories, a number of considerations may help us judge the adequacy of some theories.

Economic theories may be looked upon as sets of partially connected sample relations that operate within a changing environment. Such relations should be credible. Sample relations based on hypotheses that constantly flout experience are likely to be poor samples. Thus the realism of assumptions matters. Theories of the type considered may be useful in that the sample relations are helpful in the discovery of specific relations in specific contexts that we hope will work frequently in a loose-fitting servo-mechanistic type of arrangement. Such theories enable us to diagnose existing difficulties and fashion corrective policies. Although they cannot be expected to work universally, these theories do work often enough, in terms of directional changes, to be of interest.

3 X-Efficiency versus Allocative Efficiency

Conventional microtheory is concerned with allocative efficiency. Accumulating empirical evidence suggests that the problem of allocative efficiency is trivial. Yet it is hard to escape the notion that efficiency in some broad sense is significant. The essence of the argument is that microeconomic theory focuses on allocative efficiency to the exclusion of other types of efficiencies that in many instances are much more significant.

Allocative Inefficiency: Empirical Evidence

Some of the studies useful in assessing the importance of allocative efficiency are summarized in Table 1. These are of two types. On the one side are the works of Harberger and Schwartzman on the "social welfare cost" of monopoly.[1] On the other side we have a number of studies, including those by Johnson, Scitovsky, Wemelsfelder, and Janssen, on the benefits of reducing or eliminating restrictions to trade.[2] In both cases the computed benefits attributed to the reallocation of resources turn out to be exceedingly small.

In the original Harberger study the benefits for eliminating monopoly in the United States would raise income no more than 1/13 of 1 percent. Schwartzman's study, which recomputes the benefits of eliminating monopoly by comparing Canadian monopolized industries as against counterpart competitive United States industries, and vice versa, in order to determine the excess price attributable to monopoly, ends up with a similar result. Similarly, the benefits attributed to superior resource allocation as a consequence of the Common Market or a European Free Trade Area are also minute—usually much less than 1 percent.

The calculations made by Scitovsky of the benefits to the Common Market (based on Verdoorn's data) led him to conclude that "the most striking feature of these estimates is their smallness. The one that is really important (for reasons to appear presently), the gain from increased specialization . . . which is less than one-twentieth of one per cent of the

Table 1. Calculated "welfare loss" as percentage of gross or net national product attributed to misallocation of resources.

Study	Source	Country	Year	Cause	Loss (percent)
A. C. Harberger	*A.E.R.* 1954	United States	1929	Monopoly	0.07
D. Schwartzman	*J.P.E.* 1960	United States	1954	Monopoly	0.01
T. Scitovsky	(1)	Common Market	1952	Tariffs	0.05
J. Wemelsfelder	*E.J.* 1960	Germany	1958	Tariffs	0.18
L. H. Janssen	(2)	Italy	1960	Tariffs	0.1 maximum
H. G. Johnson	*Manchester School* 1958	United Kingdom	1970	Tariffs	1.0 maximum
A. Singh	(3)	Montevideo Treaty Countries	–	Tariffs	0.0075 maximum

Sources: (1) Tibor Scitovsky, *Economic Theory and Western European Integration* (Stanford, Stanford University Press, 1958). (2) L. H. Janssen, *Free Trade, Protection and Customs Union* (Leiden, Kroese, 1961), p. 132. (3) Unpublished calculation made by Ajit Singh, based on data found in A. A. Faraq, "Economic Integration: A Theoretical, Empirical Study," unpublished diss., University of Michigan, 1963.

gross social product of the countries involved. This is ridiculously small."[3] Wemelsfelder has calculated that the welfare gain of reducing import duties and increasing imports and exports accordingly amounts to .18 of 1 percent of national income.[4] Harry Johnson, in an article about England's gain in joining a Free Trade Area, calculates the net gain from trade at less than 1 percent, and concludes that 1 percent of the national income would be the absolute maximum gain for Britain from entering the European Free Trade Area.[5]

A study by L. H. Janssen calculates that the gains from increased specialization for the different countries of the European Economic Community would be largest for Italy, but even here the amount is only 1/10 of 1 percent of total production.* He points out that, if the production gain

* R. A. Mundell, in a review of Janssen's book, appears to reach a similar conclusion to the point made in this paper when he speculates that: "there have appeared in recent years studies purporting to demonstrate that the welfare loss due to monopoly is small, that the welfare importance of efficiency and production is exaggerated, and that gains from trade and the welfare gains from tariff reduction are almost negligible. Unless there is a thorough theoretical re-examination of the validity of the tools on which these studies are founded, and especially of the revitalized concepts of producers' and consumers' surplus, someone inevitably will draw the conclusion that economics has ceased to be important!" See R. A. Mundell, review of L. H. Janssen, *Free Trade, Protection, and Customs Union* in *American Economic Review*, 52:621–622 (June 1962).

for Italy resulting from specialization were calculated by Scitovsky's method, which he believes involves an overestimation, "the production gain in the most extreme case is still less than .4 per cent." Janssen concludes, as have others, that the welfare effects of a customs union based on the superior allocation of resources are likely to be trivial. He does, however, point to the possibility "that the mere prospect of the frontiers opening would infuse fresh energy into entrepreneurs."[6] He recognizes that certain qualitative factors may be highly important and that the consequences of growth are more significant than those of allocative welfare.

Ajit Singh has calculated the gains from trade (following the Scitovsky method) for the Montevideo Treaty Countries (Argentina, Brazil, Chile, Mexico, Paraguay, Peru, and Uruguay) and found it to be less than 1/150 of 1 percent of their combined GNP.[7] Even if we double or triple this result to allow for such factors as the effect of failing to take account of quantitative restrictions in the analysis, the outcome is still trivial.

Harberger's study on Chile, which involves the reallocation of both labor and capital, yields a relatively large estimate.[8] Harberger intends to obtain as large an estimate as possible of the consequences of reallocating resources by using what I believe to be (and what he admits to be) rather extreme assumptions in order to obtain maximum outer bounds. Despite this he comes up with a number between 9 and 15 percent. However, no actual data are employed; what are used are outer-bound estimates based on personal impressions. I suspect that a careful study, similar to that of Verdoorn-Scitovsky, would come up with numbers no larger than 1 or 2 percent.

The empirical evidence, although far from exhaustive, suggests that welfare gains achieved by increasing *only* allocative efficiency are usually exceedingly small, at least in capitalist economies. In all but one of the cases considered all of the gains are likely to be made up in one month's growth. They hardly seem worth worrying about.

It cannot be shown that the gains are small on purely theoretical grounds. But if we combine our theory with what we could agree are probably reasonable estimates of some of the basic magnitudes, it appears likely that in many cases (though not all *possible* cases) the welfare loss of allocative inefficiency is of trivial significance. The idea could be developed with the aid of a diagram similar to the one employed by Harberger (Figure 2). In this figure we assume that costs are constant within the relevant range. Curve D is the demand function. Under competition, price and quantity are determined at point A. The welfare loss resulting from monopoly, which is the same as the welfare gain if we shift to competition, equals the triangle ABC. We obtain an approximation to this amount by

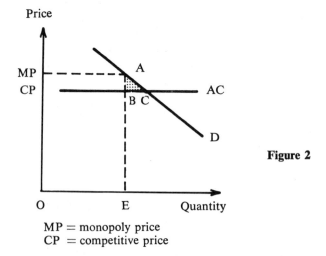

Figure 2

MP = monopoly price
CP = competitive price

multiplying the price differential AB by the quantity differential BC by one-half and multiplying this by the proportion of national income in industries involving the misallocation.

Let us play around with some numbers and see the results we get. Suppose that half of the national output is produced in monopolized industries and that the price differential is 20 percent and the average elasticity of demand is 1.5. Now the outcome will turn out to be 1½ percent. We used enormous figures for the misallocation, yet the result is small. Monopoly prices, according to estimates, appear to be only about 8 percent on the average above competitive prices. We can substitute some reason other than monopoly for the misallocation and still come out with similar results.*

Consider the cases of subsidized industries under some sort of governmental inducements to growth; and that of government-run industries. In the subsidy case the calculation would be similar. Suppose that as much as

---

* For the sake of completeness, in our estimation of consumer surplus we should take into account the income effect. It may readily be seen that this magnitude is likely to be exceedingly small. Suppose that the initial effect of a superior allocation is 1 percent; then the income effect for a noninferior good will be to shift the demand function to the right by 1 percent on the average. Thus, the addition to consumers' surplus will be 1 percent, and the consumers' surplus foregone will be roughly 1 percent of 1 percent. If we consider all consequent effects in a similar vein, then the estimated welfare loss will be $0.010101 \ldots < 0.0102$. The actual magnitude will of course be smaller because the demand will shift to the left in the case of inferior goods. For an excellent discussion of these matters see A. P. Lerner, "Consumer Surplus and Micro-Macro," *Journal of Political Economy*, 73:66ff. (February 1963).

50 percent of the industries are subsidized to the extent of a 20 percent difference in cost, and that the output point on the demand function is where elasticity is unity. This last point may be reasonable since the operators of subsidized industries might want gross revenue to be as large as possible. If, on the other hand, we assume that they are profit maximizers and restrict output to a greater extent, then we might assume a price elasticity of two. This latter is unlikely because monopoly profits are inconsistent with subsidized industries. Those who receive the subsidy would have the legitimate fear that the subsidy would be lowered if unusual profits were earned. Hence, behavior in the direction of revenue maximization appears reasonable and the calculated welfare loss is less than 2 percent.

A similar result could be achieved in the case in which the government runs industries that affect 50 percent of the national income of an economy. In all the cases we have considered, the magnitudes chosen appear to be on the large side and the outcome is on the small side.

Of course, it is possible that the magnitude of allocative inefficiency would be large if there are large discontinuities in productivity between those industries where inputs are located and those industries to which the same inputs could be moved. This in effect is the basic assumption Harberger made in his study of Chile. But if it turns out that there is a reasonable degree of continuity in productivity and that the only way shifts could be made is by simultaneously increasing either social overhead capital or direct capital in order to make the shifts involved, then a great deal of the presumed gains would be eaten up by the capital costs and the net marginal gains would turn out to be rather small. My general impression is that this is likely to be the case in a great many underdeveloped countries where differential productivities appear to exist between the agricultural sector and the industrial sector. One cannot go beyond stating vague impressions since there is a lack of hard statistical evidence on this matter.

Why are the welfare effects of reallocation so small? Allocational inefficiency involves only the net marginal effects. The basic assumption is that every firm *purchases and utilizes* all of its inputs "efficiently." Thus, what is left is simply the consequence of price and quantity distortions. Although certain specific price distortions may be large, it is unlikely that all relative price distortions are exceptionally large. This implies that most quantity distortions must also be relatively small, since for a given aggregate output a significant distortion in one commodity will be counterbalanced by a large number of small distortions in the opposite direction in quantities elsewhere. While it is possible to *assume* relative price distortions and quantity distortions that would be exceedingly high, it would be difficult to believe that, without intent, the sum of such distortions should be high. However, it is not *necessarily* so on purely a priori grounds.

One important type of distortion cannot easily be handled by existing microeconomic theory. This has to do with the allocation of managers. It is conceivable that in practice a situation would arise in which managers are exceedingly poor—that is, others are available who do not obtain management posts and who would be very much superior. Managers determine not only their own productivity but the productivity of all cooperating units in the organization. It is therefore possible that the actual loss resulting from such a misallocation might be large. However, the theory does not allow us to examine this matter because firms are presumed to exist as entities that make optimal input decisions, apart from the decisions of its managers.

X-Efficiency: Empirical Evidence

We have seen that the welfare loss resulting from allocational inefficiency is frequently no more than 1/10 of 1 percent. Is it conceivable that the value of X-inefficiency would be larger?

It is not necessary for our purposes to argue that allocative inefficiency can never be large. Suffice it to say that as calculated it frequently is not. Now we hope to show that X-inefficiency frequently is significant.

One way of examining it is to return to the problem of the welfare loss. Suppose that one-third of the industries are in the monopolized sector. Could the lack of competitive pressure of operating in monopolized industries lead to a cost 3/10 of a percent higher than would be the case under competition? This magnitude seems very small, hence it certainly seems a possibility. The question essentially is whether we can visualize managers bestirring themselves sufficiently, if the environment forced them to do so, in order to reduce costs by more than 3/10 of 1 percent. Some of the empirical evidence available suggests that not only is this a possibility but that the magnitudes involved are very much larger. As we shall see, the spotty evidence on this subject does not prove the case but it does seem to be sufficiently persuasive to suggest that X-inefficiency exists and that it frequently is much more significant than allocational inefficiency.

Eric Lundberg, in his studies of Swedish industries, points to the case of the steel plant at Horndal that was left to operate without any new capital investment or *technological change,* with maintenance and replacement kept at a minimum, and yet where output per man hour rose by 2 percent per annum. He asserts that, according to his interviews with industrialists and technicians, "suboptimal disequilibrium in regard to technology and utilization of existing capital stock is a profoundly important aspect of the situation at any time." (This is according to Göran Ohlin's summary of Lundberg's findings.[9]) If a suboptimal disequilibrium exists at any time, it would seem reasonable that under the proper motivations managers and workers could produce closer to optimality, and that under other conditions they may be motivated to move farther away from optimality.

Frederick Harbison reports visiting two petroleum refineries in Egypt less than a half-mile apart: "The labor productivity of one had been nearly double that in the other for many years. But recently, under completely new management, the inefficient refinery was beginning to make quite spectacular improvements in efficiency with the same labor force."[10] We may inquire why the management was changed only recently, whereas the difference in labor productivity existed for many years. It is quite possible that had the motivation been strong enough this change could have taken place earlier.

In a recent book on the firm, Neil Chamberlain visualizes his firms reacting to variances between forecasted revenues and expenditures and actual. He quotes from the president of a corporation: "Actual sales revenue for the fiscal year varied one per cent from the original forecast. Expenditures varied 30 per cent. The reasons were practically entirely due to manufacturing problems of inefficiency and quality. . . . The only actions specifically taken were in attempted changes in methods of production . . . [and] the use of an engineering consulting firm."[11] One would have thought that the cost-reducing activities mentioned could be carried out irrespective of the variance. Nevertheless, the quotation clearly implied that they would not have been motivated to attempt the changes had they not been stimulated by the variance.

Before presenting more empirical evidence on the possible magnitude of X-inefficiency, it is important to say something about the nature of the data. The empirical evidence does not present many unambiguous cases. Most of it has to do with specific firms or, at best, industries, not for the economy as a whole. In the evidence on allocative efficiency the entire economy was considered. It is possible that the cases considered are entirely atypical and could not be duplicated in large segments of the economy. In addition, they do not always deal with X-efficiency in a pure sense; additional inputs or reallocations are sometimes involved. Also uncertainty elements and accidental variations play a role. Nevertheless, the magnitudes involved are so large that they suggest that the conjecture that X-inefficiency is frequently more significant than allocative inefficiency must be taken seriously.

Now let us turn to Tables 1 and 2. In contrast to Table 1, where the misallocation effects are small, Table 2 shows that the X-efficiency effects, at least for specific firms, are usually large. It abstracts (in the interest of

Table 2. ILO productivity mission results (percentages).

Factory or operation	Method[a]	Increase in labor productivity	Impact on the firm (unit cost reduction)	
			Labor savings	Capital[b] savings
India				
Seven textile mills	–	5–250	5–71	5–71
Engineering firms				
All operations	F, B	102	50	50
One operation	F	385	79	79
One operation	F	500	83	83
Burma				
Molding railroad brake shoes	A, F, B	100	50	50
Smithy	A	40	29	20
Chair assembly	A, B	100	50	50
Match manufacture	A, F	24	19	–
Indonesia				
Knitting	A, B	15	13	–
Radio assembly	A, F	40	29	29
Printing	A, F	30	23	–
Enamel ware	F	30	23	–
Malaya				
Furniture	A, D	10	9	9
Engineering workshop	A, D	10	9	9
Pottery	A, B	20	17	17
Thailand				
Locomotive maintenance	A, F	44	31	31
Saucepan polishing	E, D	50	33	–
Saucepan assembly	B, F	42	30	–
Cigarettes	A, B	5	5	–
Pakistan				
Textile plants	C, H, G,			
Weaving		50	33	33
Weaving		10	9	9
Bleaching		59	37	37
Weaving		141	29	29
Israel				
Locomotive repair	F, B, G	30	23	23
Diamond cutting and polishing	C, B, G	45	31	–
Refrigerator assembly	F, B, G	75	43	43
Orange picking	F	91	47	–

[a] A = plant layout reorganized   E = waste control
B = machine utilization and flow   F = work method
C = simple technical alterations   G = payment by results
D = materials handling   H = workers training and supervision
[b] Limited to plant and equipment, excluding increased depreciation costs.

Source: Peter Kilby, "Organization and Productivity in Backward Economies," *Quarterly Journal of Economics,* 76:305 (May 1962).

conserving space) from a much more comprehensive table developed by Kilby that summarizes the results of a number of ILO productivity missions.[12] (I usually picked for each country the first three and the last items contained in Kilby's table.) Note that the cost-reducing methods used do not involve additional capital nor, as far as one can tell, any increase in depreciation or obsolescence of existing capital. They usually involve simple reorganizations of the production process such as plant-layout reorganization, materials handling, waste controls, work methods, and payments by results. The cost reductions are frequently higher than 25 percent—a result that is true for a technically advanced country such as Israel as well as for the developing countries considered in other parts of the table. If the firms and/or operations considered are representative, it would appear that the contrast in significance between X-efficiency and allocative efficiency is startling. Representativeness has not been established. However, the reports of the productivity missions do not suggest that they went out of their way to work only on cases where large savings in costs could be obtained. By comparative standards (with other productivity missions) some of the results were modest, and in some cases Kilby reports that when some members of the missions returned to firms they had worked on previously (for example, in Pakistan) they found a reversion to previous methods and productivities.

A number of other studies, in addition to those by Lundberg and Harbison, present results similar to the ILO reports. L. Rostas, in his study of comparative productivity in British and American industry, points to the finding that differences in amount and quality of machinery per worker and the rates of utilization and replacement do not account for the entire difference in output per worker in the two countries. He further states that "in a number of industries (or firms) where the equipment is very largely identical in the U.S. and U.K., e.g., boots and shoes, tobacco, strip steel (or in firms producing both in the U.K. and U.S. . . .), there are still substantial differences in output per worker in the U.K. and the U.S."[13] Clearly there is more to the determination of output than the obviously observable inputs. The nature of the management, the environment in which it operates, and the incentives employed are significant.

That changes in incentives will change productivity per man (and cost per unit of output) is demonstrated by a wide variety of studies on the effects of introducing payments by results schemes. Davison, Florence, Gray, and Ross review the literature in this area for British industry, survey the results for a number of manufacturing operations, and present illustrative examples of their findings. Their summary follows: "The change in output per worker was found to vary among the different operations all the way from an increase in 7.5 per cent to one of 291 per cent, about half the cases falling between 43 per cent and 76 per cent. Such increases in output, most of them large, from our 'first-line' case histories, and from additional evidence, were found not to be just a 'flash in the pan' but were sustained over the whole period of study."[14]

Roughly similar findings were obtained for the consequences of introducing payments by results in Australia, Belgium, India, the Netherlands, and the United States. In Victoria it was found that "soundly designed and properly operated incentive plans have in practice increased production rate in the reporting firms from 20 to 50 per cent."[15] In the Netherlands labor efficiency increases of 36.5 percent were reported. It seems clear that with the same type of equipment the working tempo varies considerably both between different workers and between different departments. Appropriate incentives can change such tempos considerably and reduce costs, without any changes in purchasable inputs per unit.

The now-famous Hawthorne Studies suggest that the mere fact that management shows an interest in a certain group of workers can increase output.[16] Management's greater interest in the group on whom the experiments were tried, both when working conditions were improved and when they were worsened, created a positive motivation ranging from 13 to 30 percent.[17] In one of the ILO missions to Pakistan an improvement in labor relations in a textile mill in Lyallpur resulted in a productivity increase of 30 percent. Nothing else was changed except that labor turnover was reduced by one-fifth.[18]

Individual variations in worker proficiency are probably larger than plant differences. Frequently the variation between the best to poorest worker is as much as four to one. Certainly improved worker selection could improve productivity at the plant level. To the extent that people are not working at what they are most proficient at, productivity should rise as a consequence of superior selection methods.[19]

Although much has been written about the importance of psychological factors on productivity, it is difficult to assess this literature because many psychologists work on the basis of high-and-low productivity groups but do not report the actual numerical differences. In general, it seems that some of the psychological factors studied in terms of small-group theory can account for differences in productivity of from 7 to 18 percent. The discoveries include such findings as: (1) up to a point smaller working units are more productive than larger ones; (2) working units made up of friends are more productive than those made up of nonfriends; (3) units that are generally supervised are more efficient than those that are closely supervised;[20] and (4) units that are given more information about the

importance of their work are more proficient than those given less information.[21] A partial reason for these observed differences is probably the
likelihood that individual motivation toward work is differently affected
under the different circumstances mentioned.

The shorter-hours movement in Western Europe and in the United
States, especially up to World War I, has some interesting lessons for
productivity differentials without capital changes. Economists frequently
assume that for a given capital stock and quality of work force, output will
be proportional to number of hours worked. Experiments during World
War I and later showed that not only was the proportionality law untrue,
but that frequently *absolute* output actually increased with reductions in
hours—say from a ten-hour day to an eight-hour day.[22] It was also found
that with longer hours a disproportionate amount of time was lost from
increased absenteeism, industrial accidents, and so on. In many cases it
would have been to a firm's interest to reduce hours below that of the rest
of the industry. Firms could have investigated these relations and taken
advantage of the findings. For the most part, governments sponsored the
necessary research on the economics of fatigue and unrest under the
stimulus of the war effort, when productivity in some sectors of the
economy was believed to be crucial. The actual reduction of hours that
took place was a consequence of the pressure of labor unions and national
legislation.

In this connection it is interesting that Carter and Williams, in their
study of investment in innovations, found a high proportion (over 40
percent) of "passive" character—that is, resulting from either "direct
pressure of competition" or "force of example of firms (etc.) other than
immediate rivals."[23] Unfortunately it is difficult to find data representing
the obverse side of the coin and suggesting the degree to which firms do not
innovate through lack of a sufficient motivating force, such as competitive
pressure. However, there is a great deal of evidence that the delay time
between invention and innovation is often exceedingly long (sometimes
more than fifty years),[24] and the time lag between the use of new methods
in the "best practice" firms in an industry and other firms is also often a
matter of years. Salter points to the following striking example. "In the
United States copper mines, electric locomotives allow a cost saving of 67
per cent . . . yet although first used in the mid-twenties, by 1940 less
than a third of locomotives in use were electric."[25] Similar examples are
cited by Salter and others. A survey of industrial research undertaken by
seventy-seven companies showed that one-third were carrying on research
for "aggressive purposes," but that two-thirds were "forced into research
for defensive purposes."[26]

The relation between the "cost" of advice or consulting services and the return obtained has not been worked out for the ILO productivity missions as a whole. In one case (in Pakistan) the savings effected in three textile mills as a consequence of the work of the mission was about twenty times the entire cost of the mission that year. Although the study does not indicate how representative this result was, the impression one gets is that rates of return of rather large magnitudes are not entirely unusual.

John Johnston studied the return to consulting services in Great Britain. For the class of jobs where it was possible to make a quantitative assessment of the results (six hundred jobs were involved), it was found that on the average the rate of return was about 200 percent on consulting fees. This work is of special interest because it is a very careful study and the magnitudes of increases in productivity are of the same order (although the variations are less extreme) as those obtained in underdeveloped countries. The nature of the consulting was not dissimilar to that carried out by the ILO teams. On the whole it involved improvements in general management, plant layout, personnel, production procedures, selling organization, management, and budgeting and accounting systems. For the consulting jobs whose consequences were quantitatively assessed, the average increase in productivity was 53 percent, with the lowest quartile showing an increase in 30 percent and the highest 70 percent.[27]

The studies mentioned deal with examples that are more or less of a microeconomic nature. In recent years we have had a number of studies that are their *macro*economic complements. The work of Solow, Aukrust, Denison, and others shows that only a small proportion of increase in GNP is accounted for by increases in inputs of labor or capital. The "unexplained residual" covers from about 50 to 80 percent of growth in advanced countries.[28] The residual comprehends a greater range of "noninput" growth factors (for example, technological change and education of the labor force) than was covered in the examples we considered, but the motivational efficiency elements may account for some fraction of the residual. (Johnston estimates that one quarter of the annual increase in product is accounted for by consulting services.)

What conclusions can we draw from all of this? First, the data suggest that there is a great deal of possible variation in output for similar amounts of capital and labor and for similar techniques, in the broad sense, to the extent that technique is determined by similar types of equipment. However, in most of the studies the nature of the influences involved are mixed, and in some cases not all of them are clear to the analyst. In many instances there appears to have been an attempt to impart knowledge, at least of a managerial variety, which accounts for *some* of the increase in output. But should this knowledge be looked upon as an increase in inputs of production in all instances? Although the first reaction might be that such attempts involve inputs similar to inputs of capital or labor, I will argue that in many instances this is not the case.

It is obvious that not every change in technique implies a change in knowledge. The knowledge may have been there already, and a change in circumstances simply induced the change in technique. In addition, knowledge may not be used to capacity just as capital or labor may be underutilized. More important, a good deal of our knowledge is vague. A man may have nothing more than a sense of its existence, and yet this may be the critical element. Given a sufficient inducement, he can search out its nature in detail and get it to a stage where he can use it. People normally operate within the bounds of a great deal of intellectual slack. Unlike underutilized capital, this is an element that is very difficult to observe. As a result, occasions of genuine additions to knowledge are hard to distinguish from those circumstances in which no new knowledge has been added but in which existing knowledge is being utilized to greater capacity.

Experience in United States industry suggests that adversity frequently stimulates cost-reducing attempts, some of which are successful, within the bounds of existing knowledge.[29] In any event, some of the studies suggest that motivational aspects are involved entirely apart from additional knowledge. The difficulty of assessment arises because these elements are frequently so intertwined that it is difficult to separate them.

Let us consider types of instances in which the motivational aspect appears fairly clearly to play a role. The ILO studies discuss a number of cases in India and Pakistan in which, when demonstration projects were revisited after a year or more, there had been a reversion to less efficient techniques. This seems to have occurred both in India and in Pakistan.[30] Clearly, any new knowledge was given to the management by the productivity mission at the outset and new management methods were installed at least for the period during which the productivity mission was on hand, but there was not sufficient motivational force for the management to maintain the new methods. The "Hawthorne effects" are more clear-cut. Here an intentional reversion to previous methods still led to some increases in output simply because the motivational aspects were more important than the changes in the work methods. The ILO mission reports also mention with regret the fact that techniques applied in one portion of a plant, which led to fairly large increases in productivity, were not applied to other aspects of the production process, although this could quite easily have been done. In a sense we may argue that the knowledge was available to the management but that somehow it was not motivated to transfer techniques from one part of a plant to another.

Studies which showed increases in output as a consequence of introducing payment by results clearly involved motivational elements. For the men subjected to the new payment scheme economic motivations are involved. For the management the situation is less clear. In many instances the firms may not have been aware of the possible advantages of payment by results until they obtained the new knowledge that led to the introduction of the scheme. However, it seems more likely that the scheme is so well known that this often is not the case. Management probably had to be motivated to introduce the scheme by factors either within the firm or within the industry. In any event, these studies suggest that for some aspects of production, motivational elements are significant.

Both the ILO reports and the Johnston study speak of the need to win the acceptance of top management for the idea of obtaining and implementing consulting advice. In addition, the ILO studies make the point that low productivity is frequently caused by top management's concern with the commercial and financial affairs of the firm rather than with the running of the factory. The latter was frequently treated as a very subordinate task. Whether this last aspect involves a lack of knowledge or a lack of motivation is difficult to determine. But it seems hard to believe that if top-management people in some of the firms in a given industry were to become concerned with factory management and achieve desirable results thereby, others would not follow suit. Johnston makes the point that, "without the willing cooperation of management the consultant is unlikely to be called in the first instance or to stay for long if he does come in."[31] The ILO missions make similar remarks.

Consulting services are profitable not only to consultants but also to many of the firms that employ them. It is surprising that more of these services are not called for. Part of the answer may be that managements are not motivated to hire consultants if things appear to be going "in any reasonably satisfactory rate." There are numerous personal resistances to calling for outside advice. If the motivation is strong enough, for example, a threat of the firm's failure, then it is likely that such resistances would be overcome. But these are simply different aspects of the motivational elements involved.

Recent Empirical Evidence

Since I first presented (1966) the main materials in this chapter a considerable amount of empirical evidence has been brought out. To my mind the new evidence supports the earlier assertions, especially the idea that a high degree of X-inefficiency exists at the firm and industry level. While the caveats made because of the methodological difficulties underlying the evidence presented earlier would have to be repeated for many items that would be included in a detailed survey, there are now some studies at the national and industry level for which the previously mentioned difficulties do not hold, or do not hold to the same extent.

A study by J. P. Shelton compared owner-operated franchised restaurants with manager-operated units in which the franchises were held by the parent company. All the restaurants were directed in such a way by the franchise-issuing company that an unusual degree of uniformity existed with respect to menus, optimal recipes, manuals for waitresses, and so forth, so as to achieve standardized services as well as standardized book-keeping and record-keeping operated through the parent company's computers. Despite the very high degree of standardization, and despite the fact that there was only a slight advantage in sales volume for the owner-operated franchises, the owner-operated units had a profit margin of 9.5 percent whereas the manager-operated units averaged only 1.8 percent. In only two of the owner-operated units were there losses, but almost half of the manager-operated units showed losses. A company executive summed up the results with the remark, "This is because franchise-owners just watch the little things closer; they utilize the cooks and waitresses better: *they reduce waste*" (italics mine).[32]

A careful study by W. J. Primeaux, Jr., compared cities which had more than one electric power company (there are forty-nine such cities in the United States) with those that had a single electric power monopoly. He found, after taking economies of scale into account, "that average cost is reduced, at the mean, by 10.75 percent because of competition. This reflects a quantitative value of the presence of X-efficiency gained through competition; or an estimate of the loss caused by the absence of competition in a regulated environment."[33]

T. Y. Shen studied technological diffusion as an element that influenced cost in four thousand Massachusetts plants (data from 1935–1959) and found that "it is necessary to recognize the presence of a further systematic influence that also affects the change of input-output combinations of manufacturing plants over time. . . . We find the observed behavior pattern is better explained by the prevalence of 'X-efficiency' rather than by substitution . . . this tentative finding is put to a further test by a perusal of the nature of factor intensity change. Once more the X-efficiency hypothesis turns out to be more consistent with the data. We conclude that a technological change model based on diffusion requires the estimation and incorporation of X-efficiency. Until this step is taken, the use of the extended diffusion model for explaining growth is of dubious validity."[34]

Shepherd, in a study of 21? American firms, concludes that "size carries a negative co-efficient, perhaps owing to X-inefficiency of large absolute scale." For a group of "fifty firms in mature slow-growing homogenous . . . industries," he found that "the 50-firm group comes closest to fitting the umbrella-pricing hypothesis. The odds are that the observed decline in profitability above market shares of 27 per cent arises at least partly from relative X-inefficiency, as other evidence about steel and meatpacking firms has cumulatively suggested."[35]

Bergsman, in a study on the effects of protection (which reduces competition), found that "X-inefficiency plus monopoly returns are larger than the costs of misallocation, and tend to be large enough to matter. Of the six countries studied, they are about 5 or 6 per cent of GNP in two countries, and between 2 and 3 per cent in three others. These effects seem to depend only on the level of protection; size of domestic markets does not seem to affect them."[36]

A body of evidence on the relation between extent of ownership in management and profits that has bearing on X-efficiency is gradually accumulating. Because cost comparisons are not made directly, the implications of these studies are difficult to assess, although the results can be interpreted as conforming with the X-efficiency hypothesis. To a very high degree studies by Monsen, Chiu, and Cooley, Hindly, and Masson, and especially by Radice, Palmer, and Nyman, support the contention that where the ownership component in management is higher, profit rates are higher; and some of the writers interpret this to mean that efficiency is higher.[37] In fact the relation between ownership and efficiency may be stronger than ownership and profits, since according to the Baumol and Marris hypotheses, there may be a profits-growth trade-off to some degree.

As for recent British experience, the consequences of the introduction of the three-day week, under the Heath government (1974), were such that many industries reported that, although firms operated only 60 percent or less of normal time, output was 70 to 80 percent normal.[38]

Summary and Conclusions

The main burden of these findings is that X-inefficiency exists and that improvement in X-efficiency is a significant source of increased output. In general we may specify four elements as significant in determining what I have called X-efficiency: individual motivational efficiency; intraplant motivational efficiency; external motivational efficiency; and nonmarket input efficiency.

Neither individuals nor firms work as hard or search for information as effectively as they could. The importance of motivation and its association with degree of effort and search arises because the relation between inputs and outputs is *not* a determinate one. There are four reasons why given inputs cannot be transformed into predetermined outputs: contracts for labor are incomplete; not all factors of production are marketed; the production function is not completely specified or known; and interdependence and uncertainty lead competing firms to cooperate tacitly with each other in some respects, and to imitate each other with respect to technique, to some degree.

The conventional theoretical assumption, rarely stated, is that inputs have a fixed specification and yield a fixed performance. This ignores other possibilities. Inputs may have a fixed specification that yields a variable performance, or they may be of a variable specification and yield a variable performance. Some types of complex machinery may have fixed specifications, but their performance may be variable depending on the exact nature of their employment. The most common case is that of labor services of various kinds that have variable specifications and variable performance— although markets sometimes operate as if much of the labor of a given class has a fixed specification. Moreover, it is exceedingly rare for all elements of performance in a labor contract to be spelled out. In considerable part this is the result of the inherent complexity of labor as an input. A good deal is left to custom, authority, and whatever motivational techniques are available to management as well as to individual discretion and judgment.

Similarly, the production function is neither completely specified nor known. There is an experimental element involved so that something may be known about the current state—say the existing relation between inputs and outputs—but not what will happen given changes in the input ratios. In addition, important inputs are frequently not marketed or, if they are traded, they are not equally accessible (or accessible on equal terms) to potential buyers. This is especially true of management knowledge. Managers are available in well-organized markets in many areas of the world. But even when available, their capacities may not be known. One of the important capacities of management may be the degree to which managers can obtain factors of production that are not marketed in well-organized markets or on a universalistic basis. In underdeveloped countries the capacity to obtain finance may depend on family connections. Trustworthiness may be similarly determined. Certain types of market information may be available to some individuals but not purchasable in the market. Obviously it is one thing to purchase or hire inputs in a given combination; it is something else to get a predetermined output out of them.

Another possible interpretation of the data is in connection with the "residual" in economic growth analysis. The residual manifests itself in three basic ways: through cost reduction in the production of existing commodities without inventions or innovations; the introduction of innovations in the process of production; and the introduction of new commodities or, what is the same thing, quality improvements in consumer goods or inputs. The data suggest that cost reduction that is essentially a result of improvement in X-inefficiency is likely to be an important component of the observed residual in economic growth. In addition, and perhaps more important, in some of the cases of reduced cost knowledge was conveyed to the firms involved—knowledge already available—and this too is part of the residual. Such knowledge involved knowledge dissemination rather than invention.

Both competition and adversity create pressure for change. If knowledge is vague, *if the incentive is strong enough,* there will be an attempt to augment information so that it becomes less vague and possibly useful. Where consulting advice is available, relatively few firms buy it. Clearly motivations play a role in determining the degree that advice is sought. Where motivation is weak, firms will not seek cost-improving methods. Cyert and March point to cases in which costs per unit are allowed to rise when profits are high.[39] I have just cited cases in which there was a reversion to less efficient methods once the consultants had left. Thus we have instances where competitive pressures from other firms or adversity lead to efforts toward cost reduction, and the absence of pressures allows costs to rise.

I suggested four reasons for X-inefficiency connected with the basic notion of variable performance for given units of the inputs: contracts for labor are incomplete; the production function is not completely specified or known; not all inputs are marketed or, if marketed, are not available on equal terms to all buyers; and the *effective* utilization of an input depends on the degree of motivational pressure, as well as on other motivational factors. The responses to such pressures, whether in the nature of effort, search, or the utilization of new information, may be a significant part of the residual in economic growth. These facts suggest an approach to the theory of the firm that does not depend on the assumption of cost-minimization.

One idea that emerges is that firms and economies do not operate on an outer-bound production possibility surface consistent with their resources. Rather, they actually work on a production surface well within that outer bound. For a variety of reasons people and organizations normally work neither as hard nor as effectively as they could. Two general types of movements are possible. One is along a production surface toward greater allocative efficiency and the other is from a lower surface to a higher one that involves greater degrees of X-efficiency. The data suggest that in a great many instances the amount to be gained by increasing allocative efficiency is trivial, while the amount to be gained by increasing X-efficiency is frequently significant.

4 Bandwagon, Snob, and Veblen Effects in the Theory of Consumers' Demand

"Bandwagon" and "Snob" immediately suggest interdependencies in behavior, and observation suggests that this includes consumption behavior. This chapter treats the reformulation of some aspects of consumers' demand theory in order to include such interdependencies. Such an approach will allow us to relax one of the basic implicit assumptions of the current theory—that the consumption behavior of any individual or household is independent of the consumption of others.

In taking account of consumers' motivations usually not incorporated into the theory, we will consider the desire of people to wear, buy, do, consume, and behave like their fellows; the desire to join the crowd, be "one of the boys," and so on—phenomena of mob motivations and mass psychology either in their grosser or more delicate aspects. This is the type of behavior involved in what I call the "bandwagon effect." On the other hand, we will take account of the search for exclusiveness by individuals through the purchase of distinctive clothing, foods, automobiles, houses, or anything else they may believe will in some way set them off from the mass of mankind—or add to their prestige, dignity, and social status. Over all, we shall be concerned with the impact on the theory created by the potential nonfunctional utilities inherent in many commodities.

The Literature

The literature on the interpersonal aspects of utility and demand can be divided into three categories: sociology, welfare economics, and pure theory. Sociological writings deal with the phenomena of fashions and conspicuous consumption and their relation to social status and human behavior. This treatment of the subject was made famous by Veblen—although Veblen was neither the discoverer nor the first to elaborate upon the theory of conspicuous consumption. John Rae, writing before 1834, has quite an extensive treatment of conspicuous consumption, fashions, and related matters pretty much along Veblenian lines. He attributes many of these ideas to earlier writers, going so far as to find the notion of conspicuous consumption in the Roman poet Horace, and a clear statement of the "keeping up with the Joneses" idea in the verse of Alexander Pope.[1] An excellent account of how eighteenth- and nineteenth-century philosophers and economists handled the problem of fashion is given in Norine Foley's article "Fashion."[2] For the most part, these treatments are of a "sociological" nature.

The economist concerned with public policy will probably find the "economic welfare" treatment most interesting. Here, if we start with the more recent contributions, then work backward, we find examples of current writers believing they have stumbled upon something new, although they had only rediscovered what had been said many years before. Thus, M. W. Reder in his treatment of the theory of welfare economics claims that "there is another type of external repercussion which is rarely, *if ever,* recognized in discussions of welfare economics. It occurs where the utility function of one individual contains, as variables, the quantities of goods consumed by other persons."[3] Among earlier writers who have considered the problem to some degree are J. E. Meade, A. C. Pigou, Henry Cunynghame, and John Rae.[4]

The similarity in the treatment of this matter by Reder and Rae is at times striking. For example, Reder suggests that legislation forbidding "invidious expenditure" may result in an increase in welfare by freeing resources from "competitive consumption" to other uses. In a similar vein, Rae argues that restrictions on the trade of "pure luxuries" can only be a gain to some and a loss to none, in view of the labor saved in avoiding such production. It is clear from the context that what Rae calls "pure luxuries" are the same as Reder's commodities that enter into "competitive consumption."[5]

One reason why the interpersonal effects on demand have been ignored in current texts may be the fact that Marshall did not consider the matter in his *Principles,* although we know from his correspondence, that he was aware of it.[6] Both Cunynghame and Pigou pointed out that Marshall's treatment of consumers' surplus did not take into account interpersonal effects on utility, apparently feeling it would make the diagrammatical treatment too complex. Recently, Reder and Samuelson noticed that external economies and diseconomies of consumption may vitiate (or, at best, greatly complicate) their "new" welfare analysis; hence, they assume the problem away.[7]

The only attack on the problem from the point of view of pure theory that I could find[8] is a short article by Pigou. In this he sets out to inquire under what circumstances the assumption of the additivity of the individual demand curves "adequately conforms to the facts, and, when it does not so conform, what alternative assumption ought to be substituted for it." It is obvious that the particular choice of alternative assumptions will determine whether a solution can, given the existing analytical tools, be obtained, and whether such a solution is relevant to the real world. Pigou's treatment of the problem is, unfortunately, exceedingly brief. He attempts to deal with nonadditivity in both supply and demand curves within the confines of six pages. In examining the additivity assumption he points out that it is warranted when the demand for the commodity is wholly for the direct satisfaction yielded by it or where disturbances to equilibrium are so small that aggregate output is not greatly changed. After briefly suggesting some of the complexities of nonadditivity he concludes that the "problems, for the investigation of which it is necessary to go behind the demand schedule of the market as a whole, are still, theoretically, soluble; there are a sufficient number of equations to determine the unknowns."[9] This last point, which is not demonstrated in Pigou's article, is hardly satisfying, since it has been shown that the equality of equations and unknowns is not a sufficient condition for a determinate solution, or indeed for any solution, to exist.[10]

The Approach and Limits of the Ensuing Analysis

It should, perhaps, be pointed out at the outset that the ensuing exposition is limited to statics. In all probability, the most interesting parts of the problem, and also those most relevant to real problems, are its dynamic aspects. However, a static analysis is probably necessary, and may be of significance, in order to lay a foundation for a dynamic analysis. In view of the limitations to be set, it is necessary to demarcate the conceptual border between statics and dynamics.

Because of the numerous definitions of statics, there seems to be some confusion about the matter. Accordingly, it will not be possible to give *the* definition of statics. All we can hope to do is to choose *a* definition that will be consistent with and useful for our purposes—and also one that does not stray too far from some of the generally accepted notions about statics. Since we live in a dynamic world most definitions of statics imply a state of affairs that contradicts our general experience. But this is of necessity the case. What we must insist on is internal consistency, but we need not, at this stage, require "realism."

Our task is to define a static situation—a situation in which static economics is applicable. Ordinarily statics are thought to be in some way "timeless." This need not be the case. For our purposes a static situation is not a "timeless" situation, nor is static economics timeless economics. It is, however, "temporally orderless," so I shall define a static situation as one in which the order of events is of no significance. We, therefore, abstract from the consequences of the temporal order of events.[11] The above definition resembles, perhaps on a slightly higher level of generality, Hicks's notion that statics deals with "those parts of economic theory where we do not have to trouble about dating."[12]

To preserve internal consistency it is necessary to assume that the period of reference is one in which the consumer's income and expenditure pattern is synchronized. And, we must assume too that this holds true for all consumers. In other words, we assume that both the income patterns and the expenditure patterns repeat themselves *every* period. There is thus no overlapping of expenditures from one period into the next. This implies that the demand curve reconstitutes itself every period.* The foregoing implies also that only one price can change only from period to period. A disequilibrium can, therefore, be corrected only over two or more periods.

Functional and Nonfunctional Demand

The demand for consumers' goods and services may be classified, according to motivation, into functional, nonfunctional, and speculative. Functional demand refers to that part of the demand for a commodity resulting from the commodity's inherent qualities. Nonfunctional demand is that portion of the demand for a consumers' good which results from factors other than the qualities inherent in the commodity. Probably the most important kind of nonfunctional demand is caused by external effects on utility. That is, the utility derived from the commodity is inhanced or decreased because others are purchasing and consuming the same commodity or because the commodity bears a higher rather than a lower price tag. I divide this type of demand into the "bandwagon" effect, the "snob" effect, and the "Veblen" effect.† The bandwagon effect refers to the extent to which the demand for a commodity is *increased* because others are consuming the same commodity. It reflects the desire to purchase a commodity in order to get into "the swim of things," in order to conform with those they wish to be associated with, in order to be fashionable or stylish. By

* The above assumptions are necessary in order to take care of some of the difficulties raised by Oskar Morgenstern in "Demand Theory Reconsidered."

† These terms will be used in the special sense here defined; hence hereafter the quotation marks will be deleted.

the snob effect I refer to the extent to which the demand for a consumers' good is *decreased* owing to the fact that others are consuming the same commodity (or increasing their consumption of that commodity). This reflects the desire of people to be exclusive, to be different, to dissociate themselves from the "common herd." The Veblen effect refers to the phenomenon of conspicuous consumption, to the extent to which the demand for a consumers' good is increased because it bears a higher rather than a lower price. The distinction I make between the snob and the Veblen effect is that the former is a function of the consumption of others, the latter is a function of price.*

The Bandwagon Effect

Our immediate task is to obtain aggregate demand curves of various kinds for cases in which individual demand curves are nonadditive. First we shall examine the case where the bandwagon effect is important. In its pure form this is the case where an individual will demand more (less) of a commodity at a given price because some or all other individuals in the market also demand more (less) of the commodity. One difficulty in analyzing this type of demand involves the choice of assumptions about the knowledge each individual possesses. This implies that everyone knows the quantity to be demanded by each individual separately or that demanded by all collectively at any given price—after the reactions and adjustments that individuals make to each other's demand has been made. If we assume ignorance on the part of consumers about the demand of others, we have to make assumptions as to the nature and extent of the ignorance. A third possibility, and the one that will be employed at first, is to devise some mechanism whereby the consumers obtain accurate information.

Another problem is the choice of assumptions to be made about the demand behavior of individual consumers. Three possibilities suggest themselves. First, the demand of consumer *A* (at given prices) may be a function of the total demand of all in the market collectively. Or the demand of consumer *A* may be a function of the demand of all other consumers both separately and collectively; in other words, *A*'s demand may be more influenced by the demand of some than by the demand of others. A third possibility is that *A*'s demand is a function of the number of people demanding the commodity rather than the number of units de-

* Some writers have not made this distinction, but have combined the two effects into what they termed "snob behavior" (see Morgenstern, "Professor Hicks on Value and Capital," p. 190). The above does not imply that my distinction is necessarily the "correct" one, but only that it is found useful in my analysis.

manded. More complex demand behavior patterns that combine some of the elements of the above are conceivable. For our purposes it is best to assume the simplest one as a first approximation. Initially, therefore, we assume that A's demand is a function of the units demanded by all others collectively. This is the same as saying that A's demand is a function of total market demand at given prices, since A always knows his own demand and could subtract it from the total market demand to get the quantity demanded by all others.

In order to bring out the central principle involved in the insuing analysis, consider the following *gedankenexperiment*. A known product is to be introduced into a well-defined market at a certain date. The nature of the product is such that its demand depends partly on its functional qualities and partly on whether many or few units are demanded. Our technical problem is to combine the nonadditive individual demand curves into a total market demand curve, given sufficient information about the individual demand functions. Now, suppose it is possible to obtain accurate knowledge about an individual's demand function through a series of questionnaires. Since an individual's demand is, in part, a function of the total market demand, it is necessary to take care of this difficulty through our questionnaires. We can have a potential consumer fill out the first questionnaire by asking him to assume that the total market demand at all prices is a given very small amount—say 400 units. On the basis of this assumption the consumer would tell us the quantities he demands over a reasonable range of prices. Subjecting every consumer to the same questionnaire, we add the results across and obtain a market demand curve reflecting the demand situation if every consumer believed the total demand were only 400 units. This, however, is not the real market demand function, assuming accurate market information on the part of consumers, since the total demand (at each price) upon which the consumers based their replies was not the actual market demand (at each price) as revealed by the results of the survey. Let us call the results of the first survey "schedule No. 1."

We can carry out a second survey, subject each consumer to a questionnaire in which each is told that schedule No. 1 reflects the total quantities demanded, at each price. Aggregating the replies we obtain schedule No. 2. Schedule No. 1 then becomes a parameter upon which schedule No. 2 is based. In a similar manner we can obtain schedules No. 3, No. 4, . . . , No. n, in which each schedule results from adding the quantities demanded by each consumer (at each price) *if each consumer believes that the total quantities demanded (at each price) are shown by the previous schedule.* The quantities demanded in schedule No. 2 will be greater than or equal to the quantities demanded in schedule No. 1 for the same prices. Some consumers may increase the quantity they demand when they note that the total quantity demanded, at given prices, is greater than they thought it would be. As long as some consumers or potential consumers continue to react positively to increases in the total quantity demanded the results of successive surveys will be different. In other words, some or all of the quantities demanded in schedule No. 1 will be less than the quantities demanded, at the same prices, in schedule No. 2, which in turn will be equal to or less than the quantities demanded, at the same prices, in schedule No. 3, and so on.

At this point it is appropriate to introduce a new principle with the intention of showing that this process cannot go on indefinitely. Sooner or later two successive schedules will be identical. If two successive surveys yield the same market demand schedules, an equilibrium situation exists, since the total quantities demanded, at each price, upon which individual consumers based their demand, turns out to be correct. Thus, if schedule No. n is identical with schedule No. n-1, then schedule No. n is the actual market demand function for the product, assuming that consumers have accurate information of market conditions.

The question that arises is whether there is reason to suppose that sooner or later two successive surveys will yield exactly the same result. This would indeed be the case if we could find good reason to posit a principle to the effect that *for every individual there is some point at which he will cease to increase the quantities demanded for a commodity, at given prices, in response to incremental increases in total market demand*. Such a principle would imply that beyond a point incremental increases in the demand for the commodity by others have a decreasing influence in a consumer's own demand; and, further, that a point is reached at which these increases in demand by others have no influence whatsoever on his own demand. It would also be necessary to establish that such a principle holds true for every consumer. It would not be inappropriate to call this the principle of diminishing marginal external consumption effect. Does such a principle really exist? There are good reasons for believing that it does. First, note that the principle is analogous to the principle of diminishing marginal utility. As the total market demand grows, incremental increases in it become smaller proportions of the demand. It sounds reasonable, and probably appeals to us intuitively, that an individual would be less influenced, and take less notice of, a 1 percent increase in total demand, than of a 10 percent increase in total demand, though these percentage increases be the same in absolute amount. Second, we can probably appeal effectively to general experience. There are no cases in which an individual's demand for a consumers' good increases endlessly with increases in total demand. If there were two or more such individuals in a market, then the demand for the commodity would increase in an endless spiral. Last but not least, the income constraint is sufficient to establish that there must be a point at which increases in a consumer's demand must fail to respond to increases in demand by others. Because every consumer is subject to the income constraint, it follows that the principle holds for all consumers.

To get back to our conceptual experiment, we would find that after administering a sufficient number of surveys sooner or later we would get two yielding identical demand schedules. The result of the last survey would then represent the true demand situation that would manifest itself on the market when the commodity was offered for sale. We may perhaps justly call such a demand function the equilibrium demand function—or demand curve. The equilibrium demand curve is the curve that exists when the marginal external consumption effect for every consumer, but one, at all alternate prices equals zero.* All other demand curves may be conceived as disequilibrium curves that can exist only because of temporarily imperfect knowledge by consumers of other people's demand. Once the errors in market information were discovered such a curve would move to a new position.

The major purpose of going through the conceptual experiment with its successive surveys was to illustrate the diminishing marginal external consumption effect and to indicate its role in obtaining a determinate demand curve. There is, however, a relatively simple method for obtaining the market demand function in cases where external consumption effects are significant. This method allows us to compare some of the properties of the "bandwagon demand curve" with the usual "functional" demand curve. It also allows us to separate the extent to which a change in demand results from a change in price from the extent to which it results from the bandwagon effect.

Given a certain total demand for a commodity as a parameter, every individual will have a demand function based on his total market demand.† Let the alternative total market demands that will serve as parameters for

* The fact that the marginal external consumption effect of one consumer is greater than zero does not affect the demand schedule, since total market demand at any given price cannot increase unless there are at least two consumers who would react on each other's demand.

† The analysis in the pages following is based on a somewhat different assumption than the *gedankenexperiment*. Each demand curve in Figure 3-7 (other than the equilibrium demand curve) is based on the assumption that consumers believe that a fixed amount will be taken off the market at all prices. There is more than one way of deriving the equilibrium demand curve. The earlier method helped to bring out the nature of the central principle involved, while the method which follows will enable us to separate price effects from bandwagon effects, snob effects, and so on.

alternate individual demand functions be indicated as superscripts, a, b, . . . n (where $a < b < . . . n$). Let the individual demand functions be d_1, d_2, . . . d_n; where every subscript indicates a different consumer. Thus, d_3^a is the individual demand curve for consumer 3 if the consumer believes that the total market demand is a units. Similarly, d_{500}^m is the individual demand curve for the 500th consumer if he believes that the total market demand will be m units. We could now add across d_1^a d_2^a d_3^a, . . . d_n^a which will give us the market demand curve D^a, which indicates the quantities demanded at alternate prices if all consumers believed that the total demand was a units. In the same manner we obtain D^b, D^c, . . . D^n. These hypothetical market demand curves, D^a, D^b, D^c . . . D^n, are shown in Figure 3. Now, if we assume that buyers have accurate knowledge of market conditions (of the total quantities demanded at every price), then only one point on any of the curves D^a, D^b, . . . D^n could be on the real or equilibrium demand curve. These are the points on each curve D^a, D^b, . . . D^n that represent the amounts on which the consumers based their individual demand curves: the amounts that consumers expected to be the total market demand. These points, labeled E^a, E^b, . . . E^n, are a series of virtual equilibrium points. Given that consumers possess accurate market information, E^a, E^b, . . . E^n are the only points that can become actual quantities demanded. The locus of all these points D_B is therefore the actual demand curve for the commodity.

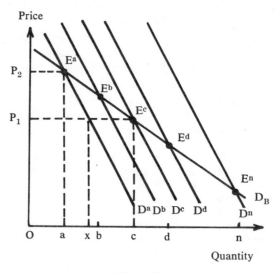

Figure 3

It may be interesting here to break up changes in the quantity demanded resulting from changes in price into a price effect and a bandwagon effect—the extent of the change resulting from the change in price, and the extent in demand resulting from consumers' adjusting to each other's changed consumption.* With an eye on Figure 3, consider the effects of a reduction in price from P_2 to P_1. The increase in demand after the change in price is ac. Only part of that increase, however, is the result of price reduction. To measure this amount we go along the demand curve D^a to P_1 which shows the quantity that would be demanded at P_1 if consumers did not adjust to each other's demand. This would result in an increase in demand of ax. Because of the bandwagon effect, however, an additional number of consumers are induced to enter the market or to increase their demands. There is now an additional increase in demand of xc after consumers have adjusted to each other's increases in consumption. The same type of analysis can of course be carried out for increases as well as for decreases in price.

Figure 3 shows something else. The demand curve D_B is more elastic than any of the other demand curves. This suggests that in general, other things being equal, the demand curve will be more elastic if there is a bandwagon effect than if the demand is based only on the commodity's functional attributes. This results from the fact that reactions to price changes are followed by additional reactions *in the same direction* to each other's changed consumption.

This result must be qualified. If the bandwagon reaction is greater for a higher price than for a lower one, the assertion about relative elasticities need not hold. Under such circumstances it is possible for the demand curve to have a positively inclined segment.

Social taboos, to the extent that they affect consumption, are in a sense bandwagon effects in reverse gear. Some people will not buy or consume certain things because other people are not buying and consuming these things. Thus, there may be no demand for a commodity with a fuunctional utility, which, apart from the taboo, would be purchased. Individual A will not buy it because B, C, and D do not, while individuals B, C, and D may refrain from consumption for the same reasons.

We can proceed as follows. Let d_1^x be the demand curve of the least inhibited individual in the market, where superscript x is the total quantity

---

* We are now in the area of "comparative statics." We defined statics and our unit period in such a way that only *one* price holds within any unit period. Thus, when we examine the effects of a change in price we are really examining the reasons for the differences in the quantities demanded at one price in one unit period and another price in the succeeding unit period.

demanded in the market upon which he bases his individual demand. Suppose that at market demand x, consumer 1 will demand at some range of prices one unit of the commodity, but at no price will he demand more. If he believes, however, that the total market demand is less than x units, he will refrain from making any purchases. Since, *ex hypothesis,* consumer 1 is the least inhibited consumer, he will at best be the only one who will demand one unit of the commodity if consumers expect the total market demand to be x units. Clearly, x units cannot be a virtual equilibrium point, since only points where the total expected quantity demanded is equal to the actual quantity demanded can be points on the real demand curve, and the quantity x cannot at any price be a point where expected total demand is equal to actual total demand. If the total expected demand were $x + 1$, the actual demand might increase, say, to 2 units. At expected total demands $x + 2$ and $x + 3$, more would enter the market, and the actual demand would be still greater since the fear of being different is considerably reduced as the expected demand is increased. With given increases in the expected total demand, there must at some point be more than equal increases in the actual demand, because if a real demand curve exists at all there must be some point where the expected demand is equal to the actual demand. That point may exist, say, at $x + 10$; that is, at an expected total demand of $x + 10$ units a sufficient number of people have overcome their inhibitions to being different so that at some prices they will actually demand $x + 10$ units of the commodity. Let us call this point "T"—it is really the "taboo-breaking point." The maximum bid (point T^1 in Figure 4) of the marginal unit demanded if the total demand were T units now gives us the first point on the real demand curve (the curve D^B).

The way in which social taboos may affect the demand curve is shown in Figure 4. Note that the price axis shows both positive and negative "prices." A negative price may be thought of as the price it would be necessary to *pay* individuals in order to induce them to consume in public a given amount of the commodity; that is, the price necessary to pay to induce consumers to disregard their aversion to being looked upon as odd or peculiar.

As indicated, T in Figure 4 is the taboo-breaking point. Point T represents the number of units at which an *expected* total quantity demanded of T units would result in an *actual* quantity demanded of T units at some *real* price. Why would not an expected demand of less than T units, say $T - 3$ units, yield an actual demand of $T - 3$ units at a positive as well as a negative price? Let the curve D^{T-3} be the demand curve that would exist if consumers thought the total demand was $T - 3$. Now, at any positive price,

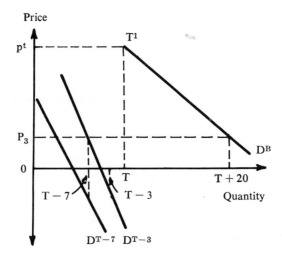

Figure 4

say P_3, the amount demanded would be less than $T - 3$, say $T - 7$. The price P_3 can therefore exist only if there is inaccurate information about the total quantity demanded. Once consumers discovered that at P_3 only $T - 7$ was purchased, and believed that this was the demand that would be sustained, their demand would shift to the D^{T-7} curve. At P_3 the amount purchased would now be less than $T - 7$ and demand would shift to a curve to the left of D^{T-7}. This procedure would go on until the demand was zero at P_3. We thus introduce a gap into our demand function and focus attention on an interesting psychological phenomenon that may affect demand. What I am suggesting essentially is that, given "accurate expectations" of the total quantity demanded on the part of consumers, there is a quantity less than which there will not be any quantity demanded at any real price. In other words, this is a case in which a commodity will either "go over big" or not "go over" at all. At P_3 zero units or $T + 20$ units (Figure 4) may be taken off the market, given "accurate expectations" of the total quantity demanded. It seems, therefore, that "accurate expectations" of the total quantity demanded at P_3 can have two values, depending upon whether people are pessimistic or optimistic about other consumers' demands for the commodity in question. If everybody expects that everybody else will not care for the commodity, then zero units would be the accurate expectation of the total quantity demanded; if, on the other hand, everybody expects others to take up the commodity with some degree of enthusiasm, then $T + 20$ units would be the accurate expectation of the total quantity demanded. The factors determining one set of expectations rather than the other are matters of empirical investigation in the field of social psychology. They may be the history of the community, the people's conservatism or lack of conservatism, the type and quantity of advertising about the commodity under consideration, and so on.

The significant point in Figure 4 is T^1, the first point on the real demand curve D^B. As already indicated, it is the point at which the maximum bid of the marginal unit demanded is P_t and the total market demand is T units. If the price were higher than P_t, the Tth unit would not be demanded and all buyers would leave the market because of the effect of the taboo at less than a consumption of T units. This is a "pure" case where all buyers are governed by taboo considerations. To summarize, if social taboos affect demand the real demand curve may not start at the price-axis but the smallest possible quantity demanded may be some distance to the right of the price-axis.

The Snob Effect

The reverse of the bandwagon effect is found in the demand behavior for those commodities with regard to which the individual consumer is a snob. Here too we assume first that the quantity demanded by a consumer is a function of price and of the total market demand, but that the individual consumer's demand is negatively correlated with the total market demand. In the snob case it is obvious that the external consumption effect must reach a limit, although the limit may be where one snob constitutes the only buyer. For most commodities and most buyers, however, the motivation for exclusiveness is not that great; hence the marginal external consumption effect reaches zero before that point. If the commodity is to be purchased at all, the external consumption effect must reach a limit, at some price, where the quantity demanded has a positive value. From this it follows that after a point the principle of the diminishing marginal external consumption effect must manifest itself. Thus, the snob effect has an opposite but symmetrical relationship to the bandwagon effect.

The analysis of markets in which all consumers behave like snobs follows the same lines as the bandwagon analysis. Because of this similarity analysis of the snob effect can be brief. We begin, as before, by letting the alternate total market demands that serve as parameters for alternate individual demand curves be indicated by the superscripts $a, b, \ldots n$ (where $a < b < n$). Let the individual demand functions be $d_1, d_2, \ldots d_n$, where there are n consumers in the market. Again, d_3^a signifies the individual demand curve for consumer 3 on the assumption that he expects the total market demand to be *a* units. By adding

$$d^n_1 + d^n_2 + \ldots + d^a_n = D^a$$
$$d^b_1 + d^b_2 + \ldots + d^b_n = D^b$$
$$\cdot \qquad \cdot$$
$$\cdot \qquad \cdot$$
$$\cdot \qquad \cdot$$
$$d^a_1 + d^a_2 + \ldots + d^n_n = D^n$$

we obtain the market demand functions on the alternate assumptions of consumers expecting the total market demands to be *a, b, . . . n*. Because of the snob behavior the curves D^a, D^b . . . D^n move to the left as the expected total market demand increases. This is shown in Figure 5. Using the same procedure as before, we obtain the virtual equilibrium points E^a, E^b, . . . E^n. They represent the only points on the curves D^a, D^b, . . . D^n that are consistent with consumers' expectations (and hence with the assumption of accurate information). The locus of the virtual equilibrium points is the demand curve D_s.

Now, given a price change from P_2 to P_1 we can separate the effect of the price change into a price effect and a snob effect. In Figure 5 we see

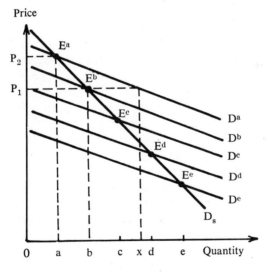

Figure 5

that the net increase in the quantity demanded by the reduction in price is
ab. The price effect, however, is *ax*. That is, if every consumer expected no
increase in the total quantity demanded, then the total quantity demanded
at P_1 would be *Ox*. The more extreme snobs will react to this increase in
the total quantity demanded by leaving the market. (The other snobs will
reduce their demand, but not by an amount large enough to leave the
market.) The total quantity demanded will hence be reduced by *bx*, with
the net result being an increase in demand of only *ab*.

All the points on the curves other than D_s (except E^a, E^b, . . . E^n)
are theoretical points that have significance only under conditions of imperfect knowledge. Figure 5 also shows that the demand curve for snobs is less
elastic than the demand curves where there are no snob effects. This is
because the increase in demand caused by reduction in price is counterbalanced in part by some snobs leaving the market because of the increase
in total consumption (that is, the decrease in the snob value of the
commodity). It should be clear, however, that the snob effect can never be
in excess of the price effect since this would lead to a basic contradiction. If
the snob effect were greater than the price effect the quantity demanded at
a lower price would be less than the quantity demanded at a higher price.
This implies that some of the snobs in the market at the higher price leave
it when there is a reduction in the total quantity demanded—patently
inconsistent with my definition of snob behavior. It follows that the snob
effect is never greater than the price effect. It follows, too, that D_s is
monotonically decreasing if D^a, D^b, . . . D^n are monotonically decreasing.

There is one final difference between the usual functional demand curve
and the D_s curve. In the usual demand curve the buyers at higher prices
remain in the market at lower prices; from the price point of view, the bids
to buy are cumulative downward. This is clearly not the case in the D_s
curve. Such terms as intramarginal buyers may be meaningless in snob
markets.

The Veblen Effect

Although the theory of conspicuous consumption as developed by Veblen
and others is a complex and subtle sociological construct we can legiti-
mately abstract from the psychological and sociological elements and consider the effects conspicuous consumption has on the demand function. The
essential economic characteristic which concerns us is the fact that the
utility derived from a unit of a commodity employed for purposes of
conspicuous consumption depends not only on the inherent qualities of that

unit but also on the price paid for it. It may, therefore, be helpful to divide the price of a commodity into two categories: the real price and the conspicuous price. The real price is the price the consumer actually paid for the commodity in terms of money; the conspicuous price is the price other people think the consumer paid for the commodity—and which therefore determines its conspicuous consumption utility. (More accurately, the conspicuous price should be the price the consumer thinks other people think he paid for the commodity.) These two prices would probably be identical in highly organized markets where price information is common knowledge. In other markets, where some can get "bargains" or special discounts, the real price or conspicuous price need not be identical. In any case, the quantity demanded by a consumer is a function of both the real price and the conspicuous price.

The market demand curve for commodities subject to conspicuous consumption can be derived through a similar diagrammatical method (see Figure 6). This time we let the superscripts 1, 2, . . . n stand for the expected conspicuous prices. The real prices are $P_1 P_2, \ldots P_n$. The individual demand functions are $d_1, d_2, \ldots d_n$. In this way d_6^3 stands for

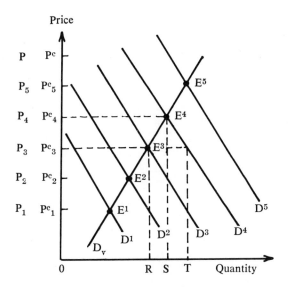

ST = price effect   −TR = Veblen effect   −SR = net effect

Figure 6

the demand curve of consumer number 6, if he expects a conspicuous price of P_3.* We can now add across $d_1^1, d_2^1, \ldots d_n^1$ and get the market demand curve D^1, which indicates the quantities demanded at alternate prices if all consumers expected a conspicuous price of P_1^c. In a similar manner we obtain $D^2, D^3, \ldots D^n$. Up to a point, the market demand curves will shift to the right as the expected conspicuous price increases. If we assume that consumers possess accurate market information, on every curve $D^1, D^2, \ldots D^n$ in Figure 6 only one point can be a virtual equilibrium point—the point where the real price is equal to the conspicuous price (where $P_1 = P_1^c, P_2 = P_2^c, \ldots P_n = P_n^c$). The locus of these virtual equilibrium points $E^1, E^2, \ldots E^n$ gives the demand curve D_v.

As before, we can separate the effects of a change in price into two effects—the price effect and, for want of a better term, the Veblen effect. Figure 6 shows that a change in price from P_4 to P_3 will reduce the quantity demanded by RS. The price effect is to increase the quantity demanded by ST: the amount that would be demanded if there were no change in the expected conspicuous price would be OT. However, at the lower price a number of buyers would leave the market because of the reduced utility derived from the commodity at that lower conspicuous price. The Veblen effect is therefore RT.

Unlike the D_s curve, the D_v curve can be positively inclined, negatively inclined, or a mixture of both. It depends on whether at alternate price changes the Veblen effect is greater or less than the price effect. It is possible that in one portion of the curve one effect may predominate, while in another portion another may predominate. It is to be expected, however, that in most cases, if the curve is not monotonically decreasing it will be shaped like a backward S, as illustrated in Figure 7 (a). There are two reasons for this. First, there must be a price so high that no units of the commodity will be purchased at that price, owing (among other reasons) to income constraint. This is the price P^n in Figure 7 (a), and it implies that there must be some point at which the curve shifts from being positively inclined to being negatively inclined as price increases. Second, there must be some point of satiety for the good. This is the point T in Figure 7 (a). It follows that some portion of the curve must be monotonically decreasing to reach T if there exists some minimum price at which the Veblen effect is zero. It is reasonable to assume that there is some low price at which the commodity would cease to have any value for purposes

---

* The expected conspicuous prices are distinguished from the real prices by adding the superscript c to the P's. Thus, to the range of real prices $P_1, P_2, \ldots P_n$, we have a corresponding range of conspicuous prices denoted by $P_1^c, P_2^c, \ldots P_n^c$.

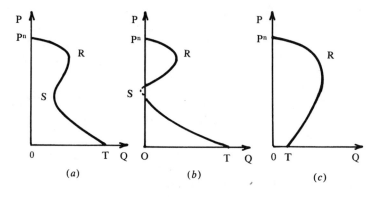

Figure 7

of conspicuous consumption. If this assumption does not hold, which is unlikely, then the curve could have the shape indicated in Figure 7 (c). Otherwise, it would have the general shape indicated in Figure 7 (a), or it might be in two segments as illustrated by Figure 7 (b).

Mixed Effects

Any real market for semidurable or durable goods probably contains consumers that are subject to one or a combination of the effects discussed heretofore. Combining these effects presents no new formal difficulties with respect to the determination of the market demand curve, although it complicates the diagrammatic analysis. The major principle still holds. For any price there is a quantity demanded such that the marginal external consumption effect (or the marginal Veblen effect) for all buyers but one, is zero. This implies that for every price change there is a point at which people cease reacting to each other's quantity changes, regardless of direction. If this is so, then for every price there is a determinate quantity demanded, and hence the demand curve is determinate.

For every price change we have distinguished between the price effect and some other, such as the snob, the Veblen, or the bandwagon effect. In markets where all four effects are present we should be able to separate out and indicate the direction of each of them that results from a price change. In other words, every price change results in two positive and two negative effects—two which, other things being equal, increase the quantity demanded and two which, other things being equal, decrease it. Which effects are positive and which negative depends on the relative strength of the

Veblen effect as against the price effect. The Veblen and the price effects depend directly on the direction of the price change. An increase in price results in price and bandwagon effects that are generally negative, and in Veblen and snob effects that are positive, provided the price effect is greater than the Veblen effect—that is, if the net result is a decrease in the quantity demanded at the higher price. If, on the other hand, the Veblen effect is more powerful than the price effect, given a price increase, the bandwagon effect should be positive and the snob effect negative. The reverse would be true for price declines.

The market demand curve for a commodity where different consumers are subject to different types of effects can be obtained diagrammatically by employing the methods developed above—although the diagrams would be quite complicated. There is no point in adding still more diagrams to illustrate this. Briefly, the method is as follows: First, given the demand curves for every individual, in which the expected total quantity demanded is a parameter for each curve, we can add these curves laterally and obtain a map of aggregate demand curves, in which each aggregate curve is based on a given total quantity demanded. Second, the locus of the equilibrium points on each aggregate demand curve (as derived in Figure 3) gives a market demand curve that accounts for both bandwagon and snob effects. This last curve assumes that only one conspicuous price exists. For every conspicuous price there exists a separate map of aggregate demand curves from which different market demand curves are obtained. Third, this procedure yields a map of market demand curves in which each curve is based on a different conspicuous price. Employing the method used in Figure 6, we obtain a final market demand curve which accounts for bandwagon, snob, and Veblen effects simultaneously.

Conclusions

Essentially, I have attempted to do two things. First, I have tried to demonstrate that nonadditivity is not an insurmountable obstacle in effecting a transition from individual to collective demand curves. Second, I attempted to take a step or two in the direction of incorporating various kinds of external consumption effects into the theory of consumers' demand. In order to solve this problem, I introduced the principle of the diminishing marginal external consumption effect. I indicated some reasons for believing that for every individual there is a point at which the marginal external consumption effect is zero. I attempted to show that, if this principle is admitted, there are various ways of effecting a transition from individual to collective demand curves. The major conclusion reached is that, under conditions of perfect knowledge (or accurate expectations), any point on the demand curve, for any given price, will be at that total quantity demanded where the marginal external consumption effect for all consumers but one is equal to zero.

A comparison of the demand curve in situations where external consumption effects are present with the demand curve as it would be were these external consumption effects absent, included three basic points. (1) If the bandwagon effect is the most significant effect, the demand curve is likely to be more elastic than it would be if this external consumption effect were absent. (2) If the snob effect is the predominant one, the demand curve is less elastic than otherwise. (3) If the Veblen effect predominates, the demand curve is less elastic than otherwise, and some portions of it may even be positively inclined.

PART TWO

New Psychological Postulates and the Basic X-Efficiency Theory

5 The Theory of Selective Rationality

In the pages that follow I will present some of the fundamental ideas on which this section of the book is based and introduce other, less basic, ones which will be developed subsequently. Because some of my ideas differ markedly from the concepts of textbook microtheory, it seems wise to introduce them in stages of gradual refinement and in juxtaposition to the main elements of the conventional theory. In a sense the existing theory may be viewed as an extreme variant of the theory to be developed—but one which is highly oversimplified. The consequences of the simplification of current microtheory is that significant elements that help to explain reality are suppressed. No book at this stage could hope to develop the theory in all its potential complex manifestations. My object, therefore, is to develop an "open theory"—one which allows or invites a great deal more manipulation and expansion in breadth, complexity, and depth.

Let me outline the psychological assumptions underlying the ideas to be developed in ensuing chapters. We assume that basically an individual effects a compromise between his desire to do as he pleases and internalized standards of behavior acquired through background and environment. Thus, we assume that individuals are influenced by others and that their psychology requires them to strike a balance between conflicting desires.

Economic Decision Units

Economic decision units or "actors"* are the basic behavioral units in current theory. Consuming units are made up of households and producing units are made up of firms. Existing theory also includes the existence of a labor market in which household members are hired by firms. However, the relation of workers to households is not developed. Workers are *of*

---

* Avoiding the term economic agents for decision units, I will use the term "actors" instead. As far as possible, I want to limit the term "agent" to its legal sense. It is useful for our purposes to distinguish between "agents" and "principals" (see Chapter 10).

households, but what they do *in* households is not part of the theory. The reason for this is clear. The basic unit is the household—not any of its components. There is a contractual relation presumed between workers and firms, but the theory speaks of no contractual relations between workers and households or among household members.

Current microtheory achieves simplicity and generality by *not* defining economic actors too explicitly. Actors or decision units may be individuals. Nothing in the theory precludes a world of single-person households, or single person firms—in fact, conventional microtheory is more defensible under this assumption than under others. Similarly, the actors may be groups where "households" and firms are made up of many individuals. But a problem exists. Much of the theory is couched in language which suggests that groups behave as if they were individuals. Although this is an interesting simplifying assumption, groups are not individuals. In order to focus our discussion let us forget for the time being the existence of single person economic actors. Consider only multiperson decision units. Should we consider how individuals are related to the economic decision units that operate as a group? This is precisely the central problem to be examined. Economic actors operate in markets. We presume to know how individuals behave in such markets. Do groups behave in the same way? If we assume that this is so, further inquiry is shut off. Instead, we can go about it in three stages. We can consider how individuals behave, next how they relate to the group, and then attempt to determine how the highly complex groups we call firms and households behave.

To be more specific, we may juxtapose the conventional firm which is *assumed* to pursue the objective of minimizing costs and choosing an output and price combination so as to maximize profits—with a theory of the firm that starts with individuals and asks how they are related to the groups called households and firms. We then examine what, if anything, could be said about the household's objectives and the firm's objectives that emerge from the objectives of their constituents.

Rationality versus Selective Rationality

Existing theory relies on extreme assumptions about individual psychology. The conventional approach may be characterized by the phrase *complete constraint concerned "calculatedness" in the pursuit of precise objectives.* What is involved in the traditional approach is a sharp division between three types of elements: (a) ends; (b) alternatives; and (c) decision techniques or procedures in choosing among alternatives in the pursuit of ends. Elements (a) and (c) involve no choice whatsoever. The theory simply disallows choice in this area. The end might be maximizing profits and the means would be what I have just referred to as complete constraint concerned calculatedness. The alternatives are divided in the most general treatments into two types of choice elements: inputs and outputs. Thus the inputs may be referred to as means, whereas the alternative outputs enter as components which are to be calculated in determining the ends.*

In contrast to the above let us consider a possible variation. Namely, we suppose that (c), "decision techniques," be looked upon as a variable. Suppose, but only for a moment, that rationality is interpreted as "calculatedness." Let us refer to two types or degrees: "tight calculation" and "loose calculation." That is, we look upon calculatedness as a variable along a dimension where at one end the degree of calculation is so sloppy as to be almost the same as a random choice within a given but fairly wide range. At the other end it is very careful and "tight," continually checked and rechecked, so that only a completely accurate answer, if possible, is tenaciously sought.† Obviously, under various circumstances people may value tighter calculations over looser ones. Equally clearly, this is not true in all instances, if a given degree of calculatedness involves *tastes* or "costs" or some mixture of the two.

In situations involving consumers' behavior the concept of "going on a spree" may reflect a deliberate choice of behavior involving a period within which calculation is rather loose. Nevertheless, "sprees" are not activities which would necessarily be viewed as either irrational or of low utility. The idea that sprees might be fun also suggests the notion that they might yield for some personalities a high degree of pleasure and should be viewed as yielding high utility. If this example is valid (and it is easy to think of others like it), then rationality does not imply perpetual and tenacious tight calculation in one's decisionmaking (or other) behavior. Outside the circles of economists, accountants, and engineers, individuals normally dislike tight calculation activity. There are degrees of calculatedness, and, for some people at least some of the time, the comfortable degree of calculatedness is not very tight.

Another area in which calculation is frequently not very tight is the use and apportionment of one's time to various activities. Since time is in one

---

* There are also alternative techniques of production. But these are reduced to calculating formulas that translate input values into output values, and we employ the formula that gives us the best score.

† Herbert Simon has stressed the distinction between rationality as viewed by cognitive psychology as against the view of economics. In cognitive psychology rationality applies to a *process* of partial calculation and choice under which the complete consequences of different options are not given at the outset.

sense exactly equally available to all individuals, and imposes the same constraints, and since a good deal of this book will be concerned with the concept of effort and the allocation of time to activities involving effort, it is important to keep the time allocation problem in mind.

Once we agree that calculatedness is a variable, we can work out a theory of economic behavior in which it enters as such. The idea behind selective rationality, in contrast to complete rationality, is that we can find dimensions which are part of the interpretation of rationality, and along which we select degrees of rationality. Tightness or looseness of calculatedness is one such dimension.

In contrast, consider our central postulate: *people behave the way they like, or they behave the way they feel they must, or they make some compromises between these elements.* This implies that there exists means of making compromises of the type just mentioned. A closely related idea is that (along any given dimension) the less our behavior takes the consequences of ignoring constraints into account the more, at some point, we will feel internal or external pressure against continuing this type of behavior.* An interpretation of this idea is that a low degree of calculatedness, and a lack of concern for given constraints, will lead to either internal or external pressure to alter such behavior.

Figure 8 contains a set of indifference curves—u_1, u_2, and u_3—which indicate how people trade off degrees of calculatedness for degrees of anticipated pressure to remain at the same utility level. If individuals have the correct anticipation of the relation between pressure and calculatedness, and if in general they dislike more calculatedness, or more pressure, then we should expect the iso-utility curves, u_1, u_2, and so on, to have the normal shape, that is, concave from the origin. We can consider the iso-utility curves which take on different shapes reflecting in part different personality types, but we need not go into detail here about the nature and possibility of such alternatives.

The arrow in Figure 8 reflects the notion that for the most part repre-

---

* We need not choose between "satisficing" versus maximizing behavior, nor do we have to debate or determine whether one is more rational than the other. This chapter is concerned with the simple notion that there are a wide variety of general behavioral rules, and that people are aware of some of these possibilities. Satisficing behavior or maximizing some variable are only two of many possibilities. If individuals are aware of alternatives, and if they do have a choice, there is no reason to impose on our theories modes of behavior which presume that people always choose either satisficing, or maximizing, or that they are limited exclusively to these two alternatives. Why presume that all firms either follow the same rule or follow a given rule all the time, or follow a simple rule? See Herbert A. Simon, *Models of Man* (New York, Wiley, 1957), pp. 241–260.

Pressure

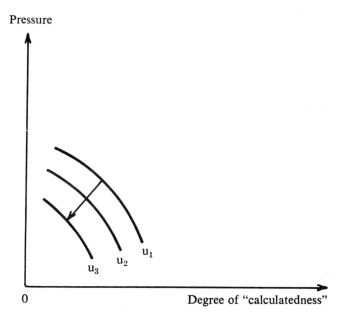

u_3 u_2 u_1

0   Degree of "calculatedness"

Figure 8

sentative individuals would like to move toward lower levels of anticipated pressure and toward more casual (less calculating) decisionmaking.

We do not have at this stage a theory of selective rationality. The diagram indicates only one narrow and special interpretation. Calculatedness is only one dimension of decision behavior—one dimension of what I shall refer to as constraint concern. A more complete theory must consider other possible dimensions, which will be examined later.

What do we mean by "calculatedness"? This is a vague term; nevertheless it is meaningful. Its vagueness arises out of the fact that different people will give different interpretations to the concept. It seems likely that for almost every individual it has ordinal meaning. The notion being more calculating versus being less calculating is obviously meaningful and communicable.

Consider the X-axis in Figure 8. How can we interpret a given point on it? We want to argue that such an interpretation does not require all individuals to have a clear-cut appreciation and sensitivity to all degrees of calculatedness. They will usually have an appreciation, sensitivity, and *capacity,* in their performance at least, to two degrees of calculatedness—and frequently many more. Suppose they distinguish between one level that we call T, implying a "tight" degree of calculatedness, and another level L, referring to a "loose" degree of calculatedness. We might readily imagine that if an individual has to decide how to spend his income he may subject a proportion α to tight calculation, and another proportion $1 - \alpha$ to loose calculation. If we can assign to T and L numbers that have ordinal significance, we can visualize the degree of calculatedness $C = \alpha T + (1 - \alpha) L$. All we are concerned with here is a possible specific interpretation that gives meaning to the idea of some felt degree of average calculatedness in a specific context.

Pressure is an equally vague but ordinally meaningful concept. Here too an index number problem is involved. What the Y-axis implies is some sense of an *average* degree of pressure. Once again there is an internal-external problem involved. For relatively normal individuals some relation will exist between the pressure they feel and stimuli imposed by the outside world, part of whose intention is to impose a sense of pressure. Examples from the area of consumption are the various "pressures" that bill collectors try to impose on those in debt. These may range from mild reproofs for not paying a bill on time, to the imposition of interest rates or other financial penalties, to threats of court actions that may force the individual to bankruptcy. At one time debtors' prisons would have been added to this list. One can readily see that a range of pressures can be imposed from the outside. A normal individual will have a sense of different degrees of felt pressure as we proceed along this range. The possibility of such pressure will depend on the degree of one's debts in relation to constraints (that is, some combination of income and wealth).

Other elements may be involved in "felt pressure." For example, the time from the present at which one may anticipate a given degree of pressure being imposed would enter. A given degree of pressure expected to be imposed far off in the future, say five years from now, would have a lesser influence on some index of pressure than the same degree of pressure imposed tomorrow.

Basic Structure of Selective Rationality

Economists use the work "rationality" as a synonym for maximization or optimization. Economic man is supposed to do as well as he can. Hence he is presumed to maximize profits, or income, or utility, or something like that. However, one can argue that there is an important sense in which non-maximizing behavior is not at all irrational. Unfortunately, in terms of clarity, there are many senses in which the word rationality is used. The main point I intend to make in developing a set of psychological postulates which are consistent with non-maximizing behavior is that such behavior need not necessarily be viewed as irrational.

With the terms "constraint concern" and "purposiveness" I shall attempt to capture and convey a host of concepts and personality traits (including "calculatedness") which form the bundle of dimensions along which individuals pursue their aims as best they can when they think in terms of maximizing behavior of the type attributed to "economic man." Consider "purposiveness." People pursue their purposes to different degrees. Hence we visualize purposiveness as a variable which fits along an ordinal dimension of "more or less." The same can be said about the degree to which individuals are concerned about the constraints that they are supposed to observe within any context. This analysis will attempt to show that *on the average* individuals try to find what is for them a *comfortable* level of constraint concern. What that particular level happens to be depends on the personalities of the individuals involved. When I use the term "constraint concern" by itself I also have in mind the other variables mentioned.

The concept of constraint concern can be viewed as a vector of personality traits. The degree of constraint concern is one component of such a vector. The other components, which will be considered in detail in ensuing sections, reflect traits along a continuum and may be interpreted as reflecting degrees of rationality. For simplicity, we may visualize that each component takes some ordinal value from zero to one. Examples of these components are degrees of (1) constraint concern, (2) calculatedness, (3) realism of context assessment, (4) independence of judgment, (5) non-reflexibility of assessments, (6) magnitude sensitivity, (7) non-deferral of decisions and actions, (8) learning from experience. This list is not exhaustive nor necessarily the most appropriate for an individual in every situation. Although constraint concern is one of the components of the vector, we also refer to the vector as a whole as "constraint concern." Unless the context implies otherwise when I refer to constraint concern, I mean the entire vector of personality traits.

If we restrict ourselves to an ordinal measure of constraint concern, then for two given degrees of constraint concern, C_1 and C_2, we can define $C_1 < C_2$ as meaning that each component in C_1 is equal to or less than the same component in C_2, and at least some components of C_1 are less than the related component in C_2. This of course would not allow us to treat the cases of different degrees of constraint concern under which some components have a higher value in one case while other components have a lower value in the other. To treat such a case we would have to move to a cardinal index and allow for trade-offs by an individual between one component and another. In that case we might be able to combine valuations of a different component and calculate an average degree of constraint concern. In principle, different degrees of constraint concern are meaningful at least to the same extent that different levels of utility are meaningful.

The structure of this theory is best expressed by Figure 9a. This figure contains a set of indifference curves which express for any particular individual the relation of degrees of constraint concern (purposiveness, and so on) and pressure (similar to Figure 8). The curves are drawn convex from above which conveys the idea that beyond some point there is a maximum amount of pressure an individual may wish to tolerate even if it may involve constraint concern, and similarly there is a maximum amount of constraint concern associated with zero pressure. We need not concern ourselves at this point whether the indifference curves which relate constraint concern and pressure will in fact touch the X and Y intercepts. The slope tangent to any point on a curve indicates the rate at which an individual is willing to trade a little less constraint concern for a little more pressure and still feel equally well off.

Thus, in Figure 9a the curves marked U_1, U_2, U_3 are indifference

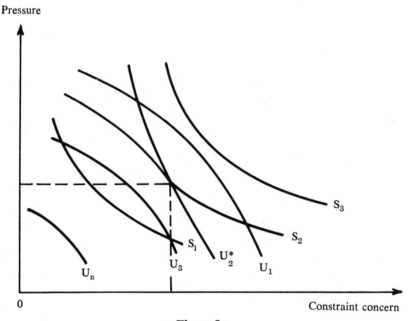

Figure 9a

curves for constraint concern and pressure. They are similar to the indifference curves shown in the previous section which associated calculatedness and pressure: $U_1 < U_2 < U_3$. This last implies that apart from other considerations such as obligation and duty, individuals, at least up to a point, will prefer both less pressure and less constraint concern.

In order to interpret these indifference curves we may use Freudian language temporarily and look upon U_1, U_2, and so on as representing the *"Id-indifference"* curves of the individual. They are intended to convey how the individual would like to behave if he had no sense of obligation, duty, or adherence to standards of some sort. We combine in the same figure a set of curves representing a person's superego, that is, the set of standards of behavior the individual would like to see himself adhering to and performing in accordance with, were it not for his "animal spirits" so to speak. Hence we show a set of indifference curves marked S_1, S_2, S_3, for which $S_1 < S_2 < S_3$, in order to convey the *standards of behavior* the individual aspires to. Curves representing the standard have a higher utility value as they move away from the origin. This represents the notion that the individual will prefer, other things equal, to see himself behave in accordance with a higher standard rather than a lower one.*

As the curves are drawn in Figure 9 there is a tangency point for the curves U_2 and S_2. This tangency point determines the most comfortable constraint concern-pressure relation for the individual. If he chose to behave in accordance with a higher standard, say S_3, he would find discomfort in the degree to which he has to be purposive, or behave under pressure, and so on. In other words, it is too high a standard to maintain for his tastes and personality. Similarly, but at the opposite end, if he chose to behave in accordance with the curve U_3 he might feel extremely comfortable in the sense of hardly noticing the constraints he was under, but he would feel psychologically uncomfortable in the sense of not living up to the standard of obligation, or sense of duty, and so on that determines his desired self-image. Hence U_2, marked hereafter as U^*, represents his optimal or most comfortable *average* behavioral curve.

The outside world does not necessarily provide an individual a job or

* For an interesting review of psychological theories of behavior by an economist see Karl A. Fox, "Combining Economic and Non-Economic Objectives in Development Planning: Problems of Concept and Measurement," in Willy Sellekaert, ed., *Economic Development and Planning* (London: Macmillan Press, 1974) pp. 111–125, esp. p. 124. It is of interest to note some similarities between the discussion of Harry Levinson's "ego ideal" concept and my superego function. See also Harry Levinson, *The Exceptional Executive: A Psychological Conception* (Cambridge, Mass., Harvard University Press, 1968).

context consonant with that person's most comfortable constraint concern relation. Thus, in Figure 9b we show U^* and three curves marked CP_1, CP_2, and CP_3. Each of these reflects the *believed* constraint-concern-pressure relation inherent in three jobs (or any other type of context) open to the individual. Let CP_1 be the relation associated with Job A and CP_2 with Job B and CP_3 with Job C. Suppose for a moment he chose Job C. For all points on U^* Job C involves greater pressure and constraint concern than the individual would comfortably like to handle. CP_3 represents a "technological" relation in a sense, that is, it says something about one of the important characteristics of handling a certain job. Clearly, with respect to the options indicated in Figure 9b the person is "best off" if he chooses Job B associated with CP_2, which is tangent to U^*. The drawing suggests that the individual would be psychologically comfortable trying to handle Job B. Job A, on the other hand, would not represent enough of a challenge to meet his "standards" or "superego," although the individual could easily handle it. This theory does not suggest that every individual would choose the equivalent of Job B—the optimal one for his constraint

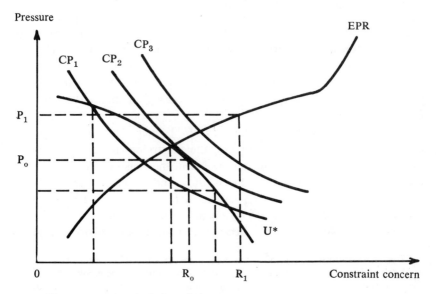

CP   = pressure-constraint relations
EPR = externally imposed pressure-response relation

Figure 9b

concern tastes. Many individuals make mistakes in this regard, and some job choices are sources of strain and unhappiness. My theory suggests that if the individual characterized by U^* chooses Job C or A he would, beyond some point, be on the lookout for superior alternatives.

In order to elucidate the structure of the theory further, suppose our individual does choose Job B, and operates within the psychological context described by U^* and CP_2, whose tangency point represents an "optimum" constraint concern level R_o and pressure level P_o. Note that these represent average levels of constraint concern and pressure. But individuals are not presumed to be inflexible. Within a firm they are expected from time to time to respond to pressures that take them beyond the *average* comfortable level R_o. Thus, Figure 9b also shows a curve marked EPR which represents the external pressure reaction relation. It indicates the extent to which the individual will undertake constraint concern levels in response to pressures from the outside, say those imposed by an authority over the individual within a firm. If the pressure level imposed is P_1 the individual moves to R_1 (greater than R_o). How should we interpret such behavior? At R_1, the individual is "stretched" beyond his comfortable level. Like a rubber band we would expect him to seek circumstances he can interpret as a relaxation of pressure so that he can "snap back" to or toward R_o.

How are points on the EPR curve determined? We assume that the individual becomes aware of pressure signals and has to provide some degree of constraint concern as a response. The response will depend on how the person feels about the disutility of a change in pressure, in either direction, compared to the utility of being on a given pressure level. If the individual wishes to remain at the perceived pressure level, he will probably respond by choosing a degree of constraint concern he expects that will neither raise nor lower the signals which imply changes in pressure. We should expect that at very high levels of pressure, the individual will choose a level of constraint concern that he expects will lead to a reduction of pressure. In general, we would expect that he is likely to choose constraint concern levels in response to pressure so that he may eventually induce those that provide the pressure signals to permit him to return toward or to his comfortable level as indicated by the curve U^*.

A voluntary movement to R_1 may represent what might be interpreted as *marginal rationality* on the part of the individual. Suppose he values his job and that not taking on more temporary responsibility would threaten his job or his superior evaluation of him on it. Obviously allowing himself to be temporarily stretched represents rational behavior. But it would not make sense for him to allow such a state of affairs to continue permanently

—hence our use of the concept of "marginal rationality" rather than "total rationality."

An important distinction can be made between marginal and "total rationality." Sensible behavior requires only marginal rationality, not rationality at every point in time. There is no need to assume that people need to stretch themselves along every dimension (calculatedness, or purposiveness, and so on) at each point in time to gain every advantage open to them. It may indeed go against their psychological make-up to do so. They need only do so from time to time when the results seem important. Otherwise it is quite sensible for them to operate at or within their comfortable bound U^*, even in cases where it may mean missing out on economic opportunities. Operating well within U^* temporarily may compensate psychologically for an earlier period of stretching.

A final aspect of the structure of the theory is that the "superego" curves S_1, S_2, and so on need not be fixed. We should normally expect an interdependence between an individual's standards and observed constraint concern levels. If the observed constraint concern level of others increases, then at least for some individuals their S_i curves (Figure 9a) should move to the right and their comfortable constraint-pressure relation U^* would also move to the right (increase) to some degree. Thus, because of the type of interdependence just described there may be drifts in the levels of U^* and R_o over time.

Other Components of Rationality

In addition to "calculatedness" other dimensions of rationality or components of constraint concern operate in a similar manner to that just described. Constraint concern and rationality are used interchangeably in this and ensuing sections.

Situation Assessment Realism. In addition to calculation, individuals in a decision situation usually have to assess the nature of the situation and the nature of the alternatives. At one extreme we can try to make as realistic an assessment as possible; at the other we can base our assessments entirely on wishful thinking. These assessments may have to do with one's own attributes, the attributes of others, or aspects of the world. For example, an employment decision may involve an assessment of one's own capacities and effort levels, as well as those with whom one will have to cooperate. Frequently wishful thinking colors one's views about some aspects of the job if other aspects appear unusually attractive. Where risks are involved people are especially prone to project wishful thinking onto the weight that they place on risk elements.

The nature of this dimension is illustrated in Figure 9c. The X-axis represents degrees of realism of the assessment and the Y-axis the anticipated pressure that can eventually occur if relatively unrealistic decision procedures are employed. Once again we reflect the idea that we can act as we like, but consideration of the constraints and the pressure that results from violating constraints forces us to take into account that, to some degree, we act as we must.

The curves marked P_1 and P_2 represent the pressure-realism relation for given constraint levels. The curve P_1 could be viewed as the appropriate component of S_i in Figure 9a. The curve marked u^* is the comfortable constraint concern pressure level for the component under consideration. Once again the tangency point between u^* and P_1 indicates the desired degree of rationality along this dimension.

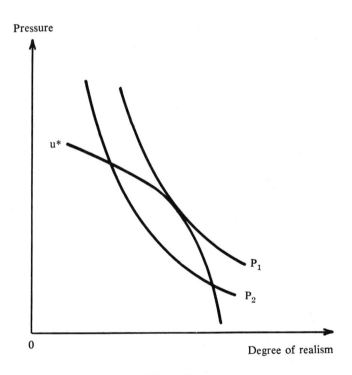

Figure 9c

Independent-Dependent Behavior. One way of making decisions is to depend on others to some degree. This may involve following the example of others in similar situations, taking the advice of others who may not have any more information than oneself, or behaving in such a way so as to please others or gain their approval. This is a contrast to what would usually be seen as decisionmaking based on independent assessments. We should keep in mind the contrast between the observations of the behavior of others simply to gain information in order to use such information for an independent decision (in which case we would look upon this procedure as one that is at the *independent* pole of this dimension) and simply following others irrespective of one's own assessment. As in Figure 9a, we can visualize a line *P* which would indicate a pressure-rationality relation where the rationality dimension flows from complete dependence on others at the zero point of the X-axis to complete independence at the other end.

Reflexive versus Non-Reflexive Assessments. Our response to an option may be completely reflexive: a "knee-jerk" type of reaction based on response to the stimuli involved in the presentation of the option. The other end of this dimension is to ignore all stimuli, many of which would be associated with past experiences, and to make assessments and choices purely on the basis of the cool appreciation of the data offered to our senses. Thus, this dimension runs from completely reflexive to completely nonreflexive behavior. Common experience suggests that highly reflexive behavior is nonrational and would eventually bring on a greater degree of pressure than nonreflexive behavior.

Magnitude Sensitivity. So far we have viewed the situation in such a way that the pressure-rationality relations and the iso-utility function were one-to-one correspondences. This implies a very high degree of sensitivity to changes in magnitude. Minute changes along the rationality dimension would result in the appreciation of changes along a pressure dimension. Actually people rarely have such high degrees of sensitivity. In terms of calculation some gain can be obtained by being more sensitive to magnitudes than less so. For example, in the purchase and sales of objects whose price may vary, let us say, between $1 and $5,000, buyers and sellers who make bids in units of $1,000, and are sensitive only to such bids, might find themselves at a disadvantage in bargaining with someone whose calculations and sensitivities are in units of $100. This is not to suggest that it always pays to bother with very small magnitudes. There may be a calculation or information costs so that small magnitude sensitivity is not worthwhile. But one who is sensitive to small magnitudes can take advantage of those situations in which it is worthwhile.

Magnitude sensitivity involves taste to some degree. Psychologically we may be either insensitive to magnitudes within certain bounds or we may find it unpleasant to be so. Hence, there may be a degree of magnitude sensitivity along the X-axis which would be reflected in sensitivity to pressure, as well as sensitivity to different degrees of utility. In Figure 10 this is indicated by drawing the P and U^* curves in terms of bands rather than pencil-thin lines which become wider as we move toward the zero point on the X-axis reflecting lesser degrees of sensitivity. This would imply that if we are not optimally sensitive, in all other rationality dimensions the curves are bands reflecting a "chosen" degree of sensitivity. In the figure $\underline{P}$ is the lower bound of the felt pressure-sensitivity relation, and $\overline{P}$ is the upper bound. The individual is insensitive, for a given magnitude on the X-axis, to points between the upper and lower bounds.

Time Deferral. Rational behavior depends in part on how we react to time. If we were "tightly" rational all the time, we would make tightly calculating decisions immediately as they arise irregardless of whether or not deferral is possible. There are situations in which more information accrues

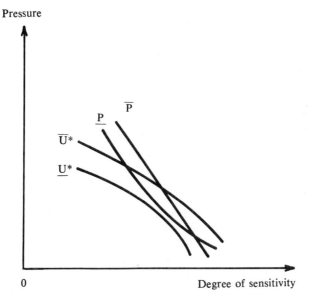

Figure 10

as time goes on, and up to a point it may pay to defer a decision in order to take advantage of the additional information. This is not the kind of situation we are considering. Rather, our concern is whether we behave in such a way that we follow "loose" procedures along various rationality dimensions because we find these procedures less irksome although the price for doing so is to defer the "tightness" of our procedures for a later period. For example, we may feel that we can safely ignore immediate pressure elements in a variety of ways and employ temporarily casual decisionmaking procedures in the hope that later we will have the taste, or find it psychologically comfortable, to force ourselves to use tight procedures.

Non-Learning versus Learning from Experience. A very significant rationality dimension is the degree to which people learn from experience. This is important in determining the procedures used and the stability of choice procedures. Clearly there is a selective element involved here. If some individuals learn only from successful experiences and blot out unsuccessful ones, the result will be quite different than if they learn from *all* experiences. Just as there is a relation between the present and the future in selective rationality, so also there is a significant relation between the past and the present. In contrast to many aspects of conventional microtheory in which bygones are only bygones and do not influence the present choice, once degrees of rationality are involved, bygones, through learning, do influence choice. Once again, nonrationality would imply nonlearning from past experience, whereas rationality would imply learning as much as possible from such experience.

Degrees of Deliberate Irrational Choice. Finally, there is the possibility that people sometimes enjoy making irrational choices. We need not go into why a taste for occasional expression of irrationality exists; I simply include it as a possibility.

The Aggregation of Rationality Dimensions

The rationality components considered are for the most part analytical categories. They represent an attempt to indicate considerations *an outsider* would use in analyzing the choice procedure of an individual. A deciding individual may have an integrated choice procedure without any sense of its analytical components. There may be some sense of some such components for more reflective individuals, but unquestionably people will ignore many components that play a role only on a semiconscious level.

For our purposes we assume that there is some sense in which individuals combine the various dimensions of rationality and test the consequences of their procedures against reality. For expository purposes we
draw an aggregate rationality curve on which we show degrees of rationality on the X-axis and pressure on the Y-axis. Figure 11 shows the area
within which the degree of rationality will be chosen. The curves $\underline{S}$ and S
indicate the lower and upper bounds of the appropriate superego curves
which allow for degrees of insensitivity. Similarly the curves marked $\underline{U}^*$
and U^* represent the lower and upper bounds of the iso-utility function
within which, for any degree of rationality, insensitivity to alternative
pressure points exist. The intersection of these two relations yields a choice
area within which the individual is indifferent as to his degree of rationality
and related degree of pressure.

The actual degree of rationality chosen will depend on specific historical
circumstances, but it will fall, on the basis of taste considerations, between
the points R_1 and R_2 on the X-axis. I will leave until later chapters the
consideration of how historical circumstances lead to the choice of a
specific position within a set of indifferent positions. The analysis at this
juncture does not require that we limit ourselves to situations within which
a unique degree of rationality is determined. Rather I wish to emphasize
the idea of separating the area within which there are acceptable degrees of

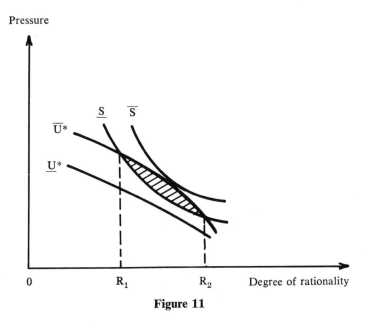

Figure 11

rationality, as against other areas in which the degrees of rationality are associated with unacceptable degrees of pressure, or involve unacceptably high degrees of rationality.

Patterned Contexts, Present Position Preference, and Ratchet Rationality

Economic theory usually does not distinguish explicitly between one-time-only situations, daily, weekly, or hourly repeated contexts, or a variety of contexts whose appearance over time is in a clear-cut pattern (in many endeavors or professions, for example, there are seasons for this, that, and the other thing). Some of the economies of specialization arise as a result of redefining and reassembling effort components so that they appear in repetitive contexts. An extreme example is the assembly-line worker who is asked to carry out the same motion every few minutes or seconds. Is rational behavior different in some sense under repetitive or patterned contexts compared to one-time-only contexts? By repetitive contexts I refer to situations where the person does not know a choice problem of a similar nature will repeat itself.

If contexts are periodic, individuals may work out a simplified decision procedure in which they find it convenient to repeat their behavior pattern time after time. Let us refer to such modes of behavior as a position. It seems likely that for many individuals there will exist present position preference. In other words, if the choice context repeats itself, it is unnecessary for an individual to go through complex decision processes in the same way, and to the same degree, and with the same information and exploratory costs, on each occasion. In fact, after a while, once it is noticed that the contexts are almost identical, or resemble each other to a considerable degree, it is necessary only to make slight adjustments for the slight variations that the periodic choice contexts present. In some cases it may even appear profitable to ignore slight variations in the context and behave as though the context repeated itself in every detail. A person may discover that the loss in such a lack of responsiveness may be very small.

Consider the person who eats each evening in the same restaurant and chooses from the same twenty-item menu. Suppose that every once in a while, on a random basis, one or two of these items are altered. The customer who ignores the menu changes may feel that he is better off not having to worry about the choice problem every evening. This will depend in part on whether or not the person has a strong preference for novelty. The main point of this discussion is to suggest that individuals in situations where contexts are repeated are likely to have present position preference. Such a mode of behavior might be called "ratchet rationality." The individual works himself into a behavioral groove, so to speak, which he finds comfortable, and which he would prefer not to leave unless the potential gain of moving out of the groove, or the potential loss of not moving, are beyond some given threshold values.

A variety of reasons come to mind why movements from one well-grooved decision procedure to another may involve real or emotional costs. To begin with, there are likely to be uncertainty elements in any new set of repeated contexts as against the existing set. Similarly, if the move involves changing the response in existing contexts in which a high degree of interdependence between individuals is involved, again uncertainty enters. The greater the extent to which people have worked out their own "position," the greater the likelihood that they have present position preference. They avoid the cost of search of new positions, the cost of learning new responses, the cost of possibly breaking existing social relationships, or the cost of forging new social relations, or costs of any other type of uncertainties that may exist in new contexts.

In many contexts where people have to dovetail their activities with those of others there is an awareness of the value of predictable behavior. One's own predictability makes it easier for others to make decisions, and vice-versa. Movements away from predictability are often emotionally costly. We choose predictable behavior patterns in part because we wish to appear as consistent personalities. The Gauguins of this world, who break consistent patterns and choose completely new positions, are relatively rare. For the most part economic life is not based on such behavior. Even in Gauguin's case the new mode of life contained highly patterned responses to relatively repeated contexts. High personal productivity frequently requires such behavior.

Using the type of diagram associated with other dimensions of rationality, we can visualize on the X-axis a dimension which involves degrees of consistency in periodic repetitious contexts, and on the Y-axis pressures that arise from deviations from such consistency. We might expect that the indifference curve of many individuals would result in highly consistent patterns. Unless the gains are sufficiently large most individuals will not choose to move to new patterns. They choose to stay with an existing pattern and appear insensitive to relatively small variations in opportunities.

Selective Rationality, Interpersonal Influences, and Economic Unit Behavior

In the theory being developed the primary behavioral actors are individuals. Groups take on secondary behavioral roles, so to speak. The analytic procedures to be used are suggested in the previous pages. Strict maximizing behavior on the part of individuals will be dropped. Rather, individuals will be assumed to choose some type of selective rationality and behave in accordance with the form chosen. In a number of contexts the form of selective rationality chosen by many reduces itself to a type of "ratchet rationality." In such cases this greatly simplifies the problem of interpretation. Individuals will be assumed to interact with each other within basic behavioral units, namely households and firms, and the behavior of households and firms will be presumed to follow, or be a consequence of, individual behavior. Interpersonal relationships are supportive of the types of decisionmaking designated as selective rationality. The result is that formal economic units such as firms whose "motivations" are determined by the interaction of their members no longer behave in accordance with some extremum such as minimization or maximization.

Economic units such as firms which are groups themselves behave in larger group contexts. They operate in a specific industry market. In our analysis we also must reverse the procedure and examine the impact of the market pressures *on* the firm, and the impact of such pressures on individual behavior *in* firms. We will not only proceed from individuals to larger groupings such as the firm and the industry, and by extension to the entire economy, but also consider the consistency of an individual's behavior when we start with the largest possible group and trace its impacts on smaller groups which in turn allow for a more refined form of impact tracing to the individual.

Degrees of Constraint Concern, or Agents versus Principals

A significant consideration is the different degree of constraint concern an individual is likely to show in his behavior, depending on whether the same individual happens to be an agent acting in behalf of someone else, or, in the same circumstances, is a principal. It seems reasonable to presume that, in the same circumstances, an individual will be governed by a lesser degree of constraint concern if he is pursuing someone else's interests than if he is pursuing his own interests. In the rest of this volume, the basic assumption we make, in what may be viewed as the normal case, is that there will be a lesser degree of constraint concern governing the behavior of agents than if these persons were principals.

This is not to deny the possibility that there may be circumstances under which some individuals might not behave in the manner assumed. There may be cases where the personality of an individual is such, *and* the relation of the individual to his principal is such, that the individual identifies with his principal and devotes himself or herself to the principal's aims to a greater degree than the principal would on his own. These may involve cases where the agent feels that he must in some way "prove" himself or herself to the principal in question. We need not probe the depth psychology of such instances. For the purposes of this volume we are concerned with the general case in which the degree of constraint concern is less when an individual acts as an agent than when he acts as a principal. This is especially likely to be so in cases in which the principal is diffused among a number of owners. The actual degree of constraint concern of an agent is likely to depend on the incentives that exist in the context in which decisions and actions take place. Such incentives depend in part on the degree to which principals can make their interests actually, or in appearance, coincidental with the agent's interests, and the extent to which the principal is able to employ other motivators that may be at hand.

Motivational Transmission and Game-Theoretic Rationality

Part of the problem of organization is the transmission of incentives and objectives from some individuals to others, within hierarchical levels, and especially from higher to lower levels in a hierarchy. How does selective rationality enter into the attempts various individuals make to resolve this problem? It may help if I summarize some of our ideas briefly. Rationality has components. Individuals are willing to forego some of the advantages of "extreme levels of rationality" (or of specific components of rationality) because of the costs of the decision process. In addition, they are willing to bear the pressure costs of behaving under less than full rationality.

The main question at this juncture is whether individuals transmit the same degree of rationality from themselves to others, or whether the degree of constraint concern becomes weaker, as it were, as successive transmissions take place. Under some circumstances constraint concern may be augmented in the process of transmission. What are these circumstances? We cannot answer these questions at this stage. It is necessary to identify some characteristics of various organizational contexts before the exact nature of the transmission problem can be worked out. The point is no more than to alert the reader that there is a relation between selective rationality, or degrees of constraint concern, and what happens in the process of the transmission of motivation.

Intraorganization decision contexts frequently involve situations which resemble games of strategy, situations in which the outcome depends not only on the decider's choice (the consequences of the alternatives presumed given) but on other people's simultaneous choices or reactions.

These are "non-parametric" situations. The games known as "prisoners' dilemma" and "chicken" are two especially interesting examples of such situations.[1] There is one set of outcomes if the interacting decisionmakers act cooperatively, and another if they make decisions which engage them in conflict, and especially in situations in which each has the option to attempt to obtain a superior outcome at the expense of the other.

Within both the household and the firm interpersonal relations are frequently of the essence. Such relations generate situations in which cooperation or conflict are possible alternative modes of behavior. Whether or not individuals react in one mode or the other depends not only on the "payoffs" but also on the utilities they associate with cooperation or conflict as such. As a consequence, in our extension of the concept of selective rationality to this class of decision problems we have to consider the utility gain or the utility cost of alternative mixtures of cooperative and conflict stances.

There is a similarity between this approach and the position taken earlier in this chapter. The degree of constraint concern depends not only on the nature of payoffs resulting from the non-parametric choices, but also on the nature of the utilities associated with the mode of decisionmaking itself. The figures following indicate two possible ways in which such situations can work out.

In Figure 12a the ordinate represents a degree of concern about the payoff. The possibility of "worse" payoffs creates more pressure. We need not define "better" and "worse," but simply assume that each "player" has a means of assessing his feeling about the payoff possibilities involved in each strategic choice or choice procedure. Point 0_a represents the zero point for player A and 0_b for B. Now A_1 and A_2 are indifference curves that reflect trade-offs between "better" payoffs and less cooperation and

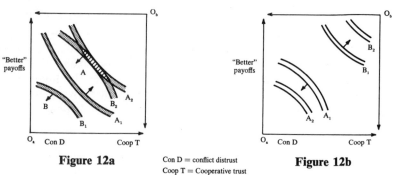

Figure 12a   Con D = conflict distrust   **Figure 12b**
                        Coop T = Cooperative trust

Arrows indicate direction of preference of indifference curves
from "lower" to "higher" curves.

vice-versa. The convex (from the origin) nature of the curves implies that A prefers more to less cooperation. In Figure 12a player B has symmetrical preferences; A_i and B_i are drawn as bands. Clearly there are likely intersections of A_i and B_i—mutually agreeable cooperative strategies exist.

In Figure 12b each player has a much stronger preference for conflict. There are no intersections and no mutually cooperative arrangements exist. (We will discuss later actual outcomes.) The essence of the point being made is that if interacting individuals attach a high utility to cooperative decisions and behavior,* the potential outcomes will be very different than if they attach high utility to conflict. This differs from the usual view in that utility depends not only on the outcome but also on the means of achieving the outcome—that is, cooperation versus conflict.

Summary

Maximizing behavior implies that individuals will use their capabilities or capacities to the greatest degree possible in order to obtain from the context the largest economic gain. However, under our psychological postulates most individuals (perhaps all) do not behave in this manner. It is an essential characteristic of economic contexts that they impose constraints on behavior. Personality characteristics control behavior within contexts. In order to describe the characteristics that govern economic behavior it helps to distinguish among capabilities, the *desire* to use capabilities under constrained circumstances, and the desired standards that individuals want to meet. In general, individuals have to compromise between two sets of opposing psychological forces: the desire to use one's capacities outside the bonds of the constraints inherent in a context; and the desire to fulfill the demands of one's superego, that is, the desire to meet as much as possible one's internalized standards, which in part depend on the observed performance of others.

We designated the concept of "constraint concern" for the set of personality traits which determine the degree of concern an individual shows for the constraints within any economic context. Beyond some point there are limits to which an individual is willing to utilize capacities under constraining influences: for example, there are limits to which an individual is interested in being calculating, to persevere in pursuit of an objective, to assess the realism of a context, or to pay careful attention to any other constraining influence. Thus, beyond some point we postulate negative mar-

* Cooperative behavior usually requires predictable behavior. Hence for many personalities there may be a close connection between a desire to appear predictable and the desire or felt need to be cooperative.

ginal utility associated with the degree to which a capability is used under constraints.

Ignoring constraints in economic contexts usually results in some degree of felt pressure. But we assume that individuals are willing to bear some pressure rather than go beyond some point in their degree of constraint concern. As a result constraint concern-pressure tradeoffs (and counterpart indifference curves) form a basis for behavior. Similarly, there are trade-offs between meeting aspired-to standards and pressure. Hence the individual can make a compromise and choose a subset that represents a comfortable level of constraint concern-pressure tradeoffs. In ensuing chapters I will show that this compromise level of constraint concern, outside of any given context, controls behavior in specific contexts.

Conventional theory does not specify why individuals behave the way they are assumed to in specific contexts, for example, why entrepreneurs should be assumed to desire to maximize the profits or minimize the costs of the firm they are presumed to control. No set of psychological postulates, in the standard theory, explains assumed behavior. By contrast, in the approach developed in this volume I first specified the psychological outside of any particular context in order to suggest how the psychology of an individual determines behavior within economic contexts.

6 The Effort Equilibrium of the Individual

Introduction

I have referred to the degree to which actual output is less than maximum output (for given inputs) as the degree of X-inefficiency, and to increases in output with the same inputs as increases in X-efficiency. In many contexts the same idea is best expressed in value terms of both inputs and outputs.* One basic assertion of this book is that X-inefficiency exists almost everywhere and that its magnitude is significant. The existence of X-inefficiency implies that except in extreme cases firms do not minimize costs, maximize profits, or optimize the rate of technological change. An objection which has been raised regarding the X-inefficiency concept is that it has not been derived from a basic set of microeconomic assumptions. This and the next chapters attempt to deal with this deficiency.

The standard theory of production treats human and nonhuman inputs almost symmetrically, or essentially symmetrically. My theory drops this approach. One distinction is obvious: human "capital," that is, human beings as such, the source of human inputs, cannot be purchased outright. What is usually purchased are units of labor *time*. But these are not the units critical for production. What is critical is *directed effort,* at or beyond some level of skill. Directed effort, however, involves choice and response to motivation on the part of those directing their efforts.

---

* These two sentences express the main forms in which X-inefficiency manifests itself. There are conceivable situations in which these notions are not identical. Suppose a firm maximizes output (in physical quantity terms) from given inputs but chooses to produce the wrong quantity. In that case X-inefficiency should be interpreted as existing despite the fact that it may not fit the criteria under a very strict interpretation of the first sentence. In this chapter we are concerned primarily with the basic idea of X-inefficiency rather than with optimal measurement. In many contexts the best measure will be in value terms, and as a percentage of the maximum value of output, or some other value benchmark given the nature of the comparisons made. I am indebted to K. J. Blois for this and related points. See his "Some Comments on the Theory of Inert Areas and the Definition of X-Efficiency," *Quarterly Journal of Economics,* 88:689–691 (November 1974).

The assumptions on which the theory is based are as follows: (1) The firm is the organization in which, for the most part, the inducements are generated that determine effort choices. (2) Labor contracts are incomplete. (3) Not all inputs are purchasable in terms of the units in which they are used in production. (4) There is no fixed trade-off between the units on the basis of which inputs are purchased (for example, time) and those of which they are used (for example, effort). (5) Beyond some point there is diminishing utility to effort, and beyond some other point negative marginal utility. (6) Not all inputs are traded. (7) The objective function of the firm is not completely determined and specified externally to the firm. The objectives of the firm depend on the preferences for a variety of things of those in the interrelated groups which make up the organization which we call the firm.*

Because the continuous labor contract is always incomplete, and because occupational roles have to be interpreted from various behavioral acts and incomplete information, the dimensions of effort are rarely completely specified. Almost all employees have some latitude in this respect. Some examples of the possible dimensions of effort are: various physical activities; the act of choosing between different activities; scanning the "information field" inside and outside the firm; evaluating the transmitted information; looking for a new means of performance, techniques of production, and new inputs or outputs; the degree of cooperation with coworkers; and the discernment and degree of devotion to group goals.

Interesting firms possess a fairly high degree of continuity, and require from their constituents a considerable degree of continuity in internal relationships. The extent to which firms operate effectively depends in part on the degree to which the internal relations between members of the same firm are relatively stable.

The economic behavior of each individual is viewed as depending upon a choice made within a contractual arrangement that is incomplete. Contracts are "semi-continuous" and open-ended. There is enough looseness in such contracts for individuals to play a game with each other to determine their relative effort positions until they reach a set of "equilibrium" effort points. An analogy would be a chess game in which the two players eventually reach a draw and the same moves can repeat themselves indefinitely.

---

* In other parts of the theory we also assume that (8) Some aspects of the production function are not fully known to the "firm." However, this is not a necessary assumption for purposes of the present chapter.

"Employment" Contracts

I use the words "employee," "worker," and "member" interchangeably, referring to someone who "belongs" to the firm, who has a possible performance role in the production sense, and who receives remuneration for this performance. In general these words will not imply the possible subordinate or supervisory natures of the role. Mere stockholders, as such, are not members of the firm because they do not have a production role, even in the remotest sense.

A great many employment contracts are possible. Firms may be organized for fixed periods or for a fixed set of transactions. However, unless otherwise stated, I refer to those firms which continue indefinitely into the future and whose contractual arrangements with members of the firm are also of a continuous, indefinite, and somewhat open nature. Of course there are many other possibilities. A firm may be established for a single venture with a specified and brief duration. Arrangements between a firm and its employees may be for a specific performance of some sort in which the nature of the employee's effort is not as important as the specific results. If a firm hires a man to install a piece of equipment and nothing more, it may care only that the equipment be installed and be unconcerned with how the job is done. Once the equipment is installed, the contractual relationship ends. These types of relations are not of prime interest here. Nothing is lost if we assume that firms and employment relations are continuous and open-ended, although it can be argued that even in presumed specific, highly limited performance contracts, the elements we are concerned with do enter. There is usually a variable *quality* aspect to all performance.

What is involved is not only the nature of employment contracts, but simultaneously the economics of capital expenditures and the economic value of repetition and indefinite continuity of operation. Most activities involve "setting up" costs. These may have a physical manifestation, such as the cost of equipment, or simply a labor cost manifestation which involves doing things to get you started but once started do not have to be repeated very often. In essence it is economic to amortize setting-up costs over long periods or over many repeated instances. As a result, in most fields single-venture enterprises are not economic. A great deal is gained, and nothing analytically is lost, if we assume that the general case being considered is the indefinitely continuous enterprise. There is an economic advantage simply to be known as an indefinitely continuous enterprise offering certain products or services. The mere fact of such knowledge enables others to apply for trade in either the inputs or the outputs.

In addition to indefinite continuity firms usually have an external image. Others have an idea to some extent as to what the firm does. Some members of such firms have to be connected with it both in terms of the image characteristics and the indefinite continuity characteristics. But indefinite continuity allows for changes in the activities of the firm and in its image. As a consequence of these requirements it becomes impossible to have "closed" contracts which define precisely all aspects of the relation of firm members to the firm. Thus employment contracts are essentially open for at least some firm members, usually, at least in some small degree, for all firm members.

The Dimensions of Effort

The basic hypothesis upon which the X-efficiency theory rests is that there is always a degree to which effort, in its broadest sense, is a variable. This is obviously true with self-employed individuals, who can exert as much or as little effort as they wish. The fact that there are consequences, such as differences in income, related to putting forth less rather than more effort does not make it any less true. Effort is a variable.

Is effort a variable when employment relations are involved? If we examine the dimensions of effort it becomes almost inconceivable for effort not to be a variable. It might appear, at first blush, that this would depend on the nature of the job. However, I will argue that effort is a variable in all instances. This follows in part from the assumption that employment contracts are incomplete and open. Not every aspect of the job is specified in advance. This is not only a reasonable assumption based on the facts of the normal work situation, but as we shall see, in most and perhaps all instances, incomplete employment contracts are more efficient than complete ones, even where "completeness" is sought. In other words, economics dictates that such contracts be incomplete. This will become more evident as we consider the complex nature of work effort and its component parts.

We can divide work effort into four components:

A　the choice of *activities* which compose the effort;
P　the *pace* at which each activity is carried out per unit of time;
Q　the *quality* of each activity;
T　the *time* pattern and length of activity.

Assume that a worker is in no way restricted in his choice of what he can do. He begins a job and is given some information. However, the information is incomplete; it does not specify the exact detailed character of the tasks he is to perform. Hence, he is forced to interpret the job. A central notion is that an interpretation involves the choice of a specific *APQT* bundle, that is, an *activity–pace–quality–time* bundle, drawn from a set of possible *APQT* bundles. The first element of choice involves the "doings" of the job, the specific things which have to be done to perform it. We are not concerned with whether these things are satisfactory or unsatisfactory from the "employer's" viewpoint. We are concerned simply with the fact that an interpretation involves, in part, choosing a set of activities which become the performing of the job. In an extreme case each activity may be zero. The choice of no activity is a permissible interpretation—although in most instances it will not be a satisfactory one from a superior's point of view.

Once a vector of activities is chosen, the question regarding the pace at which the activities are carried out arises. The simple notion is that at least some activities can be carried out at a variety of speeds, hence, the pace can vary.

The qualitative factor is associated with the performance of each activity. To some degree quality is connected with pace. For some activities beyond some point, quality declines as the pace increases. Whatever the exact relation, there is always a quality component. In the cutting of cloth in the manufacture of clothes, the qualitative aspect involves in part the accuracy in the cutting. Speed is not the only element which enters in the determination of quality. In addition to native or acquired skills the quality component depends on the extent to which the worker aims at high quality, and the degree of concentration and attention with which he carries out his job. Environmental elements also enter; a person's diet, sleeping patterns, and the nature of his non-working life may affect the quality of his work activities.

Finally there is a time dimension in work and a time pattern. The employment contract may specify fixed hours of work; nevertheless, an employee can frequently choose to come late or to come on time. In some instances he may be able to choose to quit early, to quit exactly on time, or to stay after hours. In many instances there may be options as to whether or not an employee chooses to work on weekends. Perhaps more importantly, the time dimension enters in the choice of the rhythm of work. Work is rarely carried out continuously. There is some choice in the "stop-go" pattern. In many professions the hours of work may be freely chosen and here work time is variable.

The second component of the variable T, the time pattern of activities, involves a fairly complex set of subcomponents. Let t_i be the average time length during which activity i is carried out. The activities include periods of rest between periods of work. We readily visualize ordering the activities i into a specific sequence $s(t_i)$. Such a sequence will determine the length of the total working period. This formalization gives the appearance of a much more rigid and routinized work pattern than seems to be the case for many individuals. But we are concerned here with average values for t_i. Flexibility can be introduced by visualizing upper and lower bounds for t_i, say $t_{i\ min.}$ and $t_{i\ max.,}$ so that the actual time put in on any activity depends on circumstances. It is the sequence of average values of the time lengths of the activities which we capture by the variable T in the job interpretation denoted by an *APQT* bundle. Needless to say, we do not intend to capture work reality in all its fine-grained texture in this particular fashion. Once again, we are not concerned with the relation between time put in and remuneration. Our concern for the time being is that the *interpretation* of a job (an employment contract) involves the choice of an *APQT* bundle.

Preset versus Free-Choice APQT Bundles

An employee either chooses his own *APQT* bundle or has it chosen for him by someone in the firm. A major distinction exists between preset *APQT* bundles and partially free-choice bundles. In the former, all aspects of work performance are determined in advance and the employee simply agrees whether or not to perform in the preset mold. My hypothesis is that some complete or partial free-choice *APQT* bundles are likely to be more efficient than preset ones. Although preset *APQT* bundles are possible, they are likely to be far from optimal. For instance, some activities may be carried out with a greater degree of precision than others, or with more care, or with greater attention to details. The employer can choose to specify the required activity-pace-quality-time bundle. However, if this is not to be done arbitrarily, then the managerial capacity and knowledge of techniques would have to be of a very high order indeed for the specified *APQT* bundles to approximate an optimal bundle. The alternative is to allow the workers to learn on the job and to choose an appropriate *APQT* bundle. Whether workers choose well or not will depend upon their overall capacities and the incentives they face in the work context. It seems likely that in most circumstances the employer may, in various degrees of explicitness, offer some categories of workers a higher wage, provided they learn and carry out, as well as choose, *APQT* bundles which are superior to the acceptable $APQT$ bundles specified in advance by the employer. Employees who explicitly or tacitly accept this bargain receive a higher wage in return for which they agree to work more effectively.

To preset the $APQT$ bundles normally requires a fantastic amount of knowledge of operations, exceptionally close supervision of the individuals carrying out the activities, and detailed quality control of the results. Presetting $APQT$ bundles is likely to require very high information costs, supervisory costs, and quality-control costs, as compared to non-preset or partially preset bundles. In addition, the psychic costs on employees working under preset conditions must be considered. These psychic costs often include elements of boredom, low morale, and a high degree of irritation, which is a common reaction to close supervision and detailed control. The non-preset mode of operation, based on incentives for individuals to choose reasonably good $APQT$ bundles and on the internalization of some of the firm's production values, is apt to be more productive than the completely preset alternative.

A completely predetermined $APQT$ bundle set requires extreme assumptions concerning "management." The assumption is that there is a clearcut dichotomy between those who give and receive orders (between management and labor), and a special dichotomy between the internalized values of management and those of labor. In essence this dichotomy must be a false one, except perhaps in the rare case of the one employee–one owner–manager firm. In general, managers are employees. In the pure preset situation, the managers' $APQT$ bundles must also be preset. In fact, managers would have no more freedom than those they supervise. Their own activities would have to be closely supervised and controlled, and all the strictures made about the psychic costs on those supervised would apply to the supervisors as well. We fall into an almost infinite regression, culminating with the "boss," who knows all and directly or indirectly sees all, supervises all, controls all. This vision of a work situation is as much in the realm of fantasy as its alternative, in which everyone has complete, free, and unconstrained choice of his $APQT$ bundle and in which such choices are untrammeled by adverse consequences of any sort. Not only are extreme information requirements implied in the pure preset case, but it is doubtful that managers would wish to function in this manner; their jobs would be too unpleasant. It follows that considerable free choice exists for $APQT$ bundles in almost all situations. Such choices are likely to be constrained in some degree by an "incentive-penalty" system and, for some aspects of the work, by supervisory and quality controls as well. Clearly, the existence of some controls does not eliminate the existence of choice.

A completely specified work contract, dependent upon a control system, would have to specify in detail not only the penalties for unsatisfactory work but the means of supervision and the detection of unsatisfactory work, as well as the methods of its assessment. A detailed consideration of the difficulties involved in setting up a pure preset *APQT* bundle work situation illustrates the difficulties of specifying a complete employment contract.

There are certain advantages to a non-preset work scheme. Such a scheme uses interpersonally specified and diversified knowledge quite efficiently.* It avoids the very high cost of detailed supervision and the low morale and personal irritation generated by highly detailed supervision. Managerial and entrepreneurial roles with no preset work schemes are made possible for many individuals, arrangements which do not impose the burden of possessing the unusual amount of knowledge required under preset schemes. Such non-preset schemes make working life tolerable. If preset arrangements were imposed and costs were minimized by setting Stakhonovite standards, work would take on a degree of monotony and irksomeness which might be avoided or kept under control in the non-preset case. Obviously the existence of choice makes it possible for people to choose job interpretations which avoid unusual psychic stress.

A typical employee is visualized as being faced with a host of *APQT* bundles. To interpret his job he must choose a particular bundle or effort point. (The terms *APQT* bundle and effort point are used interchangeably.) Initially an employee experiments with a number of bundles before determining which one he likes. At the outset he or she usually has only very limited knowledge of the range of choices available. As a result, the employee may not know the degree of satisfaction obtainable from the various *APQT* bundles. Almost every job involves some degree of search. Trial and error experiences in which the satisfaction involved in carrying out various activities cannot be assessed beforehand. In this sense the utility-effort relations are unstable at the outset. This is especially true when some component of utility is associated with novelty itself. Initial experiences in work situations may be more or less satisfying than when they have become stable and the trial and error process has been virtually eliminated. For now we are concerned with stable utility-effort relations, with employees who know the experience of interpreting their jobs in a specific way. The novelty and learning aspect can be considered later.

---

* That preset *APQT* bundles are inefficient is dramatically illustrated by recent British experience under which railroad workers have discovered that they can carry out the equivalent of a strike simply by "working to rule." Anyone familiar with bureaucracies knows that the rigorous enforcement of rules can depress productivity precipitously.

An employee in a stable employment situation will associate every *APQT* bundle with a given degree of utility. Can anything be said further about the utility relations of sets of alternative *APQT* bundles? To start with, let us ignore the activity choice aspect. Consider the question of pace. It is obviously meaningful to speak of greater and lesser pace. Figure 13 shows three alternatives.

The curve *A* assumes that the greatest utility is associated with a zero *pace* of effort, and utility decreases as pace increases. For curve *B* a zero utility is associated with zero pace. Utility increases as pace increases. The utility function rises and then falls in the situation shown in curve *C*. It is immaterial (as we shall see later) whether in *C* we start with a zero utility for zero pace or a positive or negative utility. Curve *C* differs from the others in that the utility function is not monotonic throughout its length. Curve *C* is likely to reflect the case for almost all individuals. Beyond a certain point utility cannot indefinitely increase as pace increases, or workers woud die of exhaustion. Some might prefer a zero pace of work to any given pace. But this is unlikely to be true for all activity bundles.

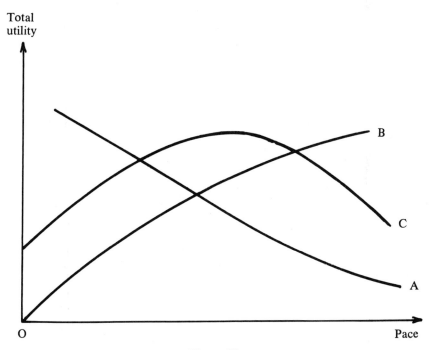

Figure 13

Frequent casual observations lead me to believe that in any stable working situation, some activity choice is apt to be made which yields more satisfaction than not working at all. We assume that the utility pace function is initially monotonically increasing, and beyond some point monotonically decreasing.

Assuming that the quality dimension can be assessed in terms of greater or lesser, there is probably an optimum quality level at which people will want to perform any chosen set of activities. If the quality is exceptionally low, carrying out the activities will reduce their meaningfulness and yield little satisfaction. However, carrying out the activities at a very high quality level involves a degree of concentration and a concern with detail that many personalities would find onerous. Hence, here too the type of utility function depicted in curve C is usually the normal one.

The relations between utility and activity are likely to be parallel to what we normally assume to be the utility relation for commodities. In general (up to a point) individuals prefer a variety of activities to a single activity. Beyond a certain point some diminishing marginal utility per unit of activity exists. For any two given activities we would expect a diminishing marginal rate of substitutability of activity A for activity B, at least beyond some point. As a result, isoquants which reflect constant utility contours for two activities would have more or less the same properties.

Although the foregoing may apply to most individuals, extreme cases cannot be ruled out. For some, indeed for almost everyone, there are some sufficiently unpleasant activities which are not chosen, irrespective of the mix of other activities. The range of activities actually chosen in a great many work situations is actually very limited. Production activities are much more highly specialized than the range of consumption goods an individual typically consumes. Narrow specialization reflects not only the taste for carrying out these activities, but perhaps more importantly, the relatively high rewards of specialization.

The work context normally involves constraints. To some degree employers or others expect certain minimal standards of performance which most individuals interpret as constraints. Thus, certain activities will not be chosen irrespective of the utility associated with them, simply because they are very clearly perceived as not being part of the job. Other activities will be avoided because they appear unpleasant, although they may be perceived as *possibly* within the job situation, but not *necessarily* so. In most cases an activity mix will be chosen which reflects a relatively high degree of utility for that mix. At the margin at which the actual mix takes place, we assume that there is an almost constant rate of substitutability among the different activities. In other words, small shifts in the ratio of activities have little effect on total utility. If two activities are involved, the utility surface may be visualized as an upside-down, relatively flat bowl, and the choice actually made is in the neighborhood of the relatively flat portion of the bowl.

The material rewards for effort must be included as part of the utility of effort. Most individuals receive a wage or salary for a job as well as the utility obtained from the actual work. The wage or salary is normally given for "adequate performance," hence, above some minimal level of effort, the wage adds a constant quantum of utility to the utility as such. Thus, the marginal utility relations of the components of effort are not affected by the utility of the reward for effort.

An individual's choice of the $APQT$ bundle determines the value added to the product of the firm. (In extreme cases the value added may be negative.) If the firm presumably maximizes profits and minimizes costs, then it would be in its interest to induce employees to choose $APQT$ bundles which would maximize value added. Firms are, however, unlikely to operate in this manner, so let us assume that there is a sense in which every $APQT$ bundle chosen by an individual is associated with a net value added to the firm. This is obviously true for those cases in which the firm can assess the value of the contribution, or even when it can assess it in principle and does not do so. We assume that a contribution to value of product exists.

Diagrammatic Illustration

Some of the ideas presented are further developed with the aid of Figure 14a. The curves A_1 to A_4 are indifference curves which reflect the choice of an individual between two production activities α and β for a given pace of effort. (Thus, α and β are members of A in the $APQT$ bundle.) Q_1 to Q_4 are quantities that identify the isoquants of value added to output. P_1 represents pace level 1, and so on. The locus OA of tangencies A_iP_i indicates the optimum activity distribution for different pace levels for an individual. The locus MQ of tangencies P_iQ_i indicates the activity bundles for different pace levels which maximize value added to the firm. As illustrated, the preference activities locus and the maximum output locus are not the same. What the individual wants to do does not lead to maximum output.

The activity indifference curves A_1 to A_4 are drawn so that they reflect a preference for less rather than more pace, and the existence of a trade-off between a worse distribution of activities and a lower pace. However, for indifference curves close to the origin, a greater pace may be preferred to a lesser one, and in that area, portions of the curves would be concave to the origin.

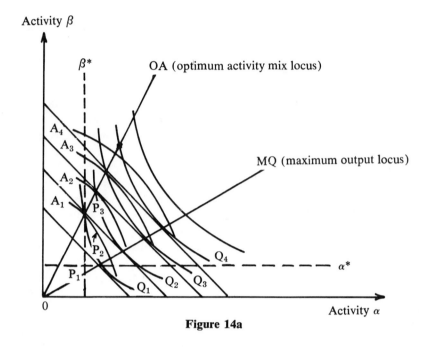

Figure 14a

We ignore for the present the relation between pace and leisure. However, a low pace on the job is not the same as, or a substitute for, leisure in terms of time away from the job. Nor is utility a simple function of pace. For cooperating individuals, utility in the aggregate may not fall if pace is increased, for within some range an individual's primary concern may be that his pace should be equal rather than slower or faster than those with whom he must cooperate.

For many individuals attached to a firm certain minimum performance levels are usually agreed to implicitly, and the "violators" may believe themselves subject to some sort of discipline. This may even involve the firing of an individual. Of course, various degrees of vagueness may exist in the implicit or even explicit agreement concerning minimum "required" performance levels. In Figure 14a levels α^* and β^* are the minimum performance levels. As already noted, MQ is the maximum performance locus, and OA represents the locus of activity mix α and β most desired by the individual for alternative pace levels.

In Figure 14b the curve $U(OA)$ indicates the utility-effort relation for the individual who operates on the locus OA. (The utility includes the utility of income, marked UY in Figure 14b; for simplicity we assume that

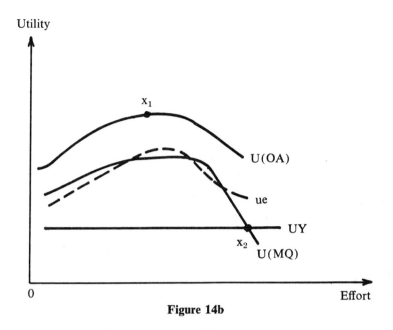

Figure 14b

effort does not influence income.) On OA every value of α is associated with a given β. Similarly on the X-axis we assume for every value of α the related value of β. (For simplicity we assume the ratio of α to β is constant for all points on OA.) The curve $U(MQ)$ indicates the utility-effort relation for the individual if he is operating on the quantity maximizing locus MQ. A later section will show why an individual will not necessarily nor usually choose the effort point x_1 that maximizes his utility from effort and income. There is no reason for him to choose x_2 which maximizes the value of output to the firm, and at which the utility of income is counterbalanced by the disutility of effort.

The Flat-Top Hypothesis

A typical utility-effort index relation $U(OA)$ is shown in Figure 14b. Two major shapes seem likely. In the figure it is assumed that up to a point the individual prefers more effort to less effort, that is, all things being equal, he is not happiest when he is not working. Beyond some point it is assumed that he prefers less effort to more. This suggests that there is a limit to which effort is enjoyed for its own sake and that beyond some point it becomes onerous.

The utility curve $U(OA)$ of Figure 14b, has a relatively flat top. A "comfortable effort range" exists, within which people do not mind working somewhat harder or less hard, hence, total utility does not change markedly. We assume that this is true for most employees.

Before continuing this discussion of effort-utility relations, consider briefly what we mean by "effort." Unfortunately this cannot be done with precision at this point, so the matter will have to be considered in detail later. Effort may be thought of in terms of pace or time dimension or some combination of the two for given A's and Q's. This view is clear-cut and in most cases will be adequate.

When it is inappropriate, we can view trade-offs between activities and so forth in terms of the value contributed to output of units on each dimension and use that to compose an index of effort. It is immaterial whether it is practical to carry out this exercise since our concern is meaning, and when possible I shall use "effort" in the former rather than the latter sense.

In some sense "increased effort" means "working harder," even if we do not necessarily increase the pace level. It may imply an increase in attentiveness, in concentration, in the degree of worrying about details, or in some combination of these elements.*

The effort-utility relation reflects an individual's personality. Highly rigid individuals desire very specific effort levels. A "Stakhanovite" type would seek to maximize his effort level and keep it close to physical exhaustion. We need not dwell on the peculiar personality types. Rather, I shall argue on behalf of our "flat-top" assumption that the flexibility requirements of most individuals, as well as the requirements of the organization of which they are a part, make it desirable that most employable individuals possess some degree of relative flexibility in their effort levels.

Some arguments in favor of the relative generality of the "flexible" flat-top utility-effort function are as follows: (1) Those who "cope well" with variations in the external demands on a person's effort have a flat-top function. (2) People who have many nonwork activities of approximately equal marginal utility have such a function: they can shift from nonwork activities to work activities without greatly altering their total utility. (3) The more varied and complex the firm and the more some people's activities must be dovetailed with those of others, the greater the extent to which selection processes will choose flexible types. (4) Because the cost

* Effort points should be distinguished from *effort levels,* or degrees of effortfulness. (See Appendix II for a discussion of meaning and measurement of effort level.) For ease of exposition we asume in Figure 14b, and in Figures 15–19, that for each effort level shown on the abscissa there is only one effort point. This need not be the case but to allow for that would unnecessarily complicate the discussion at this juncture.

of supervision is high, flat-top types are desirable. Management can count on changes in the pace of work to meet external circumstances without detailed supervision. (5) Low-effort, rigid people are often rejected by the firm in periods of crisis. (6) Inflexible individuals (those with peaked and atypical utility-effort relations) will be isolated from groups when effort dovetailing is desired. They are likely to be moved to jobs which require little or no dovetailing, and in which influence is minimized. (7) Rigidly high-effort people are apt to be rejected by their peer groups through various formal and informal small group processes. Groups find ways of rejecting or disciplining the "rate-buster."

Effort-utility functions are influenced to some degree by interpersonal cooperative relations. We would expect cooperative workers to approximately equalize their combined work effort rates whenever it is necessary for them either to dovetail their work or to get along in the small group culture. This implies that the utility of A's effort level will depend to some degree on B's effort level if A is cooperative. It also implies a further flattening of A's effort curve if A takes into account alternative levels of B's effort and vice-versa. Thus, not only are the formal and informal selective processes likely to select in favor of flexible "flat-top" types, but the effort range of the flat-top is likely to be similar for different individuals within the same groups.

Consider briefly the effect of earnings. If all earnings are a function of time, then the "flat-top" effort range will be retained. In Figure 14b the total utility of income is shown by the line UY. The utility-effort relation, excluding income, is marked ue. Adding ue and UY we obtain the total utility for money earned and effort, $U(OA)$. Because the total utility for earnings of effort do not change with effort, the shape of the sum of the two relations will be basically similar.

It may be useful at this juncture to recall some of the basic psychological postulates developed in the preceding chapter. If we visualize an individual at successively higher levels of constraint concern beyond the optimal level U^*, then the marginal utility associated with higher level of constraint concern decreases. This notion has implications for the shape of the effort utility function UE in Figure 15. Beyond some point we should expect that increases in effort involve greater constraint concern, especially in those cases where greater effort implies greater productivity, and as a consequence, increased effort levels would be associated with declines in the utility from effort. Hence, to some degree the shape of the UE curve follows from the notion of incomplete constraint concern, as well as the notion of a most comfortable level of constraint concern U^*.

We must also recall that the concept of constraint concern includes

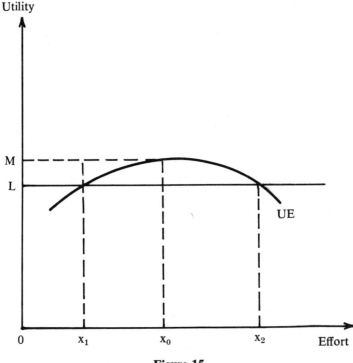

Figure 15

components which involve a sense of obligation to the individual's self-interest, and simultaneously less than complete obligation to the interests of the firm. This would imply in Figure 14b that an individual would not seek to achieve a maximum point on the curve $U(MQ)$ rather than on the curve $U(OA)$. In part this is related to the earlier discussion in which I argued that an individual acting as an agent has a different utility effort function than he would have if a principal. Of course if the individual acted as a principal he would be receiving additional income from increased effort and this aspect would have to be included in the utility-effort relation.

Effort Points and Effort Positions

In calling any $APQT$ bundle an effort point, I had in mind a very specific exertion of effort whose values along the four dimensions ($APQT$) were unique. Individuals normally do not see their efforts in quite such precise terms. In most instances jobs are interpreted so that a little more or a little less of an "outlay" of effort along a given dimension does not make much difference. Hence, we must distinguish between an effort *position* and an effort *point*. What is chosen from a somewhat longer-run viewpoint by an individual is an effort position. By this I have in mind a set of effort points or a neighborhood of effort points which are adjacent to each other and within which an individual is willing to extend his effort without any significant change in the motivations involved. For example, an individual may be willing to work ten minutes more or less per day without any change in motivations, but to work an extra hour might require more than the normal hour's compensation as an inducement. The same may hold for the other dimensions of effort. Thus, an individual may interpet his job as operating within this neighborhood of effort points, but he may visualize that a different *neighborhood* of effort points implies a different interpretation.

One reason for emphasizing the contrast between effort positions and effort points is the nature of the signals that indicate demands for effort in most economic contexts. Effort is usually called for by a signal (a verbal request, a written request, an order, a complaint, and so on). Such signals are usually interpreted as calls for effort of a given type and magnitude: and such interpretations, when heeded, trigger what the individual believes to be the appropriate effort response. There may be work contexts where it appears that individuals are given a certain task which they perform day in and day out, and in which there is little evidence that they are responding to any flow of signals. However, even in such instances emergencies arise—equipment may break, a piece of material may appear defective. Such aspects of the work context which they could not anticipate or be expected to respond to may be viewed by some individuals as signals to change effort, or may be ignored entirely. In the absence of complete certainty it seems best to generalize and visualize individuals choosing effort *positions* within which they choose effort points in response to their interpretation of changing signals.*

The Theory of Inert Areas and the Equilibrium of the Individual

The inert area idea reflects a fairly common set of experiences: those in which it is possible to improve a situation in some respects but not worth the effort to do so. By an inert area, I have in mind a set of effort points

* Such an approach is especially useful in interpreting the concept of bureaucracy in the negative sense in which there exist effort positions too narrow to respond to the range of signals which create the appropriate demands on the organization.

whose associated levels of utility are not equal, but in which the action required to go from a lower to a higher utility level involves a utility cost that is not compensated for by the gain in utility. Thus, there are a number of effort points, some preferable to others, but all of which an individual is willing to hold because shifting is too costly.* This is illustrated in Figure 15. The difference between the maximal utility level M and the lower line L represents the cost of shifting from one effort point to another. Clearly, within the range of efforts shown by the segment x_1, x_2 it would not pay for a person who was not at his optimal effort point x_0 to shift to it. The flatter the "flat-top" portion of the curve, the larger the inert segment. Any point in the segment x_1, x_2 can be an equilibrium effort for the individual.

The critical element in the theory is the concept of inert areas. For the individual, the fact that there is a utility cost in a shift from one position to another implies that there is an area within the utility cost bounds which will not induce any change. Opportunities for change which do not lead to a gain in utility (or an evident loss of utility) greater than the cost of the shift in utility will not be entertained seriously. The inert area idea could be transferred from one individual to a number of individuals. If several individuals' activities are interconnected, such as is the case where there is a continuous flow of work, then the choices made must somehow be reconciled with the given interconnections. Individuals cannot maximize their utilities in the choice of activity bundles without taking heed of the extent to which they interfere with choices made by others, setting in motion approval, disapproval, and social sanction mechanisms. If all individuals in a tightly interconnected work situation attempted to maximize the utilities in the choice of their activities, then all of their time might be spent in conflict rather than in productive performance. By recognizing inert areas, employees may avoid some of the more debilitating conflicts that might arise.

The inert area concept is related to human inertia. A very broad concept of utility cost is envisioned in which the elements that contribute to inertia are an indifference range between effort utilities, an insensitivity range, the uncertainty of the utility of a new point over the existing one, as well as over its "effortfulness," exaggerated assessments of the temporary cost of moving, the fear of newness, and fear of disappointment, and so on. In some contexts it may be especially useful to distinguish two separate components of the cost of moving: the utility cost of moving *away* from the present position—that is, that part of the utility cost reflected in present

---

*Both the costs of moving and the expected gains may be flows. After a move is made its cost consequences may continue since the move many continue to receive disapproval from some individuals. Thus, to make comparisons, individuals may have to consider long-run consequences on both the cost and gain side.

position preference; and the utility cost of getting set up and settling in, so to speak, into a new position. I touched upon some of these matters in Chapter 5 and will consider them in greater detail later.

How does an individual get into an inert area? Usually by trial and error. An individual chooses an effort position from what he believes are *known* and *allowable* positions. He associates this effort position with a certain utility. Will he move to another effort position from which he can derive a higher utility? This depends on the utility cost of moving and the utility gain from such a move. We can visualize a set of points where the utility costs of shifting from any one point within the set to any other within or outside that set involves a utility cost that is less than the utility gained. Such a set of points is an "inert effort area." Thus, an individual normally finds himself through a process of trial and error in his *optimal* inert effort area. He rarely chooses a maximum utility effort position.*

Formally we should distinguish "internal inert areas"—sets of points within which any move from any point to any other involves a greater utility cost than utility gain—from a proper inert area (or optimal inert area)—a set of points for which any movements from a point in the set to any believed allowable point inside or outside the set involves a utility loss from moving greater than the utility gain.

The basic behavioral assumption is that if the initial effort position is not in a proper inert area, an individual will move to his proper or optimal inert area. Once he lands on a point in the optimal inert area he will stay there even if the effort position chosen does not maximize his utility.

The theory of inert areas suggests the essential equilibrium condition for the individual. In equilibrium the individual takes up an effort point or position in his optimal inert area. As long as the conditions determining the inert area persist there is no reason for him to move. Essentially this

---

* The inert area theory applies to information-gathering as well as to other activities. The theory of decisionmaking under uncertainty is bypassed. What is posited in its place is what might be called the principle of temporarily sufficient information. Although decisions are made in the face of intrinsic uncertainty, individuals may find it convenient to use less information than is available. Suppose that a catalog of the world's reaction to almost every option exists, and that it is dismembered and the pages distributed randomly in various known locations. Decisionmakers gather information to discover responses to options, but the process involves a cost. At some point in the gathering process they think they know enough to predict a positive reward. They face a choice: they can gather more information or they can stop. We assume behavior to be such that they stop when the utility cost of gathering more information is greater than the anticipated gain. The uncertainty problem is essentially avoided if, as is usually the case, they get into their inert area prior to gathering all the information available. Although risk is involved in making such decisions, the uncertainty problem need not be faced consciously and directly. See the mathematical appendix to this book for more on the treatment of information.

implies that the effort-utility relation and the cost of moving remain constant.

The equilibrium of the individual is not a knife-edge situation. If the cost of moving is sufficiently large, a great many changes could take place which would not induce the individual to change his effort position. Thus, the theory of inert areas allows for a degree of stability in individual behavior in the face of a great many changing external conditions.

Appendix I. Utility-Effort Relations under Payment by Result

In this chapter we assumed that individuals received a periodic salary that did not depend on the results of their effort. In most cases this seems a reasonable assumption. But let us consider payments by results, such as a piecework system, although there are only limited areas in which such arrangements are possible.

In Figure 16 the curve marked *UY* indicates the utility from effort that we attribute only to the income from effort in the case of payments by

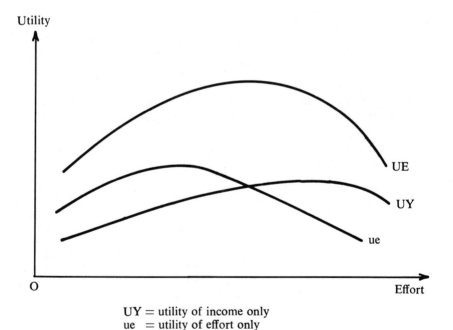

UY = utility of income only
ue = utility of effort only
UE = utility of effort inclusive of income

Figure 16

results. As effort increases, income increases, but we assume marginal disutility of income, so consequently, the curve increases at a decreasing rate up to some point. Beyond some point increases in effort may lead to actual decreases in output, since as the pace of the effort increases the quality of effort may decline, and if quality determines results to some degree then it is possible for actual income to decline beyond some point. The curve marked *ue* again reflects utility of effort apart from the payment of effort. It is reasonable to assume that this curve will reach a peak much earlier than the peak of curve *UY*. When we add the two types of utility and obtain curve *UE* we see that, although influenced by the payments by results procedure, it is on the whole not markedly different in the sense that it could have a relatively flat top. It is reasonable to presume that the peak level will be to the right of the case under which payment is on a purely time basis. In the general case the overall analysis probably would not turn out to be very different under payments by results than it would under the somewhat simpler situation in which every firm member is paid under the basis of time.

Appendix II. On the Meaning of the Effort Rate

The choice of less efficient *APQT* bundles does not imply that these bundles involve less effort. There is no necessary inverse relation between cost and effort and no necessary inverse monotonic relation between effort and its utility. Introspection and observation suggest that for many people doing something which involves more effort may be more fun than doing things which involve less effort. In addition, keep in mind the *distribution* of effort and "leisure" within the firm. If someone in a higher position in a vertical hierarchy chooses for himself a less effortful *APQT* bundle, he may do so by imposing on others more effortful bundles. Thus, even if some are able to trade effort for leisure, it may at the expense of increased effort for others.

Less effort does not necessarily imply more leisure. The clearest case of an *APQT* bundle in which effort and leisure are inversely related is with respect to the absolute amount of time on the job. If a person works fewer hours we usually assume that more leisure or potential leisure is provided. But this choice is available only to a very limited degree to most firm members. Consider quality. Doing one's job in a sloppier fashion in no sense provides time, let us say, to go fishing simultaneously.

A similar argument exists with respect to pace. Suppose activities are designated as either heavier or lighter. A man handling a lighter activity per unit of time does not provide for himself useful leisure time if he substitutes it for a somewhat heavier activity.

Effort is a complex idea. Every way of looking at it involves an index number problem. Somehow we must reduce en entity which involves at least four dimensions to a single one. We view an effort point as a vector containing $A_iP_iQ_iT_i$ components. Each component may contain a number of elements; for example, the activity component may itself contain three specific activities. Elements have to be combined to obtain a single number. One possible approximate index of effort level (or really effortfulness) may, at least in principle, be obtained in the following way. The *effortfulness* of any activity depends on the *pace* at which it is carried out, its quality and the *time* it is carried out. (Performing some activities may appear more effortful at the end of the day than earlier in the day.) Note that A_i of effort point e_i is a subset of activities that may itself contain more than one activity; that is, A_i may be composed of a_{i1}, a_{i2}, and so on, in general denoted by a_{ij}.

Now, for effort point e_i, let P^e_{ijt} represent the degree of effortfulness of the *pace* of carrying out activity a_{ij} at time t. Similarly, we can denote Q^e_{ijt} as the degree of effortfulness of the *quality* involved in carrying out activity a_{ij} at time t. In the absence of other considerations, and if we assume that the effortfulness of different elements in *additive* in order to obtain an approximate index, then the degree of effortfulness of the effort point e_i would be denoted by the expression

$$(1) \qquad \sum_j P^e_{ijt} + \sum_j Q^e_{ijt} \; .$$

There is at least another aspect to consider. Pace and quality interact in determining effortfulness. As quality increases, maintaining a given average pace may be more effortful, and vice versa. To take this into account, let α (where $\alpha \overset{>}{\leqslant} 1$) adjust the *pace* part of the algebraic expression for the average quality of performance, and let β adjust the quality part of the effortfulness component for the average pace. Hence we define an effortfulness level E_i for the effort point e_i as

$$(2) \qquad E_i = \alpha\sum_j P^e_{ijt} + \beta\sum_j Q^e_{ijt} \; .$$

Of course the components in equation (2), which is intended to yield an approximate degree of effortfulness (or degree of effort), may not be strictly additive but for ease of discussion it is helpful to assume that it is.

Pace, the most straightforward component, is usually a physical magnitude which can be externally observed since it is a function of certain number of units of an activity per unit of time. Let us consider effort as a magnitude from the point of view of the person carrying it out. An individual assesses alternatives for each component as more or less effortful; activity i may be more effortful than activity j. Other components of effort are viewed from a similar viewpoint. The final results are presumed to have only cardinal significance. The significant distinction is that the feeling of effort can be separated from the feeling of utility or satisfaction.

Each element of the effort vector requires some means of measuring it. In general the measure represents the psychological assessment of the energy required to carry out the particular element of the effort point. Where an element has a physical measure we would expect the psychological assessment to be a direct monotonic function of the physical measure. Thus, of two different activities involving weight-lifting the one requiring the lifting of a greater weight will be psychologically assessed as requiring a higher degree of effort. The same assessment can be made with respect to distances carried or lines written or calls put through or length of different types of calculations, and so on. Each different activity requires a different psychological assessment.

Quality also involves a psychological assessment. Usually a greater degree of effort "felt" may be required in order to produce a higher quality result in the sense that a greater degree of concentration, attention to detail, or some other mental aspect (frequently related to physical activity) is involved.

Time itself is readily measured in terms of clock time, but *sequences,* and the problem of setting up times, and stopping times involve a psychological assessment of different degrees of effort. There is no way of escaping the psychological assessment of each component of effort, and if we are to have an index of effort there is no way of avoiding the assignment of weights to the element of the effort vector.

At least four ways of viewing someone's effort come to mind: the point of view of the individual carrying out activities; the assessment of the effort by individuals more in vertical constraining relations with the person involved; similar assessments of effort by those in horizontal constraining relations; and to look at effort in terms of the contribution of effort to output.

In an optimally organized firm we would expect the ways of assessing effort to be as close as possible. In poorly organized firms there might be considerable disparity between these so different types of assessments. I will use the degree of such disparities in comparing the implications of different assessments of effort under various organizational circumstances. In sum, physical means frequently can help us assess degrees of effortfulness of some components of effort, but at bottom, "effortfulness" is a psychological magnitude that should be consistent with physical means where such means exist. Although distinct and separate ideas, both effort and utility are psychological notions.

7 Selective Rationality and the Effort Equilibrium of the Group

The bonds of organization depend on criteria for membership and on the extent to which individual members further the pursuance of organizational objectives. But objectives do not exist apart from beliefs about the objectives in the minds of organization members. Different individuals may have similar beliefs or highly divergent ones. Normally we expect that in effective organizations there would be considerable resemblance in the articulation of objectives by important members. This in turn should lead to a resemblance in the articulation of what key individuals believe are the main roles within the organization. Finally, we would expect the individuals playing these roles to carry out their activities in a stable enough fashion so that others would recognize that there is a fairly clear connection between the roles involved, the way they are played, and the sense of firm objectives. Hence in Chapter 6 we were concerned with the effort equilibrium of the individual. Key members choose effort positions which are in their inert areas and which in some vague way are seen as contributing to firm objectives.

The broad concept of the organization depends on the individual's effort choice. A well functioning organization requires fairly stable effort choices. Yet the choice of stable effort positions is motivated at least in part by the perception of organizational objectives. The nature of inert areas is of extreme importance in understanding how viable organizations work.

Selective Rationality and Effort Positions

I took pains in Chapter 6 to suggest that one should not jump to the conclusion that an individual would choose either the effort position that contributed most to firm output or the effort position that maximized utility. While output or utility maximization is not ruled out, such maximization achievements are viewed as extreme possibilities. The typical rational individual would not be an "extreme rationalist." That is, he would associate disutility with extreme values of some of the components of rationality. Another way of looking at the matter is to see human beings as partially driven by somewhat irrational desires and compulsions which have to be deflected and suppressed. The deflection and suppression of seemingly irrational elements are not fun. They involve a utility cost. Hence, we compromise by employing a workable but partial rationality referred to as selective rationality. This results in a compromise constraint concern outcome designated U^* in Chapter 5.

Many of the elements involved in the process of selective rationality result in degrees of insensitivity to some aspects of the choice context. To be imperfectly calculating implies by its very nature a willingness to ignore differences within some range that maximum calculatedness would take into account. The same is true of other elements such as the degree of assessment realism, of nonreflexive behavior, of magnitude sensitivity, as well as the attention to appropriate weights in the process of aggregating the components of rationality, and so on.

All this adds up to a view of the rationality-pressure relations as "bands" rather than simple curves (see Figure 17a). The band marked U^*, whose bounds are U_1 and U_2, indicates the optimal compromise constraint-concern demand curve explained in Chapter 5. Band R, whose upper and lower limits are R_1 and R_2, indicates the individual's anticipated pressure constraint-concern relation. In this case anticipated pressure is a function of the level of constraint concern chosen by the individual. If the job chosen and the job interpretation are both well selected, the R band should either be tangent or intersect with the U^* band. In other words, the job interpretation an individual is comfortable with should be one in which the pressure-constraint concern level that the individual likes is fairly close to the *anticipated* pressure-constraint concern level that he expects the firm to impose. Should these constraints not intersect, then the greater the deviation between U^* and R, the less happy the person is likely to be with his job, and the greater the chance that he will seek an alternative opportunity. Since equilibrium effort positions will be discussed, I have illustrated in Figure 17a a situation in which the U^* and R bands intersect and are of approximately the same width. (The terms "degree of constraint concern" and "degree of rationality" are used interchangeably.)

Figure 17b shows the relation EU (effort-utility), as developed in Chapter 6. On its ordinate is the connected insensitive utility range marked by the magnitude between U_1 and U_2. Initially the bands in Figure 17a appear to suggest something contrary to common sense. The thickness of U^* suggests that within this band a person is indifferent between a higher

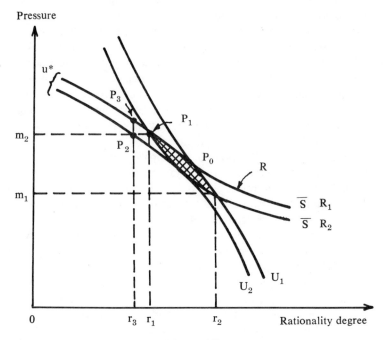

Figure 17a

utility value and a lower one. This appears contrary to the definition of an *iso*-utility curve. But we are concerned not with *ex post* recognition of utility differences but with *ex ante* appreciation. Two aspects are involved: the "sensitivity of instruments," so to speak, and the willingness to bother to use the instrument to the degree of sensitivity that it allows. Some individuals may attempt to assess their weight in single-pound differences while others may want to note only five-pound variations. Thus, a selective aspect to magnitude sensitivity results in ignored differences greater than the indeterminable differences resulting from the insensitivity of the instruments.

The intersection of curves U^* and R results in a set of points common to both. (See hatched section of Figure 17a.) The meaning of the set of points* is that the degree of rationality chosen will fall within the range r_1,

* Consider a point in Figure 17a to the left of r_1 which we designate r_3, and its related pressure level P_3. Will the triangle determined by points P_1, P_2, and P_3 be included in the insensitivity area of the type shown by the hatched section? At first it may appear that, because the person is insensitive between P_1 and P_2 and between P_2 and P_3, this area should be included. But, although an individual may be in-

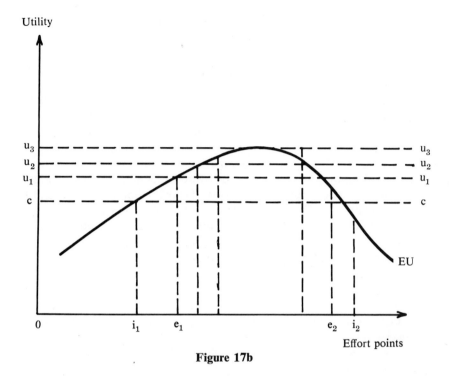

Figure 17b

r_2. (We ignore the related differences in anticipated pressure between the values m_1 and m_2.) One way of looking at it is that a shift in the pressure level within the range m_1 and m_2 will be ignored as a signal to change the degree of rationality, if that degree lies between r_1 and r_2. Similarly, in Figure 17b, if the effort *position* lies *within* e_1 and e_2 the effort position will not change within the associated utility range u_1 and u_2.*

---

different between certain pressure differences, he need not be indifferent between the utility differences associated with the pressure differences. To return to an earlier analogy, suppose utility was measured in pounds and ounces but we cared only about pound differences. Now assume the thickness of the band U^* is one pound thick. We would not choose P_3 because we could get to P_0 which is more than a pound difference. Hence P_3 is excluded. Between P_1 and P_0 there is just a pound difference and hence P_1 is on the boundary of the insensitivity area. It is important to keep in mind that insensitivity is not a transitive relation.

    * Suppose that in Figure 17a the R_2 curve is not tangent to U_2. In other words, curve R is narrower than curve U^*, which implies that the individual is more sensitive to deviations in anticipated pressure than he is to differences in the degree of constraint concern. This is quite possible. However, the outcome for our analysis

There are many ways of classifying the psychological costs that deter movement. For instance, consider the following: present position preference, the cost of making decisions, the cost of disturbing others, and the insensitivity area. An important aspect to keep in mind is that these costs are not necessarily additive. Suppose we look at present position preference as a type of inertia. Once we have paid the cost of going through the procedures to make a decision we may have had to overcome inertia and with it some of the inertia involved in overcoming present position preference. A similar argument can be put forth with respect to the insensitivity area. In other words, once we overcome some of the psychological barriers to movement we may to some extent be overcoming others. Thus, in Figure 17b the insensitivity bounds and the cost-of-moving bounds are not simply added to obtain the utility cost of moving which determines the inert area. In Figure 17b we show insensitivity bounds u_1 and u_3 and a cost-of-moving bound between u_2 and c. The "logical sum" of these bounds cu_3 now determines the inert area of effort points i_1 and i_2.

Consider the nature of the area cu_3. For effort positions whose utility values fall within this area no outward movement will be generated. We may separate costs into two: the decision cost and the moving cost. Unless the gain is greater than the combined costs, movement will not take place. The decision cost manifests itself in part in an insensitivity to pressures so that pressures to move to a different effort position would not be noticed. This is true whether the pressure is internal to the individual or external, since the internal appreciation of the external pressure is the relevant consideration. The psychological cost of moving is effective in a similar manner. There is, on the one hand, no movement within an insensitivity area, and on the other, no change that does not cover the cost of moving. An effort position movement that leads to a gain in utility greater than cu_1 does not guarantee that such a movement will take place since there may be a high degree of insensitivity to such a gain. Thus, the overall gain for an effort-position shift to take place must be greater than or equal to cu_3.

Consider some of the detailed components of rationality as elements of the overall argument. Constraint concern, a major aspect of rational behavior, depends essentially on the appreciation of pressure if there is a lack of such concern. Almost all of the other elements are in one way or another

---

remains identical. The intersection of the two curves, although somewhat smaller than in the case illustrated in Figure 17a, will still be the set of points within which the person is indifferent between different pressure-constraint concern combinations. It seems reasonable to presume that the determining aspect is the variable to which the individual has the greater degree of magnitude sensitivity.

connected to the degree of constraint concern. It is the sense of constraint and the sense of related pressure that prevents people from doing whatever they please. The efforts of individuals within an organization would be completely anarchic were there no constraint concern. One of the functions of management is to create the appropriate sense of constraint concern for firm members (including the managers themselves).

Degree of calculatedness also depends on constraint concern. If pressure is very high it generally forces individuals to be more calculating. The same is true of the degree of realism of the assessment of decision and behavior contexts. Similarly, if behavior is highly dependent it is likely to become more independent where high pressure leads to consideration of alternatives other than those that involve the emulation of others. Similar arguments can be made for the degree of reflexive behavior and for time-deferring tendencies. If pressure is high a decision may be made immediately, whereas if it is low there is the possibility and/or a sufficient feeling of ease to defer the decision. Also, learning from experience is more likely to take place where pressure is high rather than low. As we go through the various components of rationality and relate them to pressure the degree of rationality increases as pressure increases. All of the elements can be interpreted in such a way that the same directional relation holds between a component of rationality and pressure. Each results in higher insensitivity to the pressure instrument where the specific component of rationality is lower.

"Other Person" Pressure, Constraint Concern, and Inert Areas

For a member of an organization the sense of constraint concern and pressure is usually caused by others, through interpersonal relations. To include interpersonal relations into our formulation, it helps to divide the activity part of the $APQT$ bundles into those that involve other people (to be designated by A'), and those that do not (designated by A''). The A' choices involve interpersonal relations and provide the contexts in which some individuals influence or impose constraints on the set of effort bundles available to others. Many individuals are on both the giving and receiving end of interpersonal directing and constraining relations.

To formalize the interpersonal relations we distinguish categories of constraining influences R_c and different sets of effort points that both the constraining and influence relations help determine. The significant relations and categories of effort points (within the firm) are set out in Table 3.

Table 3. Scheme for influence relations within firms and sets of related effort points.

	Symbols			
(1) Constraining or influence element	(2) Both	(3) Functional	(4) Arbitrary	
Traditional	T_c	T_{cf}	T_{ca}	
Vertical	V_c $\left.\right\} = R_c$	V_{cf} $\left.\right\} = R_{cf}$	V_{ca} $\left.\right\} = R_{ca}$	
Horizontal	H_c	H_{cf}	H_{ca}	

Symbol T_c represents constraining influences deriving from the firm's history and traditions. Certain effort bundles will not be chosen because "it is not done that way" traditionally within the firm, the industry, or both. Some of these traditions may be functional in that they are desirable in pursuing the production objectives of the firm; others are arbitrary in the sense that they have outlived the context in which they were functional or were imposed arbitrarily as a consequence of the power positions of certain individuals within the firm.

The symbol V_c denotes constraints imposed through vertical relations. These involve an asymmetry in the direction of influence. Examples are vertical relations in formal hierarchical systems in which superiors give orders to transmit communications to subordinates. Once again, such constraints may be functional or arbitrary.

The symbol H_c represents horizontal relations. Essentially these are the interpersonal relations among peers which are symmetrical in that each takes the other's reactions into account in choosing his effort bundle.

For almost all firm members the environment in which they work involves directly or indirectly order giving and order taking. They may be precise and formalized—such as written instructions, blueprints, or whatever the counterpart of blueprints might be in different fields—or they may be vague and their more exact nature and intent may have to be ferreted out by the individual involved. Order giving and order taking usually supplement the incomplete nature of membership contracts. Just as the contract role has to be interpreted so does the sense of receiving orders, and the signals involved require perception and interpretation.

The sense of the employment situation is that at least in a vague way there is an order-signaling apparatus, the possibility of perceiving some of the signals, and the possibility of interpreting their nature and meaning. The interpretation of signals is part of the triggering mechanism for effort within an effort position. Some signals also contain pressure to perform in a certain direction. Thus, the order-giving apparatus does not only signal effort responses, but also frequently such signals contain pressure from others which is part of the constraint mechanism.

The simplest examples of these general ideas are supervisor-subordinate relations within an organization. In clear cases the supervisor gives precise orders and the subordinate interprets and tries to carry them out. The supervisor judges the results of the subordinate's efforts. He usually has it within his power to show approval or disapproval and sometimes to mete our rewards and punishments. But this is too specific. Although all of these aspects exist, they may be exceedingly vague; frequently no detailed reward and punishment responses are worked out as long as performance is within a broadly satisfactory range. The problem is to determine the "broadly satisfactory range." This depends on the pressures perceived by the superior that influences the subordinate's effort, and the sense of concern for these pressures.

Figure 18a resembles 17b. Curve EU is the effort-utility relation for the individual. The utility cost of decision *and* movement, indicated by c_1c_2, determines the optimal inert area, $e_1 e_3$. Add to these general ideas that of the pressures imposed by others. Part of the motivation of a representative firm member is to avoid undue pressure. Thus, we can visualize some utility deriving from such avoidance. This results in an adjustment of the EU curve. The broken line EU' indicates the new effort-utility relation, inclusive of the difference in utility resulting from pressure avoidance from superiors. Thus, for any effort point on the ordinate the difference between EU and EU' represents the utility value of pressure avoidance. For example, for very low effort levels, the adjusted utility curve is lower than the unadjusted one because of the perception that since some pressure would result this effort level should not be carried out. At relatively high levels, approval of the effort level is anticipated; consequently the adjusted utility level is higher than the unadjusted one. If we take into account the utility cost of a change, the new inert area equals e_2e_4.

Let us examine inert areas in group contexts. What is the inert area under the new circumstances where the adjusted effort-utility relation takes into account the feelings a person has about stimulations and pressures provided by others? Consider first the vertical authority relation. For the subordinate the effort area e_1e_4 in Figure 18a can be divided into three

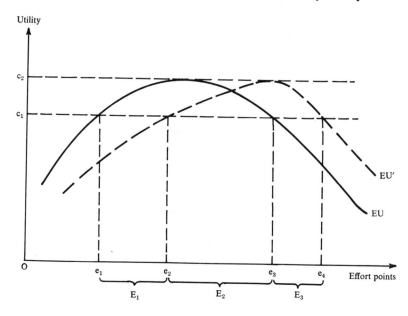

Figure 18a

segments: E_1, E_2, and E_3. Which segments, or combinations thereof, form the new inert area? Certainly E_2 is part (or all) of it, and E_2 is common to both the unadjusted and adjusted effort-utility relations.

Now consider E_1. An individual in an effort position in E_1 would certainly seek to move. The portion EU' above E_1 reflects the notion that sufficient unpleasantness is associated with the pressure that the authority is expected to impose as a result of a low effort level that he would be induced to shift to a higher one. Clearly E_1 will not be part of the group-adjusted inert area.

What about E_3? Here a serious question of interpretation deserves our attention. One might reasonably imagine that positions in E_3 reflect a different kind of feeling than those in E_2. The only reason utility is higher for effort points in E_3 than in E_2 is because the individual gets pleasure from the approval of his superior. Then the segment in E_3 should be included in the inert area. But it may be argued that E_3 reflects points where the individual is not his own master. Area E_2 is inert whether or not he is his own master, whereas E_3 would be excluded from the inert area were he his own master. It may be argued that the individual cannot feel equally well off or even better off where he is not his own master than where he is, but this merely implies that we should take into account the

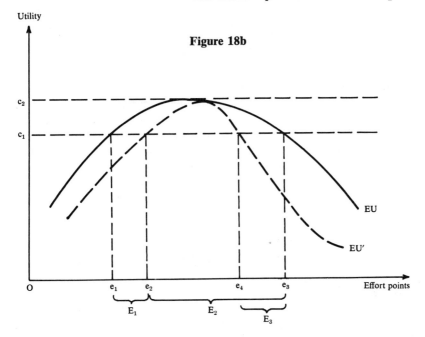

Utility

Figure 18b

disutility involved to the individual in "not being one's own master." The *net* utility of the superior's approval less the disutility of his not being his own master may still have a positive utility value. Interpreted this way the inert area in Figure 18a after adjustment is $E_2 + E_3$.

In Figure 18b we observe curve EU' in circumstances where the "not his own master" disutility is greater than the utility from the superior's approval.* In that case the adjusted EU' curve is narrowed, so to speak, by pressures from superiors. The inert area is likewise narrower; in this case it is $E_2 - E_3$. What rules in specific cases depends on the personality characteristics of those involved. We have discussed only pressures *for* performance, those which generally narrow the inert area. Pressures from peers (horizontal pressures) frequently work *against* excessive performance and in the opposite direction to authority pressures. When all indirect effects are considered it is difficult to say where the balance will be struck.

* In Figures 18a and 18b for simplicity's sake the peaks of EU and EU' are the same height. There is no reason for them to be the same height and the utility cost of moving the curves might differ. It is probably larger if a move disturbs more people rather than fewer. In fact the specter of trying to make adjustments with a number of individuals may be the main factor determining the utility cost of moving. However, the general line of analysis follows the lines indicated in the simplified case.

As a rough and ready speculation vertical relations tend to narrow the *EU′* curves, while horizontal ones tend to flatten them, to extend lower effort levels but narrow higher effort levels. This is speculation only. It would be interesting to determine the facts empirically. It seems likely (although not invariably) that vertical constraining relations work toward higher effort levels at the lower end of the effort continuum and that peer group relations work toward lesser levels at the higher end of the effort continuum. Thus, in most cases we should expect that the comparison between the unconstrained relation *EU* and the constrained relation *UE′*, when all constraints are taken into account, should turn out to be similar to that illustrated in Figure 18b—the sum of the existing constraints is likely to narrow the effort-utility relation compared to the unconstrained relation.

Multiperson Effort Points

Consider the case of two individuals who interact and have in a production sense (or a psychological sense or both) interdependent effort rates. In three-dimensional diagrammatic terms we can think of a utility surface (similar to *UE* in Figure 18a), each point of which associates a level of utility with an effort level for each of the two individuals. For each individual there is a plane *M* parallel to the effort axes tangent to the maximal utility level and another plane *L* parallel to *M* but below it by an amount equal to the effort cost of shifting from one position to another. The intersection of the *L* plane and the utility surface determines each individual's inert area. The intersection of the two inert areas yields the common inert area of the two-person group. We can try to visualize inert areas for *n*-person groups similarly.

As a shorthand let us write *IEP* for individual effort points, *IEA* for individual effort areas, and *MEP* for multiperson effort points. Thus every *MEP* is made up of a set of *IEP*'s. However, *MEP*'s are constrained in terms of the possible effort levels of those involved. Inconsistent effort levels of different individuals are not part of a *MEP*. For example, if one person worked very rapidly and another very slowly, but because their activities had to dovetail, the speed of one influenced the speed of the other, these would not be part of a two-person effort level. Or suppose a light on a worktable is shared by two individuals. Each can tilt the light to any angle he prefers, and effort levels depend on having adequate light. Here the two-person effort level cannot be the sum of the points each can achieve individually. Some tilts of the light toward *A* result in inadequate light for *B* and vice-versa. A multiperson effort point is a set of individual effort points such that each effort point is consistent with every other individual effort point and each effort point is a possible point for every individual.

Similar ideas can be expressed for effort areas. A set of multiperson effort points which contains more than one point is by natural extension an effort area.* We can think of multiperson effort *positions* in the same sense as the previously discussed individual effort position—a set of points within which individuals are willing to shift from one point to another in response to signals for changes in effort levels, without consideration of possible changes in utilities involved.

Once questions of approval and disapproval arise it is possible for a two-person effort position to be different from the sum of each individual's effort position. Approval may operate as a motivating force, one that increases the utility of the approved-of individual. An individual may include in his effort position some points he would not include if approval were not a consideration. Thus a concern for mutual approval might enlarge the combined two-person effort position. On the other hand, each person may want the other's effort area to be smaller than it is and the operation of concern for approval may result in a narrowing of the effort areas of both.

When more than two individuals are involved the situation can become extremely complex. What some approve, others may disapprove. Nevertheless, if the group is a viable one there should be some mutually agreed-upon individual effort positions so that a multiperson effort position exists. In a group with extreme dissension there is a possibility that no multi-person effort point (in the sense of positive effort) exists.†

Defined abstractly, the concept of a multiperson effort area may apply to any arbitrary collection of individuals. Within an organization the interesting groups are neither arbitrary in composition nor identical for all purposes. Because our concern is production within the firm we may think of interesting effort groups as being those which contribute to the creation of a product or a clearly defined portion of a product. Ideally, from the point of view of analytical convenience, groups should be chosen so that there are minimal influences between them, hence the effort of all the groups that

* In some contexts *continuous* effort areas would be of special interest. For any point in the effort area there is some point "next" to it in the effort area. By the sense of "nextness" we mean that the corresponding values of the components of the two points are less than some ε.

† Factions are likely to arise in certain situations. Dissension within a faction is likely to be much smaller than between factions. Group formation rules *may* allow the reconstitution of groups with reasonably like-minded individuals so that group effort positions more in accord with "firm objectives" are chosen.

make up the firm is the sum of each group's effort point. For groups chosen on this basis, an appropriate set of group effort points, one point chosen from each group effort area, produces a product. Such a set of effort points is equivalent to what in conventional theory is called a technique of production, assuming capital and other inputs as given.

Inert Areas

Interpersonal influence relations enter into the determination of multi-person inert effort areas in a critical sense. A special category of *asymmetric* influence relations includes those in which *A* cares about *B*'s effort level, but not vice-versa. This may involve the supervisor-supervisee relation in which the supervisor has to put forth effort in order to obtain *B*'s effort level (or he feels that this is the case). Or, it may involve relations in which no effort is involved in determining the other's effort level, but effort would be involved in any attempt to get the other person to change his effort level.

Members of higher levels of an organization give orders and obtain responses from those in lower levels. However, it takes effort on the part of those in higher levels of authority to change the effort choices of those in lower levels. Also it takes effort to check on other peoples' responses and performances. In Figure 19 we visualize an inert area between two layers of an organization. The curve marked *UM* represents an index of "management's" utility (given the expected efforts management has to put forth) for each level of the average worker's effort (or it may be viewed as an index of the effort level of the group) shown on the abscissa. The curve marked *UW* represents an index of "workers'" preferences with respect to alternative degrees of effort. The workers' inert effort area is indicated by e_1 and e_3, management's by e_2 and e_4. The intersection of the two inert areas e_2e_3 is the inert area for the two groups. Effort positions that fall between e_2 and e_3 do not induce any reaction for change from either management or labor.

For an *n*-person group in which the utility of a specific person's effort level depends on the levels of some or all others in the group, we visualize an inert area as a set of effort points so that for each point any person at a nonoptimal effort position will not do anything about it, since the utility cost of the effort required to change his own position or anyone else's (disturbing others, upsetting amicable interpersonal relations, and so on) is greater than the gain of making the move.

In general a two-person inert area would involve that segment of the two-person effort area containing those points for which each person feels it is

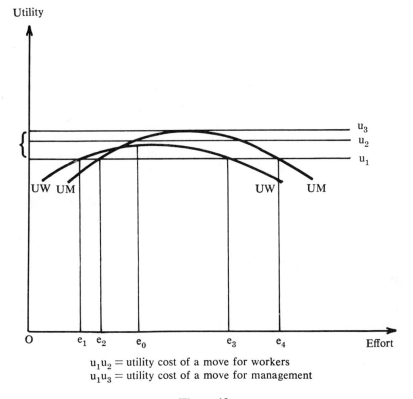

Utility

u_3
u_2
u_1

UW UM   UW   UM

O e_1 e_2 e_0 e_3 e_4 Effort

$u_1 u_2$ = utility cost of a move for workers
$u_1 u_3$ = utility cost of a move for management

Figure 19

too costly in utility terms to move to another point or to influence the other person to move to another effort point. The same idea can be generalized to n-person effort areas.

An important consideration is that as the number of individuals gets larger it may become more costly to try to influence others to move. Thus, there may be possibilities in which there would be an incentive to influence one individual to change his effort position but this would not yield much additional utility unless a second individual were also induced to so so. Thus, an n-person inert area does not in any way imply that each person is quite happy with every other person's effort position, but simply that because of the size of the group it is too effortful to try to change things yet not worthwhile for the individual to go through the costs of finding another group. The mere existence of large numbers within an interdependent group may result in a large inert effort position area, whereas the sum of smaller groups might result in a smaller inert area.

Group Size and Group Inert Areas

By making suitable assumptions it is possible to develop a theorem or generalization relating the number of interdependent members in a group and the size of the inert area. First, we define an *ATI* (above threshold interdependent) group as a group where a change in *A*'s effort position, beyond some threshold level, disturbs some or all other members of the group beyond their threshold levels. The assumptions are as follows: (1) For any two interdependent members *A* and *B* the effort of *A* influences the effort of *B*. (2) *A* change in *A*'s effort requires that *B* consider the desirability of changing his effort. (3) If *A*'s action requires *B* to change his effort beyond a given threshold level, this disturbs *B*. (4) There is a threshold disturbance level beyond which *A*'s awareness of the disturbance results in a given degree of disutility to *A* because of the disturbance. (5) The utility cost to *A* of disturbing any individual is the same as that of disturbing any other individual. (6) No addition to the group subtracts either from the utility cost of disturbing any existing member or from the number of members disturbed by an effort change, but every new member adds to the number of people disturbed by effort changes (beyond some threshold level) made by some (one or more) members. The six assumptions are somewhat abitrary and the result will not hold in some instances but the generalization hazarded seems to be an interesting possibility.

The resulting generalization is: The greater the *ATI* group, the larger the size of the group inert area. Proof depends on the following considerations: The larger the number of members in the group, the larger the number of individuals disturbed by effort changes of some members and the greater the utility cost to them as a consequence of making an effort change. The greater the utility cost of a change, the greater the individual inert area. By assumption (6) no individual's presence can reduce any utility cost. Since effort points and effort positions are interdependent by definition of an *ATI* group, the greater the individual inert areas, the greater the group inert area.

Consider an *ATI* group for which our six assumptions hold for every member of the group. Any *MEP* in the inert area will be more difficult to change the larger the group size. In many contexts it is undesirable for the effort position to be extremely rigid. But our generalization implies that the larger the group size, the more rigid any given effort position becomes. That is, it takes more of a utility gain from a change to induce the change than would otherwise be the case. The solution, in the face of seemingly rigid effort positions, in part and only in part, is to split larger groups into smaller units. This too may involve the cost of increased communication and incentive transmission between a greater number of specialized units.

Remarks on the Effort Equilibrium of the Group

In the concept of group effort equilibrium we face a difficulty we did not have to worry about in considering the individual's effort equilibrium: group membership. This involves two questions: What criteria define the group? and What aspect or aspects of membership have equilibrium properties?

A critical aspect is whether or not groups have the capacity to eject or *replace* individuals who seriously threaten the effort positions of members of the group. Initially, let us assume that the group is defined and membership is fixed and consider the question of equilibrium properties. A group effort level is a group equilibrium point if each member is in his optimal inert area, and remains in his optimal inert area for every intrapositional change that any other member may make.

One possible equilibrium property having to do with membership is that an equilibrium exists if replacements that take place one at a time normally leave the others in their inert areas. For this condition to hold requires that an individual who disrupted other effort levels sufficiently be removed from the group. He need not be removed from the firm; he may simply be shifted to another group. The group's general effort equilibrium, which would include the membership property, should be distinguished from its constant membership effort equilibrium. The membership effort equilibrium is likely to be stable in the small but not in the large. That is, if one or two members are replaced, the effort equilibrium holds, but beyond some number—say r—if $r + 1$ members are replaced, the others' effort positions are sufficiently disturbed so that some utility-effort relations are changed (since specific interdependencies are changed). Accordingly, some inert areas are changed, and some shifts in effort positions promise a gain to some individuals in the utility from effort greater than the utility cost of moving.

A final consideration is how effort positions are affected by changes in groups outside the firm. Here too the useful distinction is that between equilibrium in the small and equilibrium in the large. If small changes within other groups leave everyone within the group with effort positions within their inert areas, then the group is stable in the small. The concept of effort stability in the large follows readily.

I will hazard the following tentative generalization: For an interdependent peer group the average equilibrium effort level is likely to be below the average of the individual independent optimum effort positions since it is easier for individuals to accommodate to the lower effort levels of others than to the higher ones; lower levels usually precede higher ones historically; and the lower ones become sanctified by experience and by the defensive psychology of at least some individuals.

Conclusions

The process of selective rationality allows for the choice of decision procedures at lower effort levels than the levels implied by maximization or optimization, which in turn are responsible for bands of insensitivity to pressure. Such bands of insensitivity plus present position preference create inert areas that lubricate the relations between group members despite the high degree of interdependence that may have to exist in order to create meaningful group efforts.

The higher the degree of required interdependence, the greater the extent to which very sensitive individuals have a difficult time in an interdependent group. One of the probable requisites of the effective functioning of such groups is that some roles exist for members inside or outside the group who are empowered to remove or decrease the degree of group interdependence of those who have very narrow inert areas.

Other things equal, the larger the group size, the larger the group inert area. The larger the group inert area, the more inflexible the group effort position and the more difficult it is to introduce what may be deemed desirable changes.

The larger the group inert area, the greater the degree to which the group can contribute to X-inefficiency in production.

Group size can frequently be lowered by splitting the group into successively smaller units. However, this is likely to increase the problem of communication and incentive transmission between units.

Once our concerns shift to relations between units we are at the interface of group problems and firm problems.

8   The "Carte-Blanche" Preference Principle

Contract Terms

Not all parties to a contract have the power to negotiate all *possible* terms. Firm membership contracts are characterized by incompleteness, and by their asymmetry with respect to the details of different terms. Just as in well-organized markets, buyers and sellers are price takers, so in certain markets, buyers or sellers or both are contract term takers. How do these terms become what they are?

Consider the price takers. In perfect markets each party to a contract simply accepts the ruling price. It is precisely this ruling price that economic theory tries to explain. Other terms of economic contracts have not been equally well investigated or become part of standard theory. This is an inherently difficult problem and we can only hope to take a few steps in this direction.

To generalize the price to other aspects of contracts requires that we develop certain very broad preference generalizations. Accordingly, I will present a generalization of a very elementary and possibly obvious idea, well established in microtheory.

Grants versus Goods

It is easiest to expound my general idea through a series of simple examples involving certain types of preferences under which some parameters remain constant. My first example involves a choice between a grant in the form of money and a specific bundle of goods worth exactly the same amount. As a rule, on the basis of elementary consumption theory, individuals will prefer grants to goods. Consider the case of a father and his grown son. The father wants to buy the son a certain bundle of goods which costs $50. Will the son accept the goods or make a counteroffer? In general we should expect the son to prefer the $50 in cash if the transaction costs are trivial or zero. Given the money, the son can *at the very least* purchase the same set of goods. Or the son can buy some other bundle of goods—if such a bundle exists—that he prefers to the one the father would buy. If such a bundle does exist, then the son would clearly prefer the money grant to the goods the parent would buy.

We are not now concerned with whether the context of the offer allows the son to make a counteroffer in order that he may receive the grant rather than the goods. At this stage we are concerned with preferences rather than actual behavior. We can show that with all the possible bundles of goods the son can buy for $50 (unless the parent can guess the exact bundle the son prefers to all others), he is better off with the money grant. We may want to keep in the back of our minds the notion that parents do not feel neutral about the exact bundles of goods their children buy with the money earned by the parent. The parents may wish to exert some degree of control. But these are complications that determine the *outcome* of possible negotiations between parents and children. What we care about now are the rational *preferences* of the participants.

Figure 20 shows two commodities, *a* and *b*, and a budget line *BA* (prices given) that indicates all possible bundles of the two commodities purchasable with the outlay implied by *BA*. The parent offers to buy a bundle marked by X_1. Suppose that at X_1 the budget line is tangent to a parental indifference curve P_1. This same point is on the son's indifference curve S_1, but there is another point, X_2, which is preferred by the son. This is tangent to the son's indifference curve S_2. Now one can visualize a set of budget lines for different amounts and a set of parental indifference curves whose tangencies would yield a parental decision locus shown by the broken line *PD*. A similar set of budget lines and child indifference curves leads to a locus of tangencies which determines the son's decision locus, marked *SD*. Obviously, whatever the budget, the son is better off buying his own bundle of goods rather than obtaining the bundle of goods the parent wishes to buy for him. In other words, given a check on which the parent specifies the bundle of goods for which it can be cashed, the child would prefer a blank check (or a carte-blanche) for money with which he could buy his own choice of goods.

The identical principle emerges in other examples. The axes are called by different names, but in general the person who is to receive something of "external" value (a magnitude other than the utility value of the goods to the person involved) prefers to make his own choice rather than receive the results of someone else's choice. At the very least he can make a choice similar to someone else's, and he may be able to make one which would yield a higher utility. Thus, he could be no worse off making his own choice and he possibly could be better off.

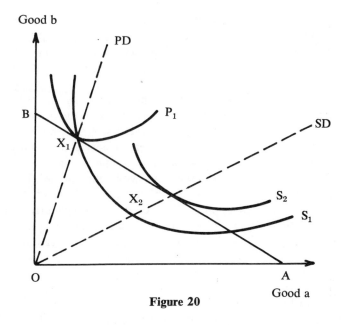

Figure 20

An interesting aspect of this elementary result is that it holds *whether or not* the recipient knows what the other person's choice will be. Thus, in the complete absence of knowledge about the other's actual choice he would still prefer his own. These general ideas could be extended to any number of goods or to any sorts of entities where choice determines personal utility.

Consider the following contrived example. Suppose a person who is to receive a sum of money can get a check for that sum negotiable at a *specific* bank, or as an alternative can receive a check of equal value negotiable at any bank within the country. Which would he prefer? The one in which the bank's name is left blank or the one in which the issuer of the check writes the name of a specific bank? Suppose he cannot ask the issuer of the check on which bank the issuer would draw it. Obviously the recipient would prefer the blank bank check to the specific bank check. He cannot be worse off with the blank check and he might be better off. In what follows I shall use the terms "carte-blanche" principle or "blank-check" principle interchangeably.

Although money grants are superior to specific goods allocations, the time period under which a given size grant (whose meaning has to be determined) is to hold and the terms under which payments are to be made present more complex problems. In discussing grants versus goods everything is known except perhaps the specific goods bundle chosen by the contributor. Once time enters, uncertainty about future values and the appropriate interest rate to obtain equal present values become part of the problem. However, for our purposes we can ignore some of the more subtle questions.

I shall concentrate on two problems: payment terms and negotiation terms. Consider two arrangements of streams of funds over a lengthy time period whose values are the same. Under the first arrangement the donor gives the recipient a fixed amount every year. Under the second arrangement the recipient can request to be paid any amount he wishes at any time up to the amount which exhausts the fund, while amounts left in the fund are credited to his account at the going interest rate. Once again the blank-check preference theorem applies. The second is the preferred arrangement: at worse the recipient can choose the same payout period as that determined initially, or he can choose payout periods that give him higher utility.

A similar argument can be put forth with respect to the renegotiation period. The donor can choose the times at which the recipient can renegotiate the grant, or the matter could be determined by the recipient—but once a renegotiation period is chosen the recipient has to stick to it. This is illustrated in Figure 21, in which the ordinate represents the frequency of

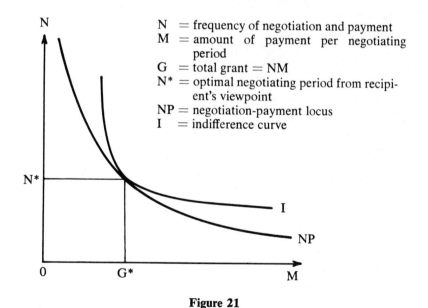

N   = frequency of negotiation and payment
M   = amount of payment per negotiating period
G   = total grant = NM
N* = optimal negotiating period from recipient's viewpoint
NP = negotiation-payment locus
I   = indifference curve

Figure 21

negotiation and the abscissa represents absolute amounts such that the negotiating period, N, and the amount to be negotiated, M, determine a sum which is the total amount under negotiation, or the total grant, G. That is, $NM = G$. The point at which the indifference curve for negotiation period I is tangent to the negotiating budget line is the optimal negotiating period for the individual. Suppose the optimal negotiating period is three years. The individual is better off under this arrangement than under one in which he is told that he must renegotiate each year, even though the present value of the two streams discounted for uncertainty would be the same. Obviously the same principle holds.

Tasks and Time

The carte-blanche principle applies also to individuals who join a firm. A variety of time arrangements are possible and a variety of tasks can be fitted into the time chosen. Suppose that hours of work are fixed in advance. The only question open is how the individual should fill these hours. He can be told what to do—his effort choice and effort position could be chosen for him by someone in the firm—or he can choose his own effort position. If he is not indifferent to tasks, other things equal, he will prefer to choose his own effort position, whether or not he knows the effort position the firm would select for him.

The same principle applies to time. For a given number of hours per week, or month, an individual would prefer to choose his own particular hours rather than have them chosen for him. He is no worse off, since he can always choose the ones that would be chosen for him, and he could be better off since he can choose a set of hours he prefers to those someone else might choose.

Another question is whether or not time should be a variable. If what is important to the firm is some specific commitment, then as long as that commitment is fulfilled the firm should not care how many hours are worked. The individual is better off choosing his own number of hours and the related pace and pressure rather than accepting those chosen by someone else. The same principle applies to innumerable other variables. For some given value agreed to by the "donor" and the recipient, the individual would prefer a blank check leaving the details up to him rather than controlled by the donor.

Why the Carte-Blanche Principle is Not Applied

Two aspects of the carte-blanche principle are relevant here: the possible application of the principle for our purposes and the fact that we can think of many instances in which it could be applied but is not. The principle says something about the basic preference of human beings. If there is some sense in which other things are equal, individuals prefer to have things their own way or to do things their own way rather than leave matters to be determined in part or in whole by someone else. If other things are not equal, the theorem suggests that individuals would be willing to sacrifice something for the right of choice. Even if completely open choices cannot be achieved, some aspects of it should be observable. In other words, there should be situations in which granting the open choice is not very costly to the grantor and is advantageous to the grantee. In the demand for jobs some degrees of open choices should be available. If this is an advantage to the grantor or employer to close some elements of choice, then the question arises whether optimal bargains have been worked out. Has the grantor closed off avenues of choice which are no real significance to him? If so, this may turn out to be a source of inefficiency.

Although it is easy to see that on the demand side the blank-check principle suggests that people want to be as free as possible to interpret how they should fill the blanks, it is not clear how those who determine the supply of "checks," whether blank or not, should feel about their offers. On a purely rational basis a check supplier should not care about the "blankness" of the check as long as the constraints or objectives that truly concern him are met. Thus, if a person is given a choice of the bank at which a check is to be cashed, the one who offers it should be indifferent as to whether or not that aspect is left blank. But there is a sense in which suppliers of "checks" also operate under the blank-check principle. They too can be no worse off by being allowed to write in as many constraints as possible, and they can be better off if they introduce a constraint whose absence could possibly make them worse off.

The word *possibly* is exceedingly important. Even if the calculated probability is very small, if it exists at all they face a potential gain in introducing the constraint. Given that both the grantor and the grantee operate under the same principle, and given even *very* small degrees of uncertainty, one can easily imagine circumstances in which the grantor imposes many constraints which are not in the interest of the grantee. Suppose for a moment that the constraints imposed are based on imaginary fears. In that case the grantor does not gain and the grantee is hurt. Suppose further that the power to impose constraints lies mostly on the side of the grantor. Then such constraints will, presumably rationally, be imposed not because the grantor gains by imposing them but because he precludes an assumed possibility of loss. Many onerous bureaucratic procedures that citizens face, and that employees face in large organizations, probably are introduced on the basis of motivations of this sort.

The concept of indifference takes on significance. On the basis of pure economic logic, in a situation in which choices are open to two parties so that those made by A are indifferent to A but make B worse off, then one would think it would be easy to persuade A not to make these choices. This is a variant of the classic Pareto possibility in which a situation exists where an arrangement can be made leaving one person better off and another person no worse off. This situation, however, is to be sharply distinguished from the classical trade situation in which both parties can be made better off. The fact that both parties can be made better off has persuasive power for them to engage in trade. In our situation the fact that B can be made better off and A no worse off by making certain choices need have no persuasive influence on A whatsoever. If cautionary constraints are free they may be imposed even though not really necessary. This is especially likely to be true if such constraints are imposed against anonymous individuals rather than directly against known and possibly cared-for individuals. The main point is that given a sense of caution, even with regard to highly improbable consequences, and given a sense of power on the part of those who impose constraints, motivation need be exceedingly weak in order to have a great many constraints imposed.

The agent-principal distinction has been emphasized at various points, and is interesting to consider the blank-check principle from the viewpoint of agents as both grantors and recipients of contracts. Agents may not share in the rewards accruing to the firm if they behave optimally from the firm's viewpoint, but they may be sensitive to certain classes of occurrences for which they could be blamed if something goes wrong. In other words, the agents offering contracts may themselves be under contracts which contain a number of potentially dysfunctional constraints. Such agents are apt to be especially cautious in order to avoid blame; though truly indifferent to various contractual provisions, they may insert constraining clauses as a cautionary device to avoid even highly improbable instances that could indirectly reflect on their performance. In this context the agents would be indifferent if they were the actual principals offering the contract. But fears arise when they are responsible to principals, and there is an asymmetry between the observability of appropriate behavior versus mistakes. Appropriate behavior is taken for granted; mistakes are noticed.

Will individuals not impose constraints if they are indifferent as to doing so and not doing so? Since most contracts are relatively complex and multitermed they can be divided into segments requiring negotiation—a segment where there are clearly opposing interests, and one containing options about which the contract supplier is indifferent. Whether this latter segment is large or small, our concern is the same. Let us refer to the latter segment as the "indifference" segment and raise the question of whether the supplier will maximize options to the recipient. If suppliers are truly indifferent there is no reason to suppose that they will impose zero constraints. It seems more reasonable that they will impose a distribution of constraints; some suppliers might impose none, others might impose about 50 percent of the constraints possible, and still others would tend to maximize constraints. On the average about 50 percent of the constraints possible will be imposed. But maximum welfare requires that no constraints whatsoever be imposed where true indifference exists. This suggests that in general more constraints than are truly necessary are imposed in various choice contexts.

A significant difference arises when there is a high degree of interdependence between those who receive blank checks and those who offer them. Suppose the gains are intermingled. The grantor gains or losses in a very direct way, depending on the behavior of the grantee. The grantee has the power to make the grantor very much better off or very much worse off. The result depends on whether the grantor can transmit motivations to the grantee so that he operates as much in the grantor's interest as possible. If the grantor believes that such motivations are indeed transmitted, he will wish to minimize constraints and offer as much of a blank check as possible. The reverse will be the case if he feels that the grantee is already motivated to work in the grantor's interest. He will then surround the grant with as many constraints as possible, although this may limit the degree to which the grantee can operate to the grantor's advantage. The foregoing is especially likely to be true in the case of contract recipients who have, in Hirschman's words, very little "voice" in the nature of the contract, and whose only recourse is either acceptance or "exit."[1]

Standard Contracts, the Carte-Blanche Principle, and Social Welfare

Can the carte-blanche preference principle explain why in small or large organizations, or in society at large, we create unnecessary inconveniences or bureaucratic hells for each other, facing at the same time situations which seem exceedingly difficult, if not impossible, to change?

Throughout this volume I have focused directly or indirectly on the fact that contracts are incomplete and imperfect. There is one type which, though incomplete in some respects, is unnecessarily detailed or constrained in others. Let us separate contract terms seen from the viewpoint of a given individual into two segments: terms about which he cares a great deal, and those about which he is largely indifferent. For purposes of exposition we limit our concern to a group of individuals all having the same division of contract terms. In other words, there is a sub-set of contract terms that every member cares about, whether they are on the supply or demand side of the contract. Any two members of this group can engage in a contract bargain and negotiate the "cared-about" terms. Now suppose that individual A is indifferent to all remaining terms, while some individuals B_1, B_2, . . . B_n are not indifferent to these terms. Let us call the A type contractors the supplier of the contracts, and the B group the recipients. At this point a simple social welfare rule suggests itself. Welfare would be maximized if the "non-bargained terms" were all left blank in accordance with the carte-blanche preference principle. Those members of the B group who cared about the specifics of this portion of the contract could fill in the blanks in accordance with their desires. The suppliers are no worse off by offering the blank checks, and some of the recipients are made better off. This seems straightforward? Is there any reason for things to work out this way? In what follows the reader should keep in mind that "bargaining power" need not be exactly equal between any two individuals negotiating contract terms.

We note a significant asymmetry in motivations. Some members of the group have a definite desire for a blank check. However, there is no equal motivation for the A group. Although they may be indifferent to blank-check terms for the non-negotiated portion, they are no worse off if these terms are specific, that is, not optimal. Let us suppose for the sake of discussion that the non-negotiated part is in some sense 50 percent non-blank rather than entirely non-blank. Referring back to the inert area idea, assume that there is a utility cost in moving from any existing standard contract to a new contract. Thus, although the suppliers would have been quite happy if the standard contract had zero constraints, they have no incentive to move to such a contract if the existing one had 50 percent constraints.

It would be difficult for any single member of the B group to convince members of the A group to violate routine procedures by giving him a special non-standard contract. Thus we have a case of a potential Pareto improvement that cannot be enforced by the recontracting of any one individual. It might also be true that it would not pay for any individual member of the B group to organize the B group in order to renegotiate a new non-standard contract. The result is that the Pareto improvement possibility which exists cannot be put into effect.

If each pair of individuals entered into a contract in which all the unique elements of the contract were considered, most of the problems we have discussed would not arise. Problems arise because detailed contracts are costly in both time and money to work out. As a result, standard incomplete contracts are used whose terms are usually interpreted by precedence, convention, or patterns of behavior. Such contracts may contain many unnecessary constraints. In such instances group efforts to remove the constraints would produce a superior result. However, no individual is willing to contribute to the group effort unless he is assured that others would contribute in a similar fashion. This point was first made by Baumol in trying to develop a rationale for the state in economic affairs.[2] It has wider applicability, however, to problems where circumstances do not allow profitable explicit trade by individuals but where individual interests are to some degree imbedded in group interests.

The fact that there is no market for small implicit trades or for explicit trades which are tied to the explicit trades of others is involved in the situation just described. We ignored the process by which blank-check portions of the contract were filled with constraints since this is really not important for present purposes. There may have been a time when there were reasons for these constraints. If the reasons no longer exist, it does not alter the fact that the constraints cannot be removed, even though such an action might result in overall social gain. We have here an equilibrium situation which is nonoptimal and X-inefficient.

Another way of looking at the whole matter is in terms of non-tradeable implicit games. Table 4 indicates the payoff of the two strategies open to each side. Suppose that contract suppliers have two choices: they can trust the contract recipient not to take advantage of blanks in the contract which might be against their interest, or they might distrust the recipient and maximally protect themselves against this possibility. Similarly, the recipients may trust the suppliers not to impose unnecessary constraints or they may distrust the suppliers and interpret the contract clauses with unnecessary specificity. The payoff matrix bears some similarity to the Prisoner's Dilemma game.[3] If both parties choose to trust each other a contract will have the maximal number of blanks and it will be optimally flexible. If one party distrusts and another trusts, then one could appear to take advantage of the other by imposing constraints on him, preventing injury to the distrusting party but imposing possible injury on the trusting party. If both parties are keen on preventing potential injury to themselves, the contract will contain the maximum number of constraints included by both sides and the most inflexible and worse possible contract will result. In this last case neither can effect a change since those who distrust cannot request the

Table 4. Two-by-two payoff matrix for contract suppliers and contract recipients.

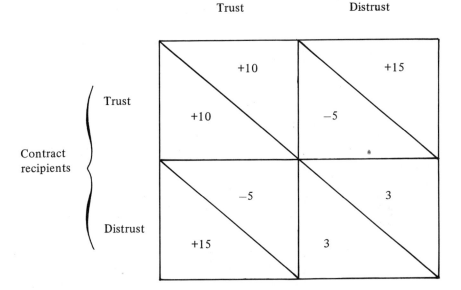

others to trust because they themselves cannot prove that they will be trusting in return.

The ideas of the two-by-two payoff matrix can be usefully expanded to a three-by-three payoff matrix (Table 5). Here the "choices" open to individuals are full trust, some trust, and full distrust. The four cells similar to the two-by-two matrix have the same value as before. The five others, however, are open to interpretation. Suppose that in some circumstances contract receivers offer *full* trust and contract suppliers offer *some* trust. If there are many more receivers than suppliers, a disequilibrium might exist which would tend to move to an equilibrium in which everyone has full trust.

The reverse case might be one in which receivers offer *some* trust and suppliers *full distrust*. This might possibly end in a movement toward complete distrust. The other possibilities are indicated roughly in Table 5. It would take us far afield to analyze all the possibilities. Enough has been said to indicate that interesting connections exist among degrees of trust, "blanks," and utility.

Table 5. Three-by-three payoff matrix for contract suppliers and contract recipients.

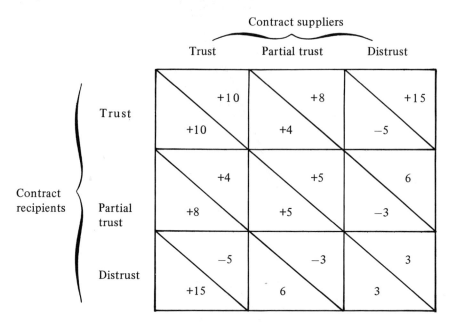

		Contract suppliers		
		Trust	Partial trust	Distrust
Contract recipients	Trust	+10 / +10	+8 / +4	+15 / −5
	Partial trust	+4 / +8	+5 / +5	6 / −3
	Distrust	−5 / +15	−3 / 6	3 / 3

A word about interpretation. What we have called the non-negotiating part of the contract may in fact traditionally have the appearance of formal negotiations. But in practice they may have fallen into disuse. It is as if the small print in some contracts exists traditionally but is never alluded to openly. This may be interpreted as an implicit trade in which for some items a blank check might be said to exist.

Elements of trade and work contracts frequently found in non-negotiated categories include customary weights and measures in which goods are sold, the nature of the packaging involved, hours of work, some aspects of conditions of work, breaks for refreshments and meals, and so on. These are standards of behavior that may be interpreted as special kinds of implicit agreements but are not actual agreements. They exist because individuals have to take these parts of the agreements on a take-it-or-leave-it basis. For various reasons the negotiated part of the contract is so important that the implicit portion cannot be renegotiated for fear of endangering the negotiated segment. Nevertheless, the implicit part may be nonoptimal and involve an amalgam of constraints which, if renegotiated, would allow individuals new sets of open choices which they would prefer.

Thus, the operation of the blank-check principle, plus the asymmetry between those who supply contracts but are indifferent to certain terms and those who receive contracts but who may not be indifferent, may lead to undesirable constraints that no one appears to be able to change in the short run.

Contracts with unnecessary constraints which operate as disincentives and which prevent some agents from acting to a greater degree than they do in the interests of the firm are sufficient reasons to create X-inefficiencies. This last is especially likely to be true if we consider the disincentives created for high levels of performance if the constraining influences produce an aura or climate of distrust as part of the on-going and incompletely specified contractual arrangements.

9 Effort Games:
"Chicken" versus "Prisoner's Dilemma"

Parametric versus Non-Parametric Decisions

Conventional economic analysis assumes that our options are parametric—that is, the consequences of our choices are either given or sufficiently known so that we behave as though they were given. Thus, the problem is reduced to situations in which we have to make the best choice, in some sense, from among alternatives of given valuations. The essence of simplifying choice is to be able to set a value on every alternative. If the consequences are not known, this cannot be done.

Is the world parametric or non-parametric?

There exists a class of situations made famous by the theory of games in which the world is *intrinsically* non-parametric. Classic examples are recreational games of strategy such as chess or checkers, in which each person makes alternate moves and no move by any individual can have a unique value since, by the very rules of the game, we cannot control the moves of the other individual.

Which approach fits economic life better? This question cannot be answered in a general sense. Situations may exist in which the non-parametric game approach yields a better fit than parametric decisions. Of course it is of little help if we seek solutions, and the game that fits has no solution. Nevertheless, theory of games, descriptions of economic situations are sometimes of interest because the theory format enables us to convey in a compact manner the essentials of two-person or two-party (each made up of many persons) decision problems. The games known as Prisoner's Dilemma and Chicken are especially apt for our purposes.[1]

The Two-Person Peer Effort Game: Chicken versus Prisoner's Dilemma

Consider a fairly simple game situation in which two individuals, whose work is interdependent, have to decide on their effort alternatives. Consider the simple case in which it is possible for one of the individuals to do all the work expected of both. How will each behave?

Let us look first at the case in which there is an acceptable minimum fixed amount the two individuals have to do as a team. Each prefers the other to do all the work. However, if neither does any work both will be fired. This is basically the game known as Chicken. If each does half the work it is superior to both being fired but inferior to each than if the other did all the work. This is a simple strategy problem. The strategies can be separated into two classes: symmetrical-cooperative and asymmetrical-uncooperative, that is, "dominating-dominated." In the symmetrical cases both parties behave the same way. In the asymmetrical cases each acts differently from the other. In the symmetrical cases the payoffs, whether high or low, are approximately the same for both individuals, while in the asymmetrical cases one gains at the expense of the other. The essence of the asymmetrical case is that the "uncooperative" player gains at the expense of the cooperative one.

Now let us get back to our simple effort problem. Suppose after a period of trail and error, or a period of discussion, each has to decide how he will behave based on assessments of how the other will behave. Suppose each is aware that the other has a strong preference not to be fired. It would seem natural, given that the game is a continuous one, to make an agreement for each party to do half of the work. This is the standard solution for this type of game. So far there is nothing very surprising about this solution.

Of special interest is that the effort game that we presumed the two peers were playing was Chicken. It is important to contrast it with the closely related game known as Prisoner's Dilemma (hereafter sometimes referred to as P.D.). To see the importance of this distinction and to illustrate the nature of the games, consider the next two payoff tables. In Table 6 we show the utilities each player associates with different outcomes. Recall that there is an externally imposed constraint of a minimal amount of work that must be produced. Square 1 shows the situation in which each works equally to meet the constraint; each receives three utils. In square 2 (moving from left to right and top to bottom) one person does the work to meet the constraint, while the other does as he pleases in order to maximize his utility; the latter receives five utils, and the former, who bends all his efforts to meet the constraint, receives none. Square 3 involves the same situation except that the other player does everything to meet the constraint. Finally, in square 4 neither meets the constraint and they risk being fired as a consequence. The important point to note is that, although the distribution of the work is determined by the two players, the constraint and the consequence of not meeting it is determined outside the two

Table 6. Payoff matrix for Chicken game.

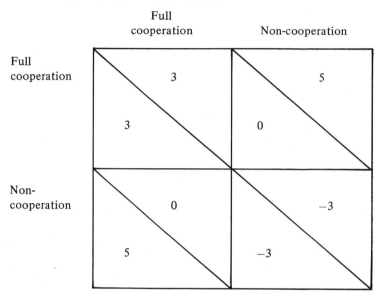

players—usually by a person or persons at a higher level in the hierarchy.

Now let us compare this with a very similar effort game which contains the P.D. characteristics. The only elements that have changed in Table 7 are the values in square 4. In this case the utils are one each. Let us assume that this results because they receive some sense of disapproval for not meeting the constraint, but they are not fired. Thus the values in square 4 depict the difference in utility between doing as they please and receiving strong disapproval. We note here that the incentives in the P.D. game are quite different. Although both are still best off if they can decide on a cooperative strategy, each has a strong incentive to do as he pleases. Even if neither takes the responsibility of meeting the constrained amount of work they are in a superior position than either would be in if he undertook to do all the work. Hence there is a strong likelihood in this situation for each individual to choose to do very little of the "required" work.

Supervisor-Supervisee Games

From management's point of view, at the next higher level in the hierarchy, Prisoner's Dilemma, as played by the lower level, is likely to lead to an outcome with a much lower effort level than Chicken. From the point of

Table 7. Payoff matrix for Prisoner's Dilemma game.

	Cooperation	Non-cooperation
Cooperation	3 / 3	5 / 0
Non-cooperation	0 / 5	1 / 1

view of the higher level, Chicken may be preferred for the lower level, if the cooperative outcomes are the same in the two situations. Table 8 indicates not only the outcomes to the peers but the productivities to the firm. Numbers in parenthesis indicate firm productivities. Let us suppose that in the P.D. game the firm productivities are lower if each player chooses a competitive strategy, but higher if each chooses a cooperative strategy.

Table 8. Payoff matrix for Prisoner's Dilemma and Chicken games on peer level.

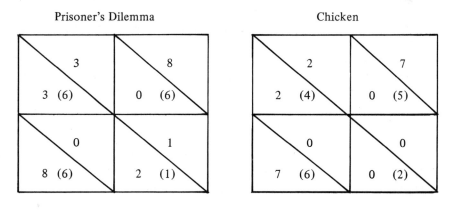

Prisoner's Dilemma

3 / 3 (6)	8 / 0 (6)
0 / 8 (6)	1 / 2 (1)

Chicken

2 / 2 (4)	7 / 0 (5)
0 / 7 (6)	0 / 0 (2)

The result is that a management which believes its workers will seek to do as little work as possible will impose a Chicken-type game on its employees. But a management which thinks it can get its employees to cooperate with each other and with management, and at the same time provides incentives for relatively high cooperative efforts without constraints, should seek a P.D. game which involves certain benefits and risks. Thus, management eliminates employee fears of being fired and, in return, hopes that its employees will find an effort level higher than the minimal effort level.

Given these ideas, let us consider the nature of the interlevel effort game. The supervisory level has two strategies: a reward-incentive strategy and a power-threat strategy. The reward-incentive strategy is similar to offering a P.D. game, whereas the power-threat strategy is similar to imposing the game of Chicken. Before proceeding further, a terminological problem should be observed. The strategies open to management are exceedingly diverse. As a consequence, it is difficult to capture in a short abstract connotation the exact set of strategies implied by the few words used, especially if, for simplicity, we restrict ourselves to a two-by-two payoff matrix.

Although the subordinates have many strategies for simplified illustrative purposes, let us try to reduce them to three basic choices: cooperation with each other and cooperation with management, to be referred to as "dual cooperation"; cooperation between peers but *not* with management—"peer only cooperation"; cooperation by one peer with management at the expense of the other peer—"vertical only cooperation." In the case of vertical only cooperation, the payoffs to the peers involved are positive for the peer who cooperates successfully with management and negative for the one who is "cooperated against," so to speak. These ideas are illustrated in the payoffs assumed in Table 9. If the subordinates are "dual cooperative" they will produce more in terms of the values of the supervisors under the P.D. game than under Chicken. If they are in partial conflict they produce less under P.D. than under Chicken. Thus, the game facing the supervisors involves a dilemma. If they are cautious and distrust workers in the belief that they will respond not to positive incentives but only to threats, they will impose the game of Chicken. Similarly, if workers are distrustful of management they will indicate that management's appraisal of their responses is correct and Chicken will again be the appropriate game (see square 5). The intertwining of the two involves a situation which suggests that the introduction of incentives, which if responded to would lead to a higher productivity than otherwise, contains the possibility of risks that can result in lower productivity than otherwise. What these simplifying game-theoretic illustrations are intended to convey is the nature of the "stick-carrot" incentive dilemmas faced by the supervisors of one level over the supervisees of another, and the possibility that what may appear as the cautious and prudent choice may turn out to be the relative X-inefficient one. The critical idea behind the valuations assumed in the illustrated payoffs is that there is a strong connection between the strength of the threat part of the incentive system, and the response to the positive reward part. Here we assume that there is an inverse relation in the sense that the larger and more effective the threat, the smaller the potential production response to the reward.*

Two-Stage Games

Let us widen the game and assume that it takes place in two stages. In the first stage the payoff matrix is that of Table 8 which reflects the simple Chicken game. The cooperative strategy is the optimal strategy for both parties because each can count on the other not to risk the dominated con-

* For some payoff matrices the higher group level may find itself in a P.D. game. Consider the following payoff matrix:

Workers' options

	Dual cooperation	Some noncooperation
P.D.	4 / 6	5 / 1
Chicken	2 / 4	3 / 3

Management options

It can readily be seen that the maximum choice by both parties leads to the distrustful Chicken-noncooperative outcome indicated in square 4. Thus, management finds that in setting the rules for those on lower levels in the hierarchy, management itself faces a P.D. type of game.

Table 9. Payoff matrix for mixed level game.

	Dual cooperation	Peer cooperation only	Vertical cooperation only
Prisoner's Dilemma	3 / 6	2 / 1	±1 / 2
Chicken	2 / 4	0 / 2	±3 / 3

(Upper level: Prisoner's Dilemma and Chicken. Each cell is divided diagonally; upper-right value listed first, lower-left value second.)

flict strategy. Hence, if they have to choose in terms of only two strategic alternatives each will choose to be cooperative. But now suppose that there is a range of cooperativeness. The more cooperative each is, and the more equally cooperative the other is, the greater the gain to both. We assume there is a set of cooperative solutions. Each member of that set is superior to an asymmetrical conflict solution. Once the players decide on a cooperative solution, will they move readily to another cooperative solution? The answer depends on which of two possibilities hold: The first is whether they can count that neither will shift to a similar cooperative strategy. The second is the possibility that if one moves out of any existing cooperative solution the other may shift to a conflict strategy. The first possibility can rarely be assured. But if circumstances allowed its assurance, individuals probably could renegotiate until they reached an optimal cooperative solution.

The basic problem facing each player is the degree of predictability of the responses of the other player. First, consider only points along the symmetric diagonal (see Table 8 and Figure 22). In this case the moves may be doubly symmetric in the sense that moves toward higher values will be responded to in the same way as moves toward lower values. If each player can count on symmetrical behavior the outcome is fairly clear-cut.

Moves will take place until a "Pareto-superior" position is reached—until it is no longer possible for one player to gain without the other losing.

The really interesting cases are those in which a point along the symmetrical diagonal is reached, neither player can count on symmetrical moves upward, only downward, and each player may choose to respond to a cooperative gesture by a competitive one. In that case there is a strong likelihood that intermediate points on the symmetrical diagonal will represent a stable equilibrium. The reason is that once such a point is achieved, the prospect of any move is not a return to that particular point but the possibility of achieving a worse point.

I have attempted thus far to describe effort situations under which it is reasonable for individuals to remain at a nonoptimal effort situation should one be achieved. Note the twin elements which operate simultaneously, the basic cooperative solution reached, and the sensitivity to maneuvering to reach a new solution because the cost of such maneuvers may lead to a worsening of the original situation. This way of describing the two-person effort problem closely resembles my discussion of inert areas in which part of the cost of moving was the potential disutility that results from disturbing a fellow worker. From the viewpoint of the game of Chicken, we can see theoretical possibilities at which the cost of disturbing a mutually arrived at position may be rather high.

In real life situations essentially non-parametric problems can be turned into parametric ones if individuals find it suitable or useful to behave in predictable ways. We want, therefore, to focus attention on those types of games in which the sets of alternatives open to each individual are such that they can be broken up into two subsets; one which involves predictable behavior and one which does not. A non-parametric decision problem can degenerate into a mutually parametric one if each party has good reason to choose among those alternatives that reveal predictable patterns of behavior to the other party.

Because the games described, by their very essence, contain elements of uncertainty, there is a strong incentive on the part of many individuals to try to interpret their decision context in such a way that the essential non-parametric nature of the context is rearranged to contain mostly routine parametric decisions. This can be achieved in two ways. Either the individual attempts to define to himself the nature of his responsibility so as to include only those alternative decisions where he need not worry about the consequences; he selects alternatives that he feels he can evaluate. Or he attempts to indicate to others that his job interpretation is one which involves predictable reactions. Hence, the nature of his effort position is such as to contain relatively infrequently game-theoretic problems.

This is a somewhat different approach. In the theory of games the nature of the games are given. In this new approach the nature of the game may to some degree be chosen by the player. Therefore, for players who do not have a taste for the uncertainties involved in game-theoretic situations, positions along the symmetric diagonal may be interpreted as approximately parametric situations. Each player essentially is telling the other that he will choose an effort position in conformity with the position on the symmetrical diagonal and that he has no desire to upset the applecart if the other can somehow evince a similar attitude.

Continuous Games

Games can be given added realism if we shift from two-by-two payoffs into games which are multivalued and contain a continuous range of alternatives. The nature of such a game is illustrated in Figure 22. On the ordinate we list the alternatives a_i and on the abcissa we list the alternatives b_i. There is a set of values along the symmetrical diagonal marked S which range from the two extreme points marked L and H. For illustration we indicate numbers, measured equidistant, which range from 1.9 to 10. The values become larger for player B as we move from point H to point VH_b, and become larger for a as we move from H to VH_a. We designate the two triangles on either side of the symmetrical diagonal by A and B. Thus, player A if he is off the symmetrical diagonal is better off in triangle A than player B is in triangle B. Consider a point in triangle B. Such a point implies the payoffs for the two players. These values can be determined if we measure the payoff for B by the value on the diagonal *plus* the horizontal distance to the point. Similarly, we obtain the payoff to A for the same point by the value from the diagonal minus the horizontal distance to the point. In triangle A we make similar measurements in order to get the payoff values for any point except that here we measure the diagonal *plus* the vertical distance to get the payoff for A and the diagonal value minus the vertical distance to get the payoff for B. The following four equations summarize how we might obtain the payoff values for every point within the square that illustrates the continuous game.

In triangle A
  (1) $V(a) = S + \alpha d'$
  (2) $V(b) = S - \alpha d'$
In triangle B
  (3) $V(a) = S - \beta d$
  (4) $V(b) = S + \beta d$
    $\alpha \geq 1, \beta \geq 1.$

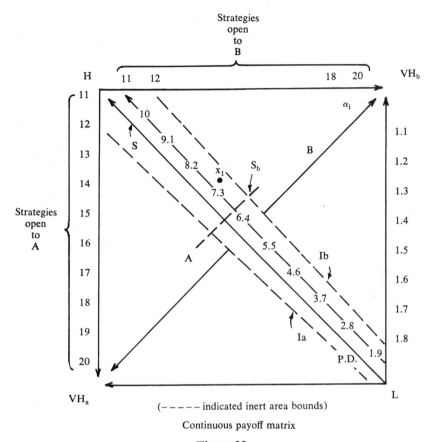

(- - - - - indicated inert area bounds)

Continuous payoff matrix

Figure 22

$V(a)$ is the valuation for player A and $V(b)$ for player B; S represents the value on the symetrical diagonal, d is the horizontal distance, and d' is the vertical distance. In the illustrations just given we assume that α and β are equal to 1, but we can generalize this by allowing α and β to stand for valuations greater than 1. The game can be further generalized by assuming different values along the symmetrical diagonal. The continuous game illustrated is Chicken. While the results obtained in general do not differ much from those considered previously there is one special element that this type of illustration allows us to include. We can incorporate the notion of inert areas to each player into the continuous game. The asymmetrical bounds are illustrated by the line I_a and I_b while the symmetrical lower bound is indicated by S_b. Here we assume that the bounds are the same for both players, but of course this need not be the case. The main conclusion is that a point surrounded by the bounds indicated and the point H will be a set of values that is in the inert area of the two players. If the game is Chicken there is little incentive for them to move to any other position. In this case a peer-group effort game with continuous values could end up in the inert area with a set of nonoptimal effort values.

However, if we interpret the game in terms of two levels in a hierarchy in which B represents the higher level, then once again the nonoptimal valuation of the point x_1 can be an equilibrium point. Consider what meaning we can attach to the nature of the payoffs in this situation. The payoffs to the lower-level members are in terms of the utilities they receive from effort and the context in which it is performed. To the managers some index of output will be one of the elements determining the satisfaction they get from the efforts of the subordinates. Suppose management utilities are a monotonic function of the subordinates' contribution to output. It would be reasonable to assume that the subordinates utility function first rises with output and then falls.

Consider three possibilities. In the first case let x_1 be a point at which the subordinate maximizes his utility but the manager does not maximize his because output is not maximized. In that case x_1 leads to an X-inefficient output, at least from the manager's viewpoint. In the second case suppose x_1 is suboptimal both for the employees and for the manager. Although output is X-inefficient no one's utility is really maximized. The third possibility is similar to the second in that employees produce more output than required to maximize their utility but not enough to maximize management's utility. Now all the points along the symmetrical diagonal are essentially points under which both parties may be seen as behaving in a similar fashion. However, the points that maximize output are the points in the area of VH_b which would also be associated with an exceedingly low utility for employees. At that point the effort required to produce that output appears so onerous that utility is much lower than it would be at point H. But of course that is not the lowest utility from the subordinate's viewpoint. In the strict Chicken game the worse situation for the subordinate is the one in which he produces the least output and receives the worst response from the superior. This is point L in Figure 22.

The game can be turned into a Prisoner's Dilemma game if we visualize the values for both players rising beyond some point on the diagonal—say the point marked P.D. We can then use identical rules to obtain the continuous payoffs except for the segment below P.D. the payoffs increase. Thus, the higher portions of the diagonal no longer dominate the game; in fact, there are some values on the diagonal for which noncooperation has a higher utility than cooperation. This would be the case if management felt that by having relatively stiff penalties for nonperformance it would at least give them assurance and—*utilities from assurance*—that a certain minimum performance level would be achieved. Similarly, for the labor (or subordinate) player the minimal constraint may at least put a floor on the performance of other players who are peers so that a higher utility is achieved from the knowledge that, while he is doing his minimal share, others are also doing theirs.

The continuous game gives a measure of realism to the analysis in the sense that, to use a well-known metaphor, it permits management a choice of strategies composed of various combinations of the carrot and the stick. To use a related metaphor, it allows the subordinates to use various combinations of attitudes to their efforts which we may designate as friend and foe. The extreme case of the "friend" attitude would be complete empathy with management, where the subordinate sees his own goals as identical with management's goals. The ultimate in "foeness" would reflect complete antagonism in which the subordinate would attempt to minimize production if that were the major aim of management. The point of attempting to describe the continuous game is to see if a shorthand way of describing the basic strategic problems and dilemmas faced by connected levels in a hierarchical system can be found.

The introduction of inert areas suggests that, both in the game between peers and in the game between different levels, nonoptimal stable solutions are possible, and likely to exist.

Summary and Conclusions

There is a sense in which the choice of effort positions involves friend-foe/carrot-stick games. It is usually possible to choose positions which conflict with those of others, and some of the others have the capacity to respond in such a way as to cause injury. Although conflicts are frequently avoided, the essence of the effort games discussed usually involves choices between cooperation and conflict within and between different levels of a hierarchy.

The payoff matrix can be broken into sets of strategies which may be designated as symmetrical or asymmetrical joint choices. In the symmetrical case, "we do unto others as others do unto us." This may involve either cooperation by both parties or equal conflicting moves by both. I indicated a way of thinking about the payoffs in continuous rather than discreet terms. A basic notion of such games as Prisoner's Dilemma or Chicken is that if each tries for an asymmetrical, "exploitive" outcome they end up with what neither sought: a symmetrical, nonexploitive outcome which is worse for both parties.

The likely outcomes are the following: If individuals at the same level play Chicken it is apt to lead to a cooperative solution between peers. This usually turns out to be at effort levels above, equal to, but *not* below, the "stick" level. That is, if the stick is sufficiently harsh, individuals will cooperate to avoid it. In Prisoner's Dilemma the "free rider" problem enters. If individuals choose between fair shares and free rides it is possible for almost everyone in a small group to choose the free-ride outcome if there are no penalties or very light penalties for such an outcome.

If we look at the problem in terms of *inter*level strategies there are reasonable distributions of the payoffs enabling a superior outcome to be achieved in the P.D. game if each party at the lower level puts forth a relatively high fair-share effort. Or, those at the higher level can avoid a symmetrical free-ride solution if in choosing between the carrot and stick they put the weight heavily on the stick side and impose a Chicken game on those at the lower level. Thus, the ones at the higher level in working out the incentive structure find that they themselves are involved in a dilemma.

In the multiple payoff situation the effort outcome along the symmetrical diagonal may be stable and X-inefficient if there is uncertainty about the nature of the reactions, and if the negative consequences of possible reactions are taken seriously. One can visualize a set of reasonable payoffs under which nonoptimal positions are stable once they have been achieved. If inert areas are introduced into the picture so that bounds of non-movement exist in the neighborhood of the symmetrical diagonal, the possibility of the existence of a nonoptimal effort outcome increases. Such effort positions may involve relatively high utility outcomes but not maximum utility outcomes.

An important aspect of the effort "solution" at a given level is the relation between effort choices and the entropy problem in Prisoner's Dilemma effort games. The degree of non-control which may be the price for potential high effort increases the possibility of a slide toward relatively disorganized effort unless "management" struggles against the potential effort entropy in the system.

10 The Firm

Firms are composed mainly or entirely of agents. It is, therefore, valuable to consider them in some detail.

The Agent-Principal Problem

Conventional microtheory builds on the notion that in every exchange both parties gain. The logic behind this view is that the parties would not exchange in the first place if each of them did not see the potential for gain. This assumes that exchange is between principals, or operates *as if* it were. However, the situation becomes much more complex once *agents* enter the scene. Legally agents act in the name of their principals but nothing forces them to have the same interests. Arrangements made between principal and agent need not necessarily provide that they have similar interests.

Consider a simple three-person case. The actors are principal A, agent A_1 (an agent of A), and principal B. If A and B carry out an exchange we might expect both to gain thereby, but a transaction carried out between B and A_1 contains three possibilities: A_1 has the interest of his principal in mind so strongly that A and B both gain; A neither gains nor loses but B gains (A_1 is happy to oblige B as long as A is not injured); A_1 may oblige B despite the fact that A is injured as long as the principal cannot control or check fully on the *specific* transaction. By using the word *cannot* I do not suggest that it is physically impossible for the principal to check on the transaction, but simply that he does not normally do so. Result: once agents enter the scene there is no need for both parties to gain in order for transactions to take place.

Complexity increases once we introduce a world in which only agents act for their principals. Add a fourth actor, agent B_1, and assume that only the agents engage in transactions. In that case it is possible for the agents to carry out transactions in which both principals lose, and to ignore transactions in which both principals would gain. The extent to which they do so depends on a number of motivating and controlling forces. One might argue that the welfare of agents depends on the welfare of their principals; therefore, agents act as their principals would. But this presumes that *every* time the principals benefit the agent benefits. In a general way the agent may be concerned that in some aggregate sense the principal remains sufficiently well off so that he retains the agent. However, there is no need for the agent to have that concern about *every* transaction. Especially likely are the cases where agents play it safe, are excessively cautious, and ignore potential transactions that would lead to the mutual gain of their principals. This may happen for various reasons, including the fact that some agents may be interpreting rules set by their principals too closely in order to avoid potential blame. Another way of formulating the point is that the high degree of risk aversion is typical of agents. Because agents usually cannot appropriate to themselves the gains due their principals, there is an incentive for them to be risk-averse where the principals are not, or in cases where the agent would not be risk-averse were he acting in his own behalf as principal.

A significant element is that explicit or implicit contractual arrangements usually contain penalties for less than minimal performance on the part of agents but not rewards for exceeding minimum performance levels. This is especially apt to be true the greater the degree to which attempts are made to articulate and formalize job specifications. Some of this results from the fact that it is easier to state minimal standards and the connection of the fulfillment of minimal standards to a penalty-compensation framework than to relate varying performance levels to monetary or other incentives in cases where there are a variety of components that are part of the effort level, the output level, or both. In any event it is possible and even probable that agents ignore opportunities that principals might find worthwhile.

We have only considered single layer principal-agent relations. The possibilities for nonoptimal agent behavior expand enormously if we think of a hierarchy of agents, all of whom can contribute or engage in transactions. Agents actually doing things may be many removes from the principals, and in fact frequently have no contact with the principals whatsoever. Extreme but ubiquitous cases involve situations in which it becomes exceedingly difficult to determine the true principals. Thus, in the modern corporation in which stock holdings are widely disbursed, or in state-owned corporations, the relation between principal and agent is so remote that the entire world is one of agents whose interests may be very different from those of the principals they are presumed to serve. In such cases, which normally involve complex bureaucratic rules, there may be a great many opportunities for mutual gain of principals which are not entered into simply because they do not easily fit the rules.

The very meaning of gain becomes diffused and tortured when there are many layers between principals and agents. In some ultimate sense we attempt to interpret gain in terms of utility, but this ceases to be a clear notion when the principals are a large group of shareholders or all the citizens of a country.

There are of course good reasons why principals should resort to agents. If an organization using agents (employees, and so on) operates well, it extends the capacity of the principal far beyond what a principal could do on his own. On the other hand, there is the possibility that the agents operate with X-inefficiency. In examining the world of the firm we are examining a structure made up largely of agents in which there exists innumerable possibilities of nonprofitable transactions and missed opportunities carried out by agents. The problem faced by the firm is how to operate in a manner that carries out the intent of the "true principals"—if that intent can be defined.

Management Functions and Entropy

As an initial step it may be useful to employ the concept that firms translate external opportunities and constraints (especially in terms of financial evaluations) into internal opportunities and constraints. These translations are part of the effort activities, hence part of the effort positions of some firm members. We thus have constructed our theory from the inside out—from the characteristics of individual members, to more complex units such as groups, to interdependent sets of groups. All groups are visualized as being strictly inside the firm. Now let us look at the firm as a whole. To use a biological analogy we may visualize the groups as surrounded by a membrane that separate one group from the other. But there is a sense in which we want to look at the firm from the *outermost* membrane, which allows for a two-way view, from that membrane inside into its component groups, and simultaneously from the membrane to the outside world.

Some set of members control and give direction to the activities of those responsible for the "outermost membrane." I will refer to this group as *management,* but its membership in our terms need not be the same as that employed in ordinary business language. Managers essentially translate signals from the outside world and attempt to articulate a sense of direction and control within the firm. Management attempts to (1) receive signals from the outside; (2) transmit signals through the organization which reflects the interpretation of management intent and in part reflects the attempt to trigger performance; (3) evaluate the performance of internal groups; (4) transmit incentives throughout the organization directly or indirectly; (5) give direction to changes in the scale of the organization over time; and (6) struggle against effort entropy.

A slightly different way of looking at the firm is in terms of its structure. I have already indicated that rigidities and inefficiencies are likely to arise if groups become very large. As a consequence it is desirable to limit group size, to give each group some sort of integrated character, and hence to have a variety of group types. A system of necessary coordination of groups leads to a hierarchical authority and signal transmission system under which, what we might refer to as the inner groups operate at various degrees of remoteness from the outer group, or its controlling members on the enveloping outermost membrane. Thus, the basic structure facilitates the major function of the organization which is to receive, evaluate, and translate signals from the outside in order to induce performance on the inside. At the same time the nature of performance on the inside has to be evaluated against the demands from the outside.

While these types of inside-outside evaluations take place the organization must also struggle against potential or actual organizational entropy. The struggle against effort entropy need not take place directly, but the degree of effectiveness with which the other functions are carried out may simultaneously operate as a retarding force on the latent effort entropy.

Consider a set of interdependent effort groups. If a sense of direction and control is not communicated to group members, gradually some of them may choose effort levels differing from those management would view as acceptable. Suppose that the management group initially articulated a purpose which more or less defines acceptable effort positions, and that it imposes controls and incentives which instill in firm members an appropriate sense of constraint concern which in turn induces them to choose acceptable effort positions. Now suppose that the controls and some of the incentives gradually disappear. The consequences of having to abide by the constraints are then seen not to exist, and pressures deriving from constraint concern are attenuated. The more onerous tasks which were part of compromise effort positions gradually cease to be undertaken. Connections between intermember and intergroup effort points are weakened and eventually disappear. Thus, effort positions are gradually changed to others that defy integration into a sense of purposefulness and meaningfulness for the organization.

Unless there is persistent exercise of very strong controls by some members of the organization on the job interpretations of others, it is likely that what were initially acceptable interpretations will be transformed into effort positions of lower acceptability in terms of the articulation of management's overall intent. Accordingly, the sense of the collective purposive aspects of the organization are gradually attenuated into effort positions that reflect temporary "private" interests and a choice of activities that loosens the connections between the effort points of different individuals. Countermeasures are called for in order to overcome the erosion of purposive into nonpurposive effort areas from the point of view of some reasonable articulation by management of the organizational intent. The nature of the phenomenon of entropy can be illustrated by Figure 23. In this figure curve UE is the utility-effort relation for the individual, and curve P is the productivity that results from the individual's effort. The curve P declines beyond some point because increases in pace may be associated with decreases in quality beyond some point. The area marked AC is the effort position of the individual. Assume that signals require responses equally from the effort segments BC and AB. If the incentives for the individual to respond effectively to signals decrease or if the monitoring of responses for the individual decreases, it is quite probable that there will be an incentive for the individual to shift responses away from the segment BC, in which productivity is higher, toward AB in which productivity is much lower. As a result, even without any shift in the effort position, we may have an entropy effect from management's viewpoint.

In addition, there exists the possibility, not illustrated in Figure 23, that higher level managers may gradually reduce their constraints so that the curve UE shifts to a slightly higher position. This shifts the UE curve out of the inert area bounds and results in a situation under which the utility gain from moving from the current effort position is greater than the utility cost. Once this occurs we should expect further increases in effort entropy.

The Inverse Signal Hypothesis

The hierarchical structure of firms requires some degree of coordination from the top and attempts on the part of firm members at one level to obtain performance of some sort from those at a lower level. This results invariably in a two-way flow of signals. I have already stressed that both within levels and between levels there exist possibilities of either cooperative or conflict relationships as well as subtle mixtures of the two. The signal flow which includes motivational signals is influenced not only by the nature of such relations but by reactions to them. Individuals contribute to production directly, and also indirectly, by contributing to the motivational environment.

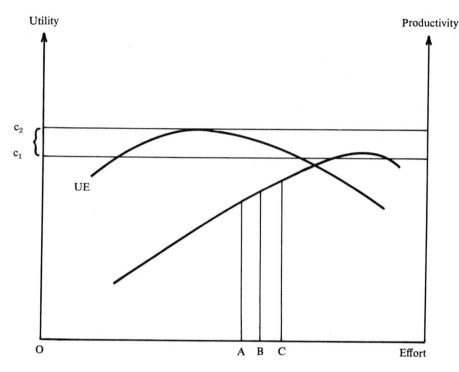

$c_1c_2 =$ utility cost of a change in the effort positions

Figure 23

Because of their dual character, signals are likely to compete. Consider signals intended to influence or trigger productive activity. We are not concerned with the nature of precise instruments used—whether written or oral or whether they involve specific orders or simply hints. What matters is that some sort of informational content with respect to the intent to influence productive activities is imparted from some people to other people.

My hypothesis is that intent signals contain a motivational message and that motivational signals frequently contain intent messages. If an individual has chosen an effort position it usually reflects a belief about the scope of his work. He is likely to expect that the intent signals will match the decision scope he has worked out for himself. If, however, the intent signals reflect a larger scope than his chosen decision area, this frequently implies considerable trust in his judgment and may operate as a positive motivating influence. If, on the other hand, signals are "excessively" specific and involve a narrower scope than he has chosen for himself, this may be interpreted as reflecting mistrust and may well have a negative motivating effect. "Mistrust" may not be the best word to convey the phenomenon involved and its potential emotional interpretations. The main idea is that the signal reveals a different scope level than that initially perceived by the one carrying out the effort. The principle I am trying to develop need not imply that this is a universal reaction, only that on the average a sense of scope diminution is likely to have disincentive consequences.

In a similar fashion we may expect direct motivating signals to convey some sense of the performance expectations. For example, specific instances of praise or blame not only convey motivational messages but may also indicate something about the expected quality of the effort. Similar inferences may be made from very direct motivating forces which may exist in terms of income increases, prizes, honors, or promotions. Not only has something of a motivating nature been done; in addition, the subject involved frequently gleans from the occurrence and the context in which it happens something about the way his superior or peer may wish him to carry out his work in the future.

There is likely to be a range within which intent signals and motivation signals do not conflict. However, on either side of this range and on the basis of the above considerations, we might hypothesize the following law: beyond some level of signal flow, the greater the detail and frequency of intent signals, the less the indirect motivating signals, and/or the less the effectiveness of any given direct motivating signals. There is an inverse relation, at least at the margin, between the quantum of intent signals and the quantum of motivation. The more the one, the less the other, and vice versa. This is not to suggest that there should be no intent signal and only motivating signals (or vice versa) but that because of the inverse signal law, should it turn out to be valid, there is some optimal mix of intent and motivating element, and management should be aware of the danger that increasing one type of signal may reduce the other.

Two reasons may be advanced for the inverse signal law. First, there is likely to be a fixed capacity of individuals to receive signals. Once this capacity is reached, performance signals drive out motivating signals and vice versa. Even below some absolute capacity for receiving and evaluating such signals the quality of evaluating one type of signal is likely to fall if there is an increase in the other type. Second, the most detailed type of information often exists at the most "local" level, that is, the level at which direct performance activities are being carried out. The more specific the signals from a higher level, the less individuals will rely on the local information available, hence the likelihood that superior information will be used if the signals coming from above are excessively specific.

Effort Standards and Choice of Technique

Although the struggle against entropy takes place within the firm, it also is influenced by the structure of the environment in which the firm operates. Within the firm the struggle depends not only on the nature of management and the signals it receives from the environment but also on the nature of the machinery and other equipment with which workers carry out their activities. The nature of signals given and the ease or difficulty of their transmission depend to a considerable degree on equipment employed. All this of course presumes that the same commodity is being produced since we are not here concerned with differences that result in organizational structure as a consequence of different commodities or different commodity mixes. The significant consideration is that the nature and degree of effort depend on the machinery. (The words equipment, machinery, and physical capital are used interchangeably.) We cannot assume that human inputs work at the same pace or effort level as we consider alternative types of equipment. Even though the wage cost *per man* may remain the same with alternative types of equipment, the wage cost per unit of effort may be very different, depending on how different types of equipment influence the intent signal flow, the motivational signal flow, and the reactions of firm members which result in changes in their effort flows.

If the wage cost per unit of effort depends on the type of equipment, it is conceivable that with increases in equipment the wage cost may at first rise but with further increases it may at some point fall. This is shown in Figure 24, where the usual production isoquant has two segments, *a* and *b,* which are the normal shape reflecting diminishing marginal rates of substitution between capital and labor. The figure also contains an intervening segment, *d,* which is concave from the origin and which reflects an increasing marginal rate of substitution. The consequence of this can be seen if we look at a small shift in the iso-cost line c_1 and note what happens as a consequence of a very small change in the wage rate (per man) indicated by the slight difference in slope of the iso-cost line of c_2. This implies that a small change in the wage rate may lead to a very significant change in the type of equipment employed, even if from a purely physical viewpoint the potential technologies involved are continuous. In other words, this result of a considerable shift in equipment need not in any way depend on extreme discontinuities in types of equipment available.

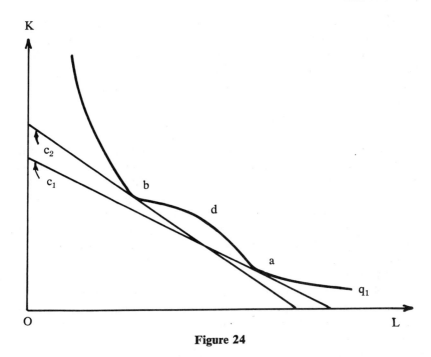

Figure 24

The way the diagram should be interpreted is that beyond a certain point more expensive equipment per man becomes *effort-stretching*. If the wage rate rises, it not only becomes worthwhile to substitute a little more capital for labor but, because of the increasing effort-stretching capacity of the more capital intensive technique, it pays to shift to much more capital per man until a point is reached where the effort-stretching capacity falls sufficiently so we get the usual equilibrium determined by the tangency of the isoquant and the iso-cost line. Rather than go into all the possible results that could occur as a consequence of the effort-stretching capacity of equipment (as well as effort-contracting consequences of other equipment), I chose one possibility simply to illustrate that once effort is a variable and is in part a consequence of the type of equipment employed, the results become much more varied than is likely to occur with conventional convex cost functions.

Firms as Price and Quantity Setters

Price and quantity decisions are among the major problems firms face. In conformity with the psychological principles postulated previously we presume that these decisions are also made on the basis of selective rationality. From this viewpoint there is no reason why the decision procedure is necessarily consistent with profit maximization. For the time being, let us concern ourselves only with the price decision. In accordance with the selective rationality principle, a great many price determining procedures would fit as long as the consequences of such procedures are taken into account.

In the early history of a firm, or in the history of the introduction of a new product, a series of experimental price-making procedures may be tried until one is chosen which achieves a degree of stability in terms of the principle of ratchet rationality espoused earlier. Such a procedure will appear satisfactory in terms of past experience and in terms of what is done elsewhere. Although not all procedures are equally good—any procedure will have to be tested in terms of its contribution to the firm's survival, and some procedures will be discarded or modified by the *pressures* created by perceived adverse results or clearly missed opportunities—the procedure that survives and persists does not have to be of the type under which price is set equal to marginal cost.

Consider one of the most frequently used procedures—average cost plus conventional markup pricing. Though such a procedure does not maximize profit, it is nevertheless a viable one if everyone in the industry uses the same markup and calculates unit costs in the same way. Once such a procedure becomes highly conventional it will not be altered as long as the results fit into the inert areas of those making the decisions or of those influenced by them. Of course, considerable adversity may lead to a reconsideration of the procedure as outcomes go beyond the inert areas.

Consider the case in which industry demand declines persistently for a period (such as occurred in the demand for seats in motion picture theaters upon the advent of television). Now consider two possible types of responses. First suppose that firms maintain constant prices. As illustrated in Figure 25, where we see the new demand curve to the left of the old one, a new demand-supply equilibrium is struck at the point consistent with the decline in demand by one-third. For purposes of argument we assume that most firms are operating under circumstances in which the sales price equals the unit cost of production. In order for such an outcome to be successful, approximately one-third of the average-size firms would have to leave the industry. The others could then operate at the same capacity as before and do roughly as well as before.

An alternative outcome to that pictured in Figure 25 is one in which each firm sees its output decline more or less proportionately. In order to stay in the industry it increases its price, say, by 50 percent. A new "equilibrium" is then struck at the price P_2 rather than P_1. Of course the output of the industry is much smaller than before. The final adjustment

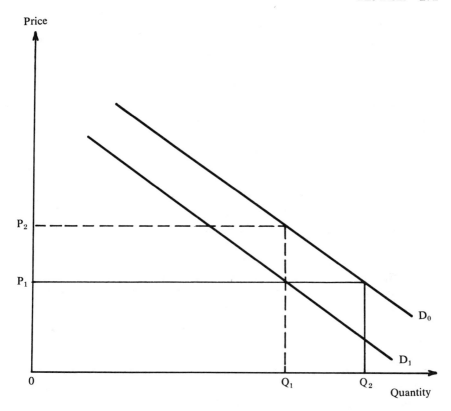

Figure 25

comes about in two ways: some firms leave the industry; and, the remaining firms operate at a much lower capacity and at a much higher price. According to our theory, both outcomes are possibilities. In the second case, were some of the firms to probe and discover the true price elasticity of demand they might lower the price and attempt to obtain a greater share of the market. However, there is no reason why such price elasticity probing should occur.

We are not concerned here with the dynamics toward a new equilibrium point in an industry. Our concern is limited to a single firm. All that is being argued is that, if the environment does not disturb an equilibrium price of P_2, it is possible for the firm to establish a price of P_2, operate at a lower capacity than before, and be in its inert area.

I have alluded to the possibility that the supply function might be a band rather than a single line; the fact of inertia may allow an individual firm to have a different price, within limits, than that which might be viewed as the ruling price in the industry. The elements likely to enter into determining the price are what the firm believes its cost per unit will be, the conventional procedures it uses for price setting, and whether or not the environment and the consequences of its procedures still result in outcomes which are within its inert areas. Thus, in the short run we visualize much greater potential variety in price setting than in the conventional theory. This should not be taken to mean that greater variety will exist in practice. Interfirm influences are an important component of behavior, and in the absence of other pressures we should expect firms to copy the conventional procedures in the industry. Thus the short-run results permit considerable deviation from the conventional profit maximizing norm. But we shall see in Chapter 12 that the long-run results, under a high degree of competition, are likely to be close to the conventional competitive outcome. The main conclusion that emerges from all this, one which need not be belabored at this stage, is that non-cost minimizing procedures and non-profit maximizing pricing are likely to occur. Furthermore they are likely to contribute to the aggregate degree of the firm's X-inefficiency.

A Note on Price Discrimination

One of the implications of conventional price theory in a world in which there is less than perfect knowledge is that it pays for sellers, whenever possible, to use price discrimination rather than uniform prices. This is a standard result, so it is not necessary at this stage to prove this assertion or to go into details. If the demand function is given, then for a given quantity sold, a higher gross revenue can always be obtained through various degrees of price discrimination and on the basis of a single price.

Price discrimination is almost an ubiquitous phenomenon in every economy. For example, in advanced economies such things as airline fares, theater tickets, medical costs, utility rates, automobile prices, and local taxes as a payment for local services all involve price discrimination to various degrees. So, in considering the various pricing formulas a firm could use, some degree of price discrimination will be involved. Since price discrimination generally increases gross revenues, it is apt to cover a higher level of costs per unit and, as a result, reduce the pressure on the firm to reduce costs. In other words, one of the means the firm could use to fight effort entropy and avoid the consequence of higher degrees of X-inefficiency is to find price discriminating formulas which pass the consequences of higher costs on to consumers.

In the next chapter I shall argue that various classes of consumers can be characterized by demand functions which are bands rather than straight lines and which implicitly contain within them inert areas. Situations of this sort allow for more possibilities of price discrimination, as well as possibilities of experimenting with discriminating formulas, than would otherwise be the case. This is especially true, if we apply Hirschman's ideas, and note that in many industries in advanced economies the buyer has almost no "voice" in price negotiations and can only resort to "exit."*

Contrary to conventional theory, I believe that firms do not make price, quantity, and *cost* decisions in one fell swoop. Rather, the firm's ongoing operations and the effort positions of its members determine the cost per unit. Given these costs, the firm uses a price determining procedure, such as cost mark-up pricing or discriminatory multipart pricing, and determines the quantity to be produced as a response to actual demand. To the extent that there are errors in estimating demand, these are in part taken care of by allowing inventories to build up or decline. Various adjustments in the inventory level are made in subsequent periods. The inventory decision itself will have X-inefficient components; as a result, it is part of the quantity decision which influences unit costs.

The pricing procedures employed depend in part on what other similar firms do. There is nothing sacrosanct about any pricing formula. As long as their outcomes are within the inert areas, the formula will be continued; if the results are outside the inert area, variants will probably be tried, or a formula may be discarded in the face of adversity or in the light of unusual opportunities for greater profits or other goals pursued by the firm.

The Theory of Impactees and Residual Adjustees

Some of the older literature on the theory of the firm employs the concept of residual claimants to explain the return to either entrepreneurs or

---

* A. O. Hirschman, *Exit, Voice, and Loyalty* (Cambridge, Mass., Harvard University Press, 1970). A recent paper by W. J. Adams and J. L. Yellen, "Commodity Bundling and the Burden of Monopoly" (Harvard Institute of Economic Research Discussion Paper #402, February 1975), presents an interesting variant on the price discrimination formulas. They argue that one way in which firms increase revenues is through "commodity bundling." Instead of selling single commodities, they are combined into bundles so that individual choice is limited and the entire bundle must be purchased. By selling a variety of commodity bundles (for example, automobiles with different types of equipment as "standard equipment"), the seller obtains the equivalent of price discrimination since different bundles will presumably appeal to different classes of buyers, although sales would be very different if buyers could purchase the "unbundled" components.

manager-owners. A variant of this idea, essentially a generalization of the concept, will be useful for our purposes. The main notion is that an effort change results in a cost somewhere in the system and that cost (or gain) has an impact somewhere in the system. A basic problem is to determine who initially and ultimately pays for the consequences. Let us refer to the one on whom the cost initially falls as the effort-cost impactee. The impactee has two choices: he can either absorb the cost, or shift it elsewhere. If the absorption occurs within the impactees' inert area, nothing more happens. If not, he may try to alter the behavior of the effort changer or shift it elsewhere. If the costs are passed on they fall first on intermediate impactees but they must ultimately rest somewhere. Let us refer to those on whom the costs ultimately fall (or who ultimately gain) as the residual adjustees. We shall use the notions of impactees and residual adjustees to refer to the individuals or groups who initially or ultimately pay for the consequences of either effort point changes or less than optimal effort positions from the viewpoint of someone other than the one who puts forth the effort.

Effort shifts can take place in a number of ways. (1) The phenomenon of effort entropy, which may be a consequence of the attenuation of supervisory controls, has already been described. Clearly the cost impact of effort entropy falls on someone. (2) A similar effort shift can occur as a consequence of the normal replacement of personnel. Altered conditions outside of the firm may cause replacements to choose less productive effort positions than the ones chosen by those they replace. (3) Changed circumstances can create inducements which result in individuals' moving out of their inert areas and choosing less productive effort positions. (4) If we recall the exact definition of an effort position—which is a set of effort points where the individual involved can shift from one to another in response to what he considers legitimate demands—and that there was no presumption that the various effort points in the position are equally productive, then the consequence of a redistribution of demands for effort can result in a change in the productivity of the particular effort position. In all the cases indicated, the change in effort involves a cost (or a gain) whose impact falls on someone.

The impactees or the residual adjustees may be the managers of the firm, the stockholders, or the workers responsible for the effort change (because of salary or dismissal from positions), or it may fall on the consumers either because they receive lower quality goods or services or pay a higher price for the same quality good. In some cases the impact may fall on government and ultimately on taxpayers. This view contrasts sharply with the implicit position of the textbook theory of the firm, in which the implication is that it is only the manager-owner who is the residual adjustee, and who can do something to change the situation.

Two critical aspects for analysis are suggested by this mode of reasoning: to discover not only the cost of changing effort positions but also the distribution of both the impactees and residual adjustees; and to determine whether those who are either impactees or residual adjustees are in a position to respond to incentives and to intervene in the context in which the effort shifts took place. The distribution of residual adjustees and the incentives to which they respond, as well as the opportunities to do so, vary considerably depending on the market structure (competition, monopoly, and so forth) within the industry.

The main elements to determine in any specific analysis are (1) the path of effort change cost shifts; (2) who the residual adjustees are and the roles they play in the economy; (3) whether the cost adjustment falls into the adjustee's inert area; and (4) whether or not the cost impact on any impactee results in an attempt to change the effort positions of others. Clearly it is most important to know whether there is an intersection between impact targets and the power to make organizational changes and improvements. The potential for and rate of effort entropy depends to a considerable degree on the nature of such intersections.

The Effort Equilibrium of the Firm

The ideas considered imply three conditions for a firm's detailed equilibrium: (1) that all effort positions are within interesecting inert areas for all interacting individuals and groups; (2) that all actual effort positions are within intersecting defensible positions if defensible positions exist. By a defensible position I mean situations in which individuals have no objection to moving from an existing effort position except for the fear that, should they move, further movements will be requested; so in order to deflect such requests they refuse to budge beyond a narrow circumscribed area; and (3) if all cost impacts of effort changes fall within the inert areas of residual adjustees. If the foregoing holds for some but not all groups in the firm, then a *partial effort equilibrium* may be said to exist. Even such partial equilibriums are important, since the inert areas of the groups involved can become frictional forces inhibiting change in the face of opportunities for profitable changes.

The processes employed to induce interdependent individuals to cooperate are also likely to be equilibrating processes within the firm. If an event disrupts a group's equilibrium, the interdependent relations of its members, which depend in part on each others' effort choices, may also be upset. As a result, individuals may attempt to influence others to change their effort choices. There are various activities likely to be generated by the disequilibrium which return the group to an equilibrium level. (1) Personnel may be replaced, individuals may be discharged or shifted to other departments, or their activities may be isolated or altered so that the degree of interdependence between them and their peers is reduced. (2) People may be urged to reinterpret their existing firm roles. (3) Material or nonmaterial rewards may be offered for the acceptance of change which falls within a reconstituted inert area. (4) The group may be completely or partially broken up so that organizational regroupings take place. (5) The social processes of approval and disapproval may induce some individuals to change their effort choices to those sanctioned by such processes. (6) Finally, some individuals may alter their utility-effort relations.

The detailed equilibrium just described is unlikely to occur in reality, except perhaps in very small firms. For firms of any significant size another type of equilibrium, which I call the "macro-equilibrium" of the firm, may exist.

Before defining "macro-equilibrium" let us consider how various formal decisionmaking groups cope with the fact that they cannot carry out the detailed supervision of the efforts of others or master the detailed results of all members of the firm. The normal approach in handling such situations is for supervisory decisionmaking groups to invent or borrow various conventional summary indices of performance such as output per man or output per production unit, cost per unit of output, profits per unit, and sales per unit. For our purposes it does not matter which indices are used or what comparisons are made to determine whether or not performance has been satisfactory. What matters is that such indices are of a summary character.

In terms of such indices a decisionmaking group behaves in such a way that for some values of the indices no decisions for change are called for, that is, they do not attempt to alter the APQT bundle of others within the firm. The nature of the APQT bundles may be changing for individuals who are in a disequilibrium position, but these changes do not influence the macro indices in such a way as to cause supervisory decisionmaking groups to take any effective action. As a result, a range of values of summary indices may exist for which the firm may be said to be in macro-equilibrium. At the same time and perhaps unnoticed, however, unchecked changes are taking place in some individual's APQT bundles, which in turn affect costs, profits, demand, and other aspects of firm performance. In extreme cases a firm might find itself on the verge of bankruptcy while the formal management may not have done anything effective to alter the situation. The contrast between what we call the macro-equilibrium of the firm and the detailed micro-equilibrium (partial equilibrium) may be critical in explaining why in fact bunkruptcies occur, whereas conventional microeconomic theory has no mechanism for explaining such events.

Summary and Conclusions

The concept of partially free effort choices (interpreted as APQT choices) and the existence of inert areas imply certain conclusions about the operations of firms. These conclusions differ markedly from those obtained on the basis of the conventional theory of the firm. Three are negative and can be stated succinctly: cost per unit of output is not minimized by the firm; profits are not maximized; and observable opportunities for gain may not be pursued or avoidable situations which involve losses may not be avoided. Another interpretation of this last point is that the firm may be in a situation in which its economic circumstances are worsening, yet the formal decisionmaking groups within it do nothing to alter the conditions responsible.

The last point depends in part on the three types of organizational equilibriums I have distinguished. The first is the detailed full equilibrium of the firm in which every individual is within his inert area. A second possibility is the detailed partial equilibrium of the firm in which *some* individuals are within their inert areas. A third and special variant of the detailed partial equilibrium is the macro-equilibrium. Here formal decisionmaking groups operate on the basis of summary indices of performance of both the firm as a whole, and of the subunits under which their inert areas are determined by the particular values of the summary indices. In this last instance significant changes may be taking place within the firm but as long as they do not force the summary values of the indices to fall outside the inert areas of the formal decisionmaking groups, no action is taken.

It may seem that all of our conclusions at this stage are negative and that the theory we have developed does nothing more than point to the possibility that the conclusions resulting from conventional microtheory need not occur. Although these are the most striking for those trained in the conventional microeconomic mold, they are not the only conclusions. One basic result (albeit at a highly generalized level) is that the rate of change within the firm depends on the nature of the APQT bundles chosen, on the size of the inert area bounds, and on the rate of change of external stimuli. The conventional theory suggests that firm changes depend only on the nature and rate of change of external stimuli. In our theory, however, the relative sizes of the inert area bounds separate situations in which there is interfirm interactions as against those in which no interactions occur. They determine the degree of sensitivity of one firm to the behavior of other firms.

11 The Atomistic Theory
of Consumers' Behavior

Consumption Targets

The connection between the behavior of households that enter and operate within markets—as against the behavior of *members* of households that operate *within* that economic unit but outside markets—is not considered in conventional microtheory. Consider, for example, the connection between the affect relation (positive or negative) between household members, and the impersonal relations between the household and the market.* Let us begin by classifying various categories of household decisions and examining the possibility of treating such decisions in an expanded theory. The distinctions to be considered are: (1) ordinary goods versus "target goods"; (2) ordinary expenditures versus target expenditures; (3) independent decisions and interrelated decisions; and (4) "external" household decisions versus intrahousehold consumption decisions.

These four considerations suggest a theory of consumption in which to some degree the diminishing marginal utility postulate, *or its variants,* do not hold for all quantity segments of a commodity or of utility expenditure functions. By ignoring the distinction between preference functions for households and preferences of household members and related considerations, the traditional theory ignores that large class of behavior inconsistent with reasonable inferences from the theory. I will retain the weak ordering postulate but not retain *in all instances* the diminishing marginal rate of substitution postulate, or its equivalent formulations.

According to traditional theory, diminishing marginal utility sets in from the first microunit, so to speak, for all goods. Economists seem to believe

* Cairncross pointed out parallels between households and firms in a compact and humorous way, but the connection between intra-agent relations and agent behavior was not developed. A. Cairncross, "Economic Schizophrenia," *Scottish Journal of Political Economy,* 5 (February 1958).

that everyday experience supports this postulate. But there are types of commodities and situations for which we would not expect it to hold. Consider drug x, for which a certain minimal amount is necessary for it to be effective medicinally. In that case we would not argue that diminishing marginal utility sets in immediately. If the drug is presumed to have a curative value at some minimal amount but be ineffective below that amount, many people would consider the drug's utility zero up to the minimal "target" level, and positive beyond that. Nor should we presume that diminishing marginal utility sets in as soon as the target value is reached. There may be an optimal effectiveness level which is above the minimal target level, and diminishing marginal utility may set in only after that optimum effective level is reached. There is no reason to believe that human psychology and the nature of disease are such that this is false. The opposite is frequently true, or physicians and patients behave as if it were true.

Standards in the field of nutrition and medicine frequently involve minimal requirements. One can readily visualize a class of commodities for which minimal "target" values and optimal consumption values exist. It is immaterial whether or not these targets are based on physiological knowledge; for purposes of the theory it is sufficient that people *believe* it true.

The vulgar conception of "needs," usually employed by noneconomists (and usually argued against by economists), often may be interpreted as physiologically or psychologically (or even politically) determined target values of this sort. Human beings are a standard-creating species, even if the external material world does not impose standards. Consider education as a commodity. Most educational authorities set up artificial standards and attach more significance to marginal units necessary to reach the standard than to the intramarginal ones. University degrees and other certificates are usually treated in this way. To many it makes a considerable difference whether they have completed the course or only nine-tenths of it. The last tenth appears to add more to the total value of the experience than any previous tenth. Or, let us look at the somewhat extreme case of the degree of the medical doctor. Completing the course spells the difference between being able to practice a lucrative and fulfilling profession rather than its next best alternative—which may be very much inferior. I repeat: it is not the external valuation that matters but how individuals feel about fulfilling the standard, irrespective of its arbitrariness. External aspects do play a role, however. In foreign-language instruction there may be a minimal amount of such instruction which, if received, turns the language into a usable vehicle of communication and prior to which the limitations of knowledge are simply too great to enjoy communication. Here both the external characteristics of the commodity and its relations to internal feelings determine a standard which operates as a significant target valuation.

The same external circumstances need not create significant "target valuations" for all individuals. To return to a medical example, suppose that four small pills relieve one of headache pain completely, but that one pill relieves some of the pain and the others relieve more of it. For some people this may be an either/or situation, for others a continuum, depending on their tolerance for this particular type of pain. Those with sufficiently low tolerance will want relief from all pain if at all possible. For them, four pills constitute a significant target value. Or consider addiction. It may be easier for some to choose between smoking and not smoking *at all* than to cut down from their customary smoking standard. Most of us in some cases, and some of us in many cases, behave as though meeting a standard, whether self-imposed or partially externally imposed, is of such importance that the marginal unit that gets us over the hill, so to speak, has greater utility than submarginal units.* In addition to commodities which possess a target value quantity there are *expenditures* of this type. For example, if for some purpose there is a target expenditure on food in order to meet certain nutritive or socially determined requirements, the expenditure as such may take on this characteristic.

It is usually assumed that the nature of goods are "given" and the quantity of any good purchased is then determined by the preference map of the household and budgetary constraints. Thus, the expenditure on any commodity or class of commodities *results* from the given quality-price-income parameters. Yet an alternative approach is frequently found: a prior decision is made about the amount to be spent out of a given budget on a given category of goods or a given good. That is, we make a commitment to live in accordance with a somewhat arbitrarily determined expenditure standard. The relations between commitments, standards, and possible minimum target values is the essence. Whether or not this is a rational procedure is not a consideration. We are concerned that if a prior budgetary commitment procedure is used, we can understand it and examine its consequences.

Not all expenditure commitments have critical target values. By examining the budgeting process through which households, in full or in part, make such commitments, we can discover whether some of them have tar-

* No doubt Tenzing and Hilary received greater satisfaction from climbing the last 100 feet to the peak of Everest than any previous hundred feet. See Sir John Hunt, *The Conquest of Everett* (New York, Dutton, 1954), ch. 16.

get values similar to the type discussed under target quantities of goods. Among the main reasons for expenditure commitments are the implicit quasi-contractual arrangements often found within the family which are made in order to work out a seemingly orderly, and reasonably peaceful, family life.

The fairly universal behavior sequence involves the creation of a standard and a commitment to observe and attain it. It is silly and extremely costly to try to find out everything about every commodity in every market to determine and consider how one feels about every commodity in order to make a "rational" allocation of one's income. Hence, a seemingly reasonable procedure is to divide one's income among classes of goods—say, 25 percent for rent, 30 percent for food, and so on—and *commit* oneself to live within these boundaries. Some individuals may set unusual significance to certain standards so that utility is negative as one goes over the budget limit, but marginal satisfaction rises as we approach some predetermined standard, which may be at, or prior to, the budgeted maximum.

A more important set of situations in which goal attainment behavior may be operative are those that involve obligations to oneself or to others. Consider pensions. An individual may have a minimum target annual pension that he desires after retirement, and this may require a target expenditure each income period, the attainment of which the individual feels very strongly. Expenditure on insurance to avoid certain risks whose consequences an individual may fear is another such category. A predetermined savings rate may operate in a similar way, either because the person feels that certain minimal savings involve some sort of virtuous behavior or because it involves a minimal degree of protection for an uncertain future. The allocation of minimal funds necessary for a set of activities that one values very highly, and which involve a variety of goods, may operate in the same way: for example, a given minimum amount may be wanted to engage in some athletic activity, or in some other especially prized recreational activity.

Pervasive types of expenditure commitments that have significant target values may include such general ideas as a tithe for charity or a fixed monetary obligation to help support a relative, friend, or group. Such obligations may be quasi-contractual or may involve standards of behavior on which we set great store (such as contributions to support the arts or political causes). Some may involve obligations acquired in the past, for which we undertook a certain expenditure commitment for a time period—for example, alimony payments or remittances sent to his home country by an immigrant worker. The most important obligations usually are those that income earners have to members of their own family.

Intrahousehold Division—The Form Problem

Two aspects are involved in the household division of income: How much to whom? and What form does the income distributed take? On the latter some of the alternatives are distributions in cash, in goods, in mixtures of both, in short-term commitments, or in long-term commitments. Although some aspects of this problem were discussed in Chapter 8, I wish to reiterate to show that in general individuals prefer "target commitments" to "short-term allowances." Figure 26 shows two commodities that the contributor (or parent) wants the receiver (claimant) to have in some ratio. Assume a budget shown by B_1. The parent's indifference curve target to the budget is shown by P_1 and the claimant's indifference curves are C_1 and C_2. It is evident that the claimant wants a different allocation of the budget. If the parent's commodity mix is chosen, the claimant is on his indifference curve C_1; if the claimant is allowed to choose his own mix, he can get to a higher point on his preference function, namely C_2. In sum, if the claimants have the same tastes as contributors they are no worse off by a grant (and buy the goods themselves), but if they have different tastes they are clearly better off by a grant.

I also pointed out that claimants prefer long-term commitments to short-

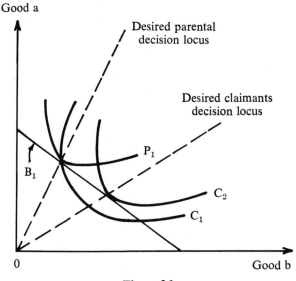

Figure 26

term grants. The claimant's long-term plans are more readily handled if he feels that he has a commitment from the contributor to a *stream* of grants. Constantly renegotiating the allowance is costly in time and frequently unpleasant. From the claimant's viewpoint a long-term commitment saves on transaction costs and reduces uncertainty. Ideally a claimant wants a situation in which there is a floor on the size of the commitment to him, and an open-end arrangement for renegotiation upward.

Outsiders also want commitments from household members. Leases, mortgages, school fee arrangements, credit payment, club memberships, and so on take the form of intermediate-length commitments to the outside world entered into by household members.

In general the proportion of household income that goes to commitments rises with increases in socioeconomic status. The reason for this is that to a considerable degree one needs to be either a commitment recipient or have a fairly high income before one can safely and easily become a commitment payer. There is a trade-off between the steadiness of income receipts to the household and the income stream that determines the capacity of the household to supply commitments to its members. A formalization and professionalization of jobs takes place as we go up the socioeconomic scale. In the world of the day laborer receiving an irregular wage there is likely to be far fewer commitments to household members than in the world of the corporate executive receiving an annual salary. A relatively stable income stream permits the household to undertake stable commitments both to its members and to the outside world, though, given the ability to borrow, a higher less stable income can substitute for a lower more stable one.

How Much to Whom?

Certain elements influence the income distribution between household members. The essence of the problem resembles the prisoner's dilemma situation developed in game theory.[1] It may be useful to explore it from that viewpoint. Each member wants as much as possible of the household income. A family member's utility depends on the amount "spent" on him or her, the form of the expenditure, and the nature of the negotiations and subsequent relations that result in the expenditure. If the payoff matrix is in terms of utility, this is not a constant sum game. The nature of intrafamily negotiations can create unpleasantness that reduces the utility of all contending members.

Cooperative and noncooperative outcomes are possible. In the simple three-by-three case illustrated in Table 10a we see that if each one wishes to maximize his or her utility the outcome will be worse for both members.

Table 10a. Payoff matrix for Prisoner's Dilemma game.

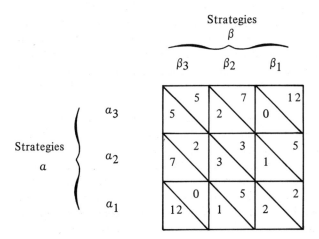

Each chooses strategies α_1 and β_1 and receives only 2 utilities each. Should each choose a maximum strategy, they also end up choosing α_1 and β_1 and receive only 2 utilities each. Within households strongly independent, noncooperative individuals reduce utility all around.

The diagonal in Table 10a forms a set of cooperative solutions. Should family members choose to be cooperative, various divisions are possible. We shall consider approaches that yield cooperative solutions later and

Table 10b. Payoff matrix for Chicken game.

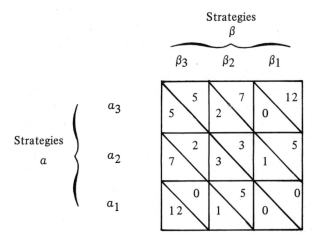

discuss the implication of noncooperative outcomes. In the original P.D. formulation the prisoners were not allowed to consult each other and only a single "play" was involved. In actual families a large number of iterations of the "game," so to speak, are possible and numerous consultations can take place. In experiments carried out by behavioral scientists almost half of the couples tested found a cooperative solution in 25 iterations or less.* Where many more iterations are allowed a higher proportion will probably find a cooperative outcome.

It is interesting that the nonoptimal cooperative outcome in which each receives 3 utils the solution is stable. If either tries to move to a better situation it is possible for the other to respond in a noncooperative way which would worsen the situation. Thus, individual A may not choose α_3 for fear that individual B would then choose β_1, which would make him worse off. This is more convincingly illustrated in the case in which the values in the payoff matrix are continuous. The arrows around the edges of Figure 27a indicate the direction of the value of the payoffs. Now suppose that the diagonal values are as illustrated in Figure 27b. In that case it would seem more likely that any local peak would be a stable cooperative solution. As long as some degree of distrust exists in which there is fear that the actions and reactions of trying to move to a new position could lead to a worsening for both, then a local nonoptimal cooperative outcome could be stable.

Another possibility is that an inert area exists for both "players" along the cooperative diagonal. This is shown by the shaded area surrounding segment I in Figure 27a. We may also visualize that the inert area extends to either side of the diagonal. In that case, if both parties choose, after a process of trial and error, a set of strategies within the inert area they will stay there, despite the fact that it is the optimal outcome for neither.

I showed in the preceding section that receivers prefer commitments to other forms in expressing their claim demands. However, on the supply side, that is, in their offers to meet claims, contributors frequently seek some other form. The nature of the situation and its possible cooperative solution is indicated in Figure 27c. Let us refer to the contending members as parent and claimant (say, a son). The curve marked P_1 indicates the parent's willingness to trade some degree of control over the expenditures of the claimant for a greater amount of the expenditure. That curve approaches an asymptote since there is a maximum amount the parent is willing to spend. The claimant's indifference curve S_1 is shaped the oppo-

---

* This was true for relatively normal couples. A much smaller ratio of couples who sought help for mental problems found cooperative solutions in similar game experiments. See J. Santa Barbara and N. P. Epstein, "Conflict in Clinical Families," *Behavioral Science,* 19:100–110 (1974).

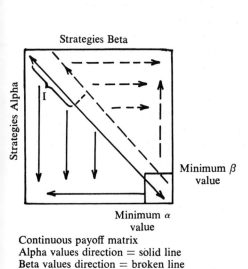

Strategies Beta

Strategies Alpha

I

Minimum β
value

Minimum α
value

Continuous payoff matrix
Alpha values direction = solid line
Beta values direction = broken line

Figure 27a

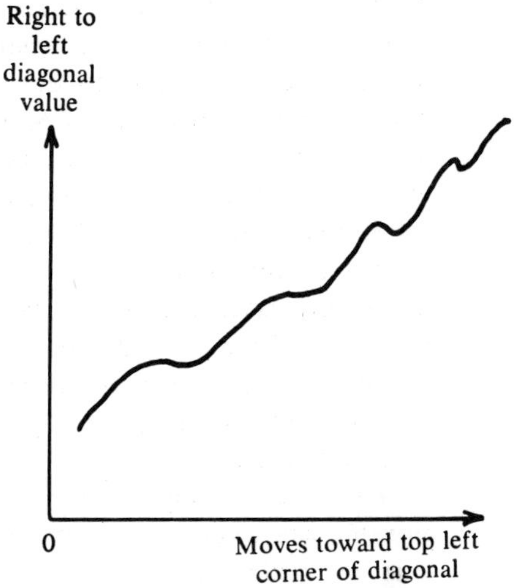

Right to
left
diagonal
value

0   Moves toward top left
corner of diagonal

Figure 27b

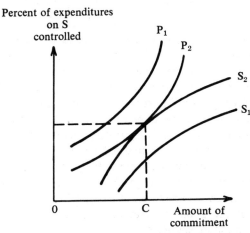

Percent of expenditures
on S
controlled

P_1

P_2

S_2

S_1

0   C   Amount of
commitment

OC = "controlled commitment" agreement

Figure 27c

site way reflecting the son's desire to give up some of the amount of the expenditure if less parental control is exercised. Each curve represents a "control-commitment" mix where no degree of unpleasantness is involved. The parent, who ultimately controls the purse strings, can always impose a solution by his willingness to undergo a high degree of unpleasantness. Thus, if curves P_1, S_1 do not have any contact points, they may be viewed as moving toward each other, but at the same time curves closer to each other involve degrees of dissatisfaction on both sides. Curves P_2, S_2 have a tangency point that reflects a cooperative solution, but it involves some degree of dissatisfaction for both parties. The significant point is that P_2 and S_2 both are functions of current family income. If income was higher the son would expect more and be dissatisfied with the existing solution and the parent would probably be willing to yield more (a movement of the P curve to the right).

A final, extremely important aspect is fairness. The form in which such appeals are likely to be made is through counterpart members of the family's social reference groups. Thus, the son would use information about grants given to children in similarly placed families as an argument for the fairness of his grant. Family income may directly or indirectly form a basis for the degree of effectiveness of such arguments. Coalitions within the family are also likely to use arguments of this type in attempts to pry larger commitments out of the net contributor.

IMU Goods or Grants and Utility–Expenditures Functions

Consider what a utility function in which there are target goods or target expenditures (commitments) looks like. Goods or grants whose utility functions contain increasing marginal utility segments will be referred to as IMU goods or grants. Assume prices are given. Each unit of a commodity is the amount that could be purchased per dollar. In Figure 28a the curves are conventional marginal utility functions. Figure 28b shows a commodity whose utility is nil for the early units (our medicine example), increases to a maximum, and then declines. Figure 28c shows a commodity whose marginal utility rises to its initial minimal target level, T, continues to rise until it approaches its optimum effectiveness point, O^*, and declines after that. Now suppose first that only goods g_1 and g_2 exist (in Figure 28a). To draw a curve which would show the marginal utility per dollar spent we chose amounts of the goods so that the marginal utility is equal for all commodities given the expenditure.

Now suppose that g_3, an IMU good, becomes part of the commodity set. Previously in allocating successive additions to our budget we simply

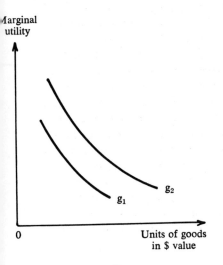

Figure 28a

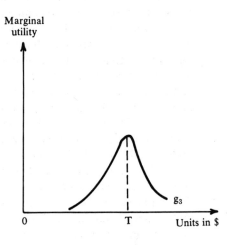

Figure 28b

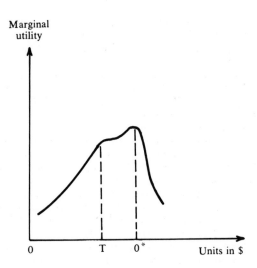

Figure 28c

asked: if we spent one more dollar which additional unit of which commodity would add the greatest utility? We can no longer do so once IMU goods are involved. As we contemplate spending successive dollars we have to ask whether there is a commodity that initially has a lower marginal utility than its competitors but which for the x-dollars spent adds more to total utility than if the same amount is spent on "normal" diminishing marginal utility goods. At each stage we must consider all the successive values of x, say for $x = \$2$, then $x = \$3$, and so on. It can readily be seen that once an IMU good or grant enters the picture the utility expenditure curve is no longer necessarily negatively inclined throughout but can have a hump of the type illustrated in figure 29b.* In this figure suppose the budget is B_1. The IMU good g_3 would not be included under this budget constraint. If the IMU good is an important target good (or grant), it seems likely that, at least for some individuals, sufficient regret or frustration could be involved as a consequence of not being able to afford g_3 so that negative marginal utility results. I shall refer to this phenomenon as "frustration disutility."†

Intrahousehold Conflict and X-Inefficiency in Consumption

In the usual microtheory treatments the allocation of goods in accordance with given household demand involves the allocational efficiency of the system. But households may not employ their purchasing power as well as possible. In accordance with usage elsewhere in this book I shall refer to

---

* In the famous article by Friedman and Savage there is a segment of their *total* utility-function which implies increasing marginal utility of expenditures. However, the authors do not appear to see this aspect nor do they develop it on the basis of individual utility function for specific goods or other expenditure components. It is invented out of the blue, as it were, in order to explain why some people buy insurance and gamble simultaneously. See M. Friedman and L. J. Savage, "The Utility Analysis of Choices Involving Risk," *Journal of Political Economy*, 56:279–304 (August 1948). One reason for IMU goods is that the consumer does not want a particular good for itself but in order to fulfill a "want category." For instance, people do not want medicines, or medical services—they want health. But a minimal targeted expenditure on medical insurance or on medical goods helps to "buy" health. A similar point is made by Wilfred Beckerman, "Environment, Needs, and Real Income Comparisons," *Review of Income and Wealth*, 19:333–339 (March 1973).

† It is not difficult to imagine situations in which the goods available but not bought can involve feelings of negative utility. Suppose that an ill individual is in pain which can be alleviated only by a treatment available in another country. The feelings of an individual who cannot afford the trip and who resents this fact bitterly can reasonably be interpreted as negative utility. The marginal utility graph of this particular good for this person starts at a negative value and rises sharply to its peak at the target cost of trip and treatment.

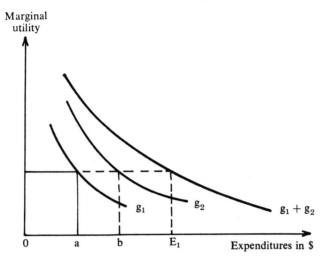

Figure 29a

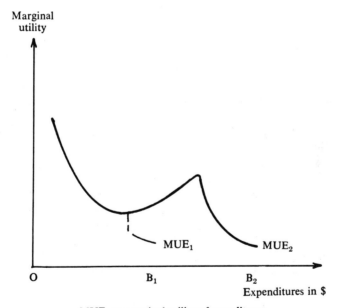

MUE_1 = marginal utility of expeditures
if budget is B_1

Figure 29b

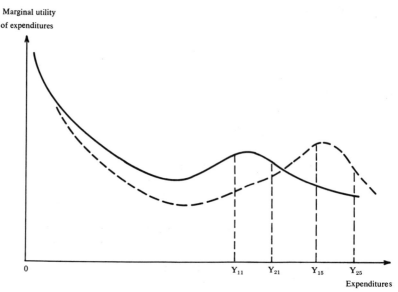

Figure 29c

intrahousehold decisions which result in a *utilization* of purchasing power that can be improved upon (without any increase in purchasing power) as X-inefficient consumption.

It is convenient to distinguish four categories of utility that an individual can obtain: own consumption utility, empathy utility, nonfunctional utility, and frustration utility. Own consumption utility refers to the satisfaction an individual receives from that part of his budget spent on himself. Empathy utility refers to satisfaction received from an income transfer spent on someone else; a parent may receive pleasure from part of his income spent on his child. Under nonfunctional utility we have in mind cases of emulative interdependencies in demand (see Chapter 4). Utility for person A depends on the ratio of A's purchases of a given good to B's purchases. Both can be made equally well-off if both reduce their competitive demands. Thus the utility value of the net opportunity cost of competitive emulation may be referred to as nonfunctional utility. Frustration utility has already been defined. The last two types of utility are likely to have negative values while the first two normally have positive values.

Now, we define the utility of distribution A as (Pareto) superior to B if it is possible under B to transfer income to A which would make some household members better off and no member worse off. This occurs if the empathy utility of the one who foregoes income is greater for him than the utility loss of the alternative uses of the income, while for the one who receives the transfer the utility from his own consumption is greater than the empathy utility foregone. Similar redistributions can be imagined which involve nonfunctional utility or frustration utility. The set of distributions that cannot be improved upon in this sense is the optimal distribution set. In this sense a "Pareto ordering" of distribution sets can be visualized. An ordinal index can be assigned to such an ordering. Let us return to the P.D. type of payoff matrix shown in Figure 27a. Assume that the distributions in the diagonal of the payoff matrix are listed in such a way so that those closest to the northeast corner have a higher or equal household utility value than those lower down. If, as seems possible, a distribution around the middle of the cooperative diagonal is chosen, and this distribution is a stable equilibrium, it follows that nonoptimal X-inefficient consumption arrangements can result as a consequence of the process of internal conflict and compromises.

As already suggested, the inert area concept can be applied to the household. Inert areas are likely to exist for various household members with respect both to the form and the value of member's receipts out of household income. Distributors and form arrangements may fall into the appropriate inert areas and persist over time, despite the fact that they can be improved upon.

Income Elasticities of Claims and Commitments

What happens to claims for commitments as income increases? In the absence of empirical studies we can only speculate on the matter, but three elements do come to mind: the nature of the resolution of conflicting claims prior to the income increases; the degree to which other households in the same social influence group have also had income growth; and competitive appeals for fairness. Undoubtedly there are others; but these enable us to imagine the degree to which competing claim pressures tend to exhaust the income growth of the household.

Let us consider claim pressure from the viewpoint of the net contributor and refer to others in the household as claimants. Suppose the initial position has left all claimants very unsatisfied. Unwelcome compromises have been imposed since all must ultimately yield to the income constraint. It is as though the contributor has built a dike to dam the wave of claims. But the dike overflows once the claimants perceive an increase in income. Claimants rush to renegotiate. The contributor must find it hard to struggle against the onslaught. There is extreme pressure for the entire income increase to be exhausted to satisfy the previously unsatisfactory condition, and the contributor may find it hard to retain his own previous level of expenditure. If we define total claim elasticity as the ratio of the increase in all claims to the increase in income, then claim elasticity is most likely greater than unity.

The extent to which the contributor yields to claims in the form of commitments determines the commitment elasticity. If the commitment elasticity is greater than 1, then the contributor's share may or may not be greater. Commitment elasticity can depend in part on the relations of family members with members of other households with whom they interact. We posit the existence of socioeconomic influence groups (SIG) to which households "belong." There are many such groups and they form a rough hierarchy in terms of social status and income range, but let us assume that a household belongs to only one such group.

Consider a case in which all households in a SIG receive an increase in income. Once the family agrees to live in a style resembling those of its SIG, many of the areas of discretion are severely narrowed. Living in the style of other members in the group implies that family members with similar demographic characteristics (age, sex) will to some extent have to be equipped with similar material goods. The very idea of belonging (and especially demonstrating belonging) to a SIG implies some similarity in expenditure patterns.

Should there be disagreements between net receivers and not contributors about the allocation of family income, the standard set by the group—or examples of specific members of the group but outside the family—are frequently invoked as reference points and arguments in appeals for "fair shares." Suppose that for family members in a SIG there is a modal allowance and a modal expenditure. For a specific household each family member argues for at least the *perceived* modal allowance and expenditure. Not receiving the allowance may be viewed as questioning whether the parents are living up to the image of the SIG to which they directly or indirectly claim to belong. Competition between households within a SIG and between demographically similar household members puts pressure on those who control household income to treat their own members no worse than they are treated in approximately similarly placed households. Thus, group standards vis-à-vis allocations of family income operate for intrafamily allocations in a way similar to that in which competition between firms in a labor market determines wage rates.

Can interdependent and interacting claim structures be explosive? Suppose all members sequentially raise their claims by some relatively small amount. If the average size allowance is used as an argument, and if some claims are met, the average allowance will gradually rise; this becomes an excuse for higher claims to be met so that we have a general upward claims drift. However, there are strict upper limits to such drifts. If many household members make such claims, competing claims soon exhaust family income and not all claims can be met. At this point some claims are not met; when enough claims cease to be met, it becomes clear that other claims are relatively excessive and the comparative appeal argument no longer works. At that point a stable equilibrium will be approached. The significant point is that the phenomenon of upward claim drifts, if it is at all generalized, frequently leads to a level of expenditures for the average SIG family which almost exhausts its income.

Competitive claim drift usually takes place in every or almost every social group. There is both a claim demand and a commitment-control offer. The outcome of the demand and supply pressures is determined on the basis of the same processes suggested by Figures 27a and 27c. Households whose incomes (after the increase) are less than the representative household's income will face more pressure than claimants than is the case for households with more than the representative income.

Consider the following polar case. There is a distribution of households in a SIG. Each receives an income increase that leaves it in the same proportionate position as before.* Assume that the marginal income elasticities of claims and commitments are greater than unity. However, the lower the household income and the lower the increase in income, the greater the marginal elasticities. In this case the share of all contributors falls. The absolute amount left to contributors from relatively low-income households may be no greater than before. To the extent that this sort of intrahousehold pressure takes place, one can see that an increase in household income, when other incomes rise simultaneously, will not yield much of a decrease in pressure from claimants.

The overall result of an income increase for the entire household is likely to depend on the strength of the following: (1) the degree to which intrahousehold claims and the nature of their resolution alters empathy utility; (2) the extent to which goods purchased are emulative and nonfunctional; (3) the extent to which net receivers gain utility when commitments to them are increased; and (4) the extent to which frustration disutility changes as options change when the household moves into a new income position.

Household Agents, Inert Areas, and Implications for Demand Functions

The ideas about selective rationality considered in Chapter 5, as well as those discussed in this chapter, lead to some implications for the nature and shape of demand functions. As noted in my discussion of Bandwagon

* Of course some households will change their relative income position. However, we might normally expect that about as many get to an improved position as those who get to a worsened position.

and Veblen effects (Chapter 4), it is possible under interdependencies of demand for a portion of the demand curve to be positively inclined. To obtain an equilibrium demand function, it is necessary to posit that beyond some point marginal changes by the entire group will not affect anybody's demand. The theory of inert areas now allows us to reinterpret this aspect in a very simple manner. If there are demand interdependencies, then at some point we might expect the interdependence effects to cease as the influences of marginal changes in some individual's quantities demand fall into the inert areas of the individuals under consideration. Thus, the equilibrium demand function is readily obtained once we note that beyond some point every individual has an optimal inert area within which he is nonresponsive to marginal change.

Many purchases made by households are made by agents. Individuals make such purchases in part or entirely for consumption by other household members. The theory of selective rationality says that such components as partial constraint concern, magnitude sensitivity, and reflexive behavior imply the existence of instances in which individuals are nonresponsive to some changes in price. Hence, we would expect that the demand function would be represented graphically, not by a curve, but by a band which captures the notion of inert areas for household members. To the extent that purchases are made by agents rather than principals, and to the extent that agents do not completely have identical interests with principals, we would expect this to be a contributing factor to the existence of a degree of indifference within a range of prices. The fact that a number of formal and informal commitments involving target quantities may exist also contributes to some degree of nonresponsiveness to price differentials.

Demand functions that are bands and that reflect degrees of inertia make it less risky for some sellers to experiment with pricing procedures involving price discrimination. It would seem reasonable to presume that the greater the width of the demand function, the less risk involved by a seller in losing buyers if, up to some point, he attempts to charge a higher rather than a lower price. Perhaps of greater interest, we shall see in a later chapter that demand functions of this type also contribute to the explanation of some aspects of the process of inflation.

Some Applications of Atomistic Consumption Theory

The Easterlin Paradox. Conventional microtheory does not explain what might be called "the Easterlin paradox." R. A. Easterlin collected thirty surveys, covering some nineteen countries, to see if there was any association between reported happiness and the per-capita income or consumption level.* What is significant about these surveys is the consistency of the results, and the fact that in terms of the existing theory of consumer behavior the results appear odd. Within any country, at a given point in time, higher income groups report a higher proportion of households as "very happy" and a lower proportion as "not happy" than do lower income groups. But when we compare the surveys of various countries, no consistent pattern emerges between low per-capita income countries and high per-capita income countries. More important, over time, according to United States data, despite significant increases in income per household, the proportion of "very happy" seems not to have changed markedly, and if anything, to have declined. The data suggests that at any one time the higher the income, the greater the probability of happiness; but over time as income rises the quantum of happiness either does not change or actually falls. If happiness is the same as utility, then utility does not seem to increase as the consumption level increases.

If we include the possibility of increasing marginal utility-expenditure segments (see Figure 29b) and the notion that the quantity targets—in terms of goods, sets of goods, or claims on family income—in turn depend on overall income, for the most part the paradox is cleared up. In general we should expect that an *inverse* relation holds between an ability to meet claims and happiness. Being at the peak of an IMU segment of the MUE curve implies that one is just able to meet the claims on him, with nothing to spare.

Figure 29c shows two marginal utility of expenditure functions. The solid line is for year 1 and the broken line for year 5. Assume that per capita income has risen by 25 percent in the interim. Nevertheless, we can readily see that for the representative household whose income is 25 percent higher, total utility need not have risen. The reason is that all target expenditures may have risen more than proportionately or even in absolute amounts to wipe out all non-target increases, so overall utility appears the same to the net contributors to household income. This is illustrated for the incomes Y_{11} and Y_{15}, contrasting the income of household #1 in years 1 and 5. In both cases the individual is at the peak of his MUE curve. He feels equally pressured for more income. All that has changed is that the curve itself and its peak have moved to a new position. As the figure indicates in both year 1 and year 5 household #2 is better off than household #1. This fits Easterlin's data.

* R. A. Easterlin, "Does Economic Growth Improve the Human Lot? Some Empirical Evidence," in *Nations and Households in Economic Growth: Essays in Honor of Moses Abramovitz* (Palo Alto, Stanford University Press, 1975).

The discussion in the preceding section of intra-family claim drift as incomes rise suggests an additional aspect of the explanation. Other target claims depending on relative status would add evidence in the same direction.*

Economic growth and inflationary pressure. Similar arguments can be employed to show why increased income per capita over time does not ease the demand side of inflation. One would think that as incomes doubled the amount saved would increase and as a result inflationary pressure from the demand side would decline. Yet there seems to be very little connection between growth and inflation. Part of this may be on the productivity side. As income increases, the ratio of services consumed frequently increases, although improved productivity in services lags behind the growth of productivity in other areas.

Our theory suggests, however, that increases in income set up very strong pressures for increases in consumption. Some of these pressures arise from the simultaneously shifting status targets discussed previously, and some from the claim drifts made by household members who are net receivers. Net receivers of household income can view their increase in claims as more or less free income, but they too are subject to interhousehold influences in making expenditures. In addition, there is a tendency for such individuals to maintain increased consumption expenditures at least equal to increased allowances; otherwise their claim of need for increases becomes suspect. In other words, commitment claimants are under pressure to spend their receipts, otherwise the size of their claims are in jeopardy. Hence, as claims increase so does the demand side of inflationary pressure. Recipients of governmental allocations, even when they themselves are governmental bodies, are subject to similar pressures.

Taxation theory. An interesting application of our theory is to the field of public finance, especially to criteria behind systems of taxation. A frequently invoked criterion is the equal sacrifice principle. The notion is that a "fair" taxation system involves approximately equal sacrifices *in utility terms* from different taxpayers. If the marginal utility of expenditure curve is negatively inclined throughout, it leads to the conclusion that equal sacrifice implies that those with higher incomes should pay more than those with lower incomes. Once we introduce the possibility that a portion of the MUE curve may be positively inclined, this last conclusion no longer necessarily holds. The felt sacrifice may now be higher for some with higher incomes compared to those with lower incomes, even if their tastes in the

---

* I have used similar ideas elsewhere to help explain modern human fertility changes; see Harvey Leibenstein, "The Economic Theory of Fertility Decline," *Quarterly Journal of Economics* 89 (February 1975), for elaboration.

broad sense were identical. In other words, even if individuals have identical MUE curves, it is possible for an equal amount of income withdrawn from a lower-income person to involve a lesser utility dimunition than the same income withdrawn from a higher-income person, if the income withdrawn from the latter includes the rising portion of his marginal utility of expenditures curve.

Fair contribution problems. Another class of problems involves situations where for some reason we believe that market prices and money incomes should not determine who pays how much for what. A prime example is the problem of determining assessments for charitable contributions. Suppose someone who runs a charity wants to determine what would be a "fair" amount to request from various contributors in different income groups. Should the fair assessment be in proportion to income? This is similar to the fair tax problem where we presume there should be equality of sacrifice. My theory suggests the possibility that a given amount taken from higher-income individuals may involve a greater sacrifice than an equal amount from some lower-income individuals. One may use the concept of consumption influence groups to help in this situation. If interhousehold relations influence claims strongly, the degree of sacrifice depends to a considerable extent on where a person is placed in his consumption influence group. In other words, sacrifice does not depend on absolute income differences but on two variables: the representative household's income of different consumption influence groups, and the placing of a specific person or household within his consumption influence group. We usually expect that households with income less than the representative household within their influence circle face claims that put more pressure on them than those whose incomes are above the representative income. On the whole, this class of situations is quite complex, containing factors that work in opposite directions, and very little could be said on an a priori level.

Other types of fair contribution problems involve rationing. Here we might consider functional versus nonfunctional interdependent demands. To the extent that the rationed goods hit largely "nonfunctional" demands, we may expect rationing to increase welfare, rather than the other way around. The problem is to determine the incidence of rationing. But one cannot argue on a merely a priori basis that rationing as such reduces welfare. If the bundles of goods chosen by individuals depend in part on the nature of those chosen by other individuals, a government-imposed reduction of items whose consumption is competitive could increase utility by allowing for the substitution of noncompetitive consumer goods within the chosen bundle.

Four basic elements characterize my theory of the firm. First, each individual is assumed to choose an effort position subject to the constraints of the utility cost of not interfering with the choice of others and the utility cost of moving from one effort position to another. Second, the consequence of the utility costs of moving imply that individuals possess inert areas within which opportunities for utility gains will not result in any action. Third, those who attach themselves to firms not only bring productive capacities with them but also direct and indirect incentive-influence characteristics which determine degrees of approval and disapproval of others' choices; standards of reward, promotions, career paths, and so forth; some sense (or lack of sense) of responsibility for others' effort levels; attitudes on the appropriateness of possible disciplinary measures and so on; and the capacity to influence other people's standards of behavior and to be influenced by the standards of others. To a considerable degree these largely nonfinancial considerations determine the incentive mechanism and atmosphere within the firm. Finally, not all inputs used are purchased—the incentive system is such an input. But the incentive system depends not only on elements internal to the firm but also on elements external to it.

To simplify matters I will speak of the inert areas as being either tight or loose, depending on the degree of pressure necessary to induce a movement to a new position. The extent of tightness depends on the willingness of other firm members to see changes made in a person's effort position and to accommodate their own activities to such changes. It also depends on the fear of future speedups, on the history of expected effort levels, on the surrounding mores of effort levels, and on the alternative career opportunities and the anticipated effort levels associated with them.

One of the most significant behavioral characteristics of firms was recognized by Hayek a quarter of a century ago when he pointed out that "the task of keeping costs from rising requires constant struggle, absorbing a great part of the energy of the manager. . . . that it is possible, with the same technical facilities, to produce with a great variety of costs, are among the commonplaces of business experience which do not seem to be equally familiar in the study of the economist. The very strength of the desire, constantly voiced by producers and engineers, to be able to proceed untrammeled by considerations of money costs, is eloquent testimony to the extent to which these factors enter into their daily work."[1]

I have already discussed the phenomenom described by Hayek as the struggle of the firm against effort entropy. The degree to which any particular firm, or particular member of it, is motivated to struggle against entropy depends, among other things, on the environment in which the firm exists and on the pressures for changes the environment imposes on it. An important part of that environment is the market structure in which the firm finds itself.

The environment provides signals indicating something about the adequacy of the firm's performance to its members. Some signals are also interpreted by firm members as pressures for changes. They may come from a wide variety of sources: market prices in well-organized markets, other firms, actual or potential consumers, government regulatory groups, potential input providers, potential competitiors from abroad, and so on. Some signals appear quite different under monopoly as against competition.

The Firm under Monopoly

Assume that the firm is in equilibrium in the sense that every member of it is in his inert area and that external conditions do not put any pressure on any individual to move out of his inert area. Monopoly provides a refuge from pressure for individuals to change their equilibrium effort positions whereas this does not hold under competition.

Among the variables the firm can control under monopoly are the quantity of output, quality, and price. The ordinate and the abscissa in Figure 30 are the price and quantity axes of elementary price theory. The curve D is the demand curve. The curve below D marked cp is a constant profit curve surrounded by a band which includes the bounds of an inert area CP related to the demand curve. Each point of cp implies a cost per unit or output, a related quantity of output, and related price on D that results in a profit rate that is the same for all points on cp. For ease in exposition, we assume that the cost function is approximately L-shaped, but we show only the flat portion of the curve. Thus, we can visualize a number of cost curves being consistent with the same profit rate. Three

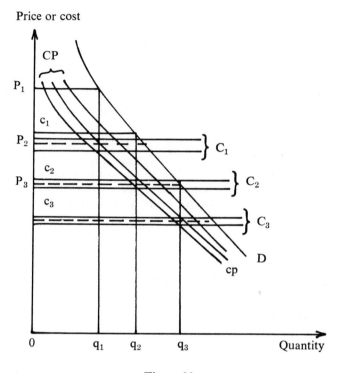

Figure 30

such curves are marked c_1, c_2, and c_3 with related inert area bands C_1, C_2, and C_3. The related quantities and prices are marked q_1, q_2, and q_3, and p_1, p_2, and p_3.

In keeping with the previous analysis, the firm is indifferent between the exact constant profit cp, or a deviation from cp but within the bounds CP, and similarly the firm is indifferent between c_1, or a cost level within band C_1. Now, to start with, assume that when the cost function is c_1 the firm can produce a quantity q_1 and charge a related price on the demand curve so that from the point of view of profitability it is no worse off than under c_3. In other words, if the band CP represents an acceptable profit rate, there is no reason why top managers should strain to achieve a lower cost per unit if c_1 is the cost that results when the various decisionmaking units of the firm are in equilibrium. According to this theory, the monopolistic firm would not seek to minimize costs, or even try to get an especially low cost. In this version of the theory, firms do not seek to maximize profits.

A basic assumption of our theory is that no one in the firm really completely controls the effort levels in terms of a choice of $APQT$ bundles contained in the effort positions chosen by different individuals. As long as the outcomes produced are in the inert areas of individual decisionmakers there is no external pressure to change the inert-area position, and there is no reason why the situation depicted under c_1 could not be a typical or representative situation under monopoly. The only external constraint is that the profit rate be more or less acceptable to those who have significant influence in the firm and for whom profits are a significant criterion of behavior. Obviously the profit rate could not be negative or very low compared to other firms under this type of equilibrium because under such low profit rates we would expect that attempts would be made to change the firm's management or ownership structure.

There are two critical questions regarding the profit rate: are the specific profit distributions in the inert areas of profit recipients? and, if not, are the profit recipients in position directly or indirectly to affect effort decisions? Suppose the profit rate and its consequent distribution is too low for some recipient, and, furthermore, that this is a consequence of low effort levels. If the recipient is a shareholder he may absorb the loss and sell his shares. Under this possibility he becomes a residual adjuster. If the individual involved is simultaneously an officer of the company, he may be able to attempt to make some alterations. But he may not have the power to do so; his role may be so constrained that despite the fact that his profit share is not within his inert area he may have no choice but to absorb what he may look upon as an implicit loss.

If the profit-sharing recipient does have a great deal of power will he necessarily attempt to increase effort levels and reduce costs? This is unlikely if he can avoid the actual loss by increasing prices and passing the loss along to consumers. The conclusion in the preceding paragraph holds not only when the costs involved are marginal but also when they are fixed costs. The profit maximization solution is the same before and after an increase in fixed costs—unlike the logic in conventional analysis in the case in which the increase in costs involves a fixed cost but no change in the marginal cost. Since profit maximization is not presumed at the outset, the initial situation could be one in which profits are below the maximum, and in which an increase in fixed costs can be shifted to consumers by increasing consumer prices. Obviously this would not be possible if consumer prices were the optimal prices to start with.

On a more general level the critical question is whether those who receive the impact of the effort change costs are in a position to effect the constraints within the firm and increase effort levels or whether they are in the position to shift the costs involved outside the firm. Under monopoly, in cases in which options exist between increasing effort-determining constraints within the firm and shifting the costs onto either stockholders or consumers, the latter course would probably be followed. These options will not hold, or would not hold to the same extent, under competition.

Now suppose we start with a disequilibrium within the firm. This implies that various individuals are in the process of altering their effort position. Consider the case in which previously imposed constraints are weakened or discontinued so that effort rates gradually decline. Whether or not effective action takes place to counter the entropy process will depend once again on whether the residual adjustees are in strong enough positions to apply countervailing constraints. Even in this case we face the possibility of disequilibrium movement of an entropy type which increase costs per unit without any coutervailing attempt to change the direction of the process. The net results may be either that certain individuals associated with the firm continue to absorb these increases in costs or that such costs may for a considerable period of time simply be passed on to consumers.

Two additional elements likely to be both inefficient under monopoly and highly resistant to change are the inherited structure of the organization, especially those aspects of the structure that depend upon hierarchical characteristics, and the arbitrary or discretionary behavior on the part of those on a higher level with respect to those in lower levels.

One reason structural characteristics usually persist is that they involve fairly well-established effort positions within the hierarchy, some aspects of which have been chosen in the past, which have been tested by experience and passed on from one occupant of the post to the next one. Consequently, some aspects of these positions are likely to yield high levels of the utility to the jobholders in question. Occupants of such posts have strong incentives to resist changes which may endanger their effort positions. They are likely to perceive a connection between the structural characteristics of the organization and the constraints within which they are permitted to interpret their jobs. Since under monopoly it is frequently possible for the impact of low effort levels (in terms of increased costs) to be passed on either to widely distributed stockholders or to consumers, there is little motivation to examine carefully the efficiency of the structural characteristics of the firm, or for those who perceive such inefficiencies to impose a high degree of pressure on others in order to achieve the necessary structural changes.

One of the rewards of being a monopoly is a certain lack of accountability compared to other market structures. This need not manifest itself only in the utility to be derived from lower effort level but may manifest itself in the jobholder's arbitrary or discretionary behavior, some at the expense of the utility of others. The options that exist under monopoly, where pressures for high levels of performance are absent, need not be only between low and high effort levels but include various degrees of arbitrariness (or "discretion") in the activities chosen by an individual in interpreting his role.

Profit Maximization versus Cost Minimization—An Aside

For some analytical purposes it may not be necessary to depart from the profit-maximization assumption. The pursuit of profit maximization need not imply cost minimization if the top management cannot control costs but can control the quantity of output and price.[2] For each alternative cost level, none of which need be a minimum cost level, profits could be maximized. The issue of the relative X-efficiency of monopoly versus competition does not depend critically on *restricted* profit maximization as just defined. Although for some types of analytical problems a model that retains restricted profit maximization may be advantageous, for general purposes it is probably desirable to drop such an assumption and recognize that the inert areas already reflect compromises between those who see their interests in terms of a larger firm size, more sales revenues, or other similar objectives, and those who see it only in terms of larger profits.

Even if the interests of some firm members would lead them to desire a higher profit rate via lower costs than the one implied by the curve c_1, this does not mean they would attempt to do anything about it. If the pressure for higher profits or lower costs is not very great they would not try to force or pressure others to increase their effort levels so that costs could be lowered and profits raised. If they did make such attempts they probably would meet with considerable (but not unanticipated) resistance from others in the firm who saw no reason to accept an increase in their effort levels under circumstances they would view as perfectly acceptable compromises in the interactions between individuals. By definition of an inert area they are already operating under a "live and let live" situation. As long as firm survival or a significant reduction in the firm's size or income are not threatened, there is no reason for all members of the firm to acquiesce in putting forth a maximum effort so that profits are maximized in the interests of outside stockholders.

Even under workers' profit-sharing schemes effort levels need not be maximized since the utility connected with a person's effort level on the job is likely to dominate whatever relatively minute higher share he might have in increased profits. There is no reason for the group to achieve consensus on profit maximization at the expense of effort even though there may be some average sense in which individuals would choose an additional share in profits in compensation for the additional effort. The most likely situation is that in which some individuals would prefer the additional profit share to some additional effort while others would have the reverse preference. There is no reason for those who prefer their original effort positions to the possibility of additional profit to allow themselves to be prodded to increase their effort levels. Thus, while slowing up the effort level affects all other individuals, the task of attempting to work out rearrangements on the basis of a given profit-sharing formula might be very much more than anyone would be willing to undertake in order to change the existing compromise effort positions—especially those effort positions that are already in inert areas.

It may be of interest to note that the entropy concept derives from the psychological assumptions postulated in Chapter 5. The firm atmosphere provides a certain amount of pressure for performance. Observed performance becomes part of the performance standards of individuals. If the pressure for performance declines, the standards of performance for some individuals are likely to decline accordingly and the standard (superego) curves S_i (see Figure 4a) of firm members moves to the left; and in response the optimal level of constraint concern also declines. In other words, if one's standard of effort depends on the performance of others, then when performance declines, one's standard also declines. Consequently, the hold visible standards have over the desire of individuals for unconstrained behavior decreases. Accordingly, entropy is encouraged.

A question that may arise is that if entropy moves in only one direction, why should we not expect X-inefficiency to increase indefinitely? A partial answer is that latent entrepreneurship of one type or another manifests itself; this in turn puts increased pressure on firms to struggle against entropy. We may view the economic opportunity space as one that is never completely filled. A number of holes exist in it. Entrepreneurs can fill some of the holes but they seldom fill them completely since certain vital entrepreneurial capacities are scarce.

The entrepreneur must be an "input completer" in the sense that he has to be able to fill all the gaps that exist, because of imperfections in the market, in order to create an entity that can compete with existing firms. Entrepreneurs must be able to find substitutes for whatever is unobtainable in the market at the time entry is considered, and do so at low enough cost to survive. However, as entropy increases and costs rise, the holes in the economic opportunity space grow larger and entrepreneurs find it easier to enter successfully.* In addition, the persistent growth of knowledge increases the size of the economic opportunity space and provides potential substitute commodities for those produced by existing partial monopolies, which in turn creates pressure on firm members to attempt to struggle against entropy somewhat more assiduously.

Competition

Under monopoly there is no need for especially low costs to exist in order for the firm to get along and survive. Under competition, however, various types of pressure create a situation so that the level of costs that is convenient and comfortable for the internal organizational structure of the firm is not the level that external forces allow.

Competition creates more pressure and incentives than monopoly does. External pressure is felt by an individual if, in response to an external signal, he visualizes a reduction in utility unless he alters his choice of activities within an effort position or shifts to a new effort position. Internal pressure if, in response to a signal from another firm member, an individual anticipates a possible loss in utility if he does not change activities or shift to a new position. These pressures influence the effort points that can be chosen. For present purposes we associate with every effort point its contribution to output (product) and its utility to the one who puts forth the effort on a *ceteris paribus* basis.

Initially competitive pressure operates through the price mechanism. If a firm offers lower prices, it increases its share of the market and induces other firms to sell at equally lower prices or face the consequences of continually falling sales which in turn create pressures on firms to reduce costs and/or to seek means of doing so. The quest for lower costs transmits itself to individuals, at various levels within the firm, whose sense of success requires that the firm stay profitable or at least solvent, and of whom it is believed, or who themselves believe, that they can influence costs. These pressures translate themselves into attempts to eliminate non-functional activities, to eliminate low productivity effort points from various individuals' choice sets, to seek high productivity points which were previously in the constrained choice set or were previously unknown.

Monopoly gives license for a high degree of discretionary behavior. It is a license for some in powerful positions to be arbitrary, sloppy, bureau-

* For a fuller treatment of this view of the nature of entrepreneurship, see Harvey Leibenstein, "Entrepreneurship and Development," *American Economic Review,* 63:72–83 (May 1968).

cratic, arrogant and nonresponsive to the internal demands of other members of the firm. Competitive pressures do not eliminate such possibilities but they reduce the area of discretionary behavior. The obverse of license is obligation. Monopoly does not provide a sense of obligation for the monopolist to be considerate to fellow employees or to customers. Strictly speaking, neither does competition, but indirectly competition does provide pressures and incentives to do so.

Competitive pressures translate themselves in various ways: (1) in a search for higher productivity effort points; (2) in decreases in the operation of arbitrary constraints; (3) in the search for new effort points previously undiscovered (some of which may be high productivity–high utility effort points); (4) in the elimination of unfounded beliefs about constrained effort points which in fact were unconstrained. (Competitive pressures lead to the testing of the believed choice set, and to the determination of whether or not the believed effort options are in fact permissible and realistic. Thus, high productivity points in the constrained set, some of which may also be high utility points, will no longer be constrained.) Also (5) in attempts by workers to choose working conditions which in turn create pressures toward the reduction of *arbitrary* vertical constraints; and (6), in the choice of firms by workers which allows them to choose firm environments that have high utility to them. Thus, surviving firms will turn out to be those which possess interdependent relationships conducive to low absence rates, low employee turnover rates, relatively low supervisory costs, and low rates of labor conflict.

Competitive pressure requires high productivity. Obviously the appropriate effort points for this purpose are not chosen initially by all firm members. Apart from the initial *untested* choice set such high productivity effort points can only come from the constrained set of effort points open to a firm member and from the set of as-yet-undiscovered points.

If high productivity points are associated with low utility they are not especially significant since they will be resisted as actual effort choice points by employees. But should some such high productivity points be associated with high utility, then almost by definition they become likely options for choice as competitive pressure persists. Most important high productivity–high utility effort points are unlikely to be resisted. Thus, the very logic of competition brings to the fore, and into peoples' choice sets, effort points that are simultaneously highly productive and possess a high utility to those making the choice. Whereas under monopoly supervisors, through their ability to behave arbitrarily, could prevent supervisees from choosing high productivity–high utility points, the rigors of competition dampens the capacity and ardor of supervisors to behave in so arbitrary a fashion.

It is possible, if we consider a set of equi-productive effort points, that arbitrary constraining relations will eliminate some of the high utility effort points from choice sets. This is not a necessary circumstance, simply a likely one on a random basis. Functional constraints are unlikely to remove high utility effort points if these are associated with both high effort and high output. Hence, there is a random character to the choice of high utility *allowable* effort points where arbitrary constraints are involved, and a *systematic* and rational aspect in the availability of high utility *allowable* effort points that arise from functional constraints and inducements. I have already argued that under competition the functional constraints and inducements are larger, so it seems reasonable that higher utility effort points will be available under competition.* Such high productivity–high utility points can be repressed under monopoly since monopoly does not require high productivity effort positions. Furthermore, monopolistic firms can afford for some firm members to enjoy high utility at the expense of other members' low utility.

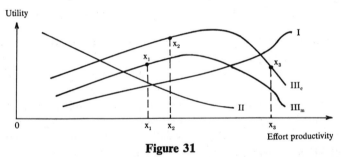

Figure 31

Figure 31 shows three possible relations between the productivity of the effort points and their utility. In case *I* higher productivity is monotonically associated with higher utility. This leads immediately to the conclusion that competition leads to higher utility and productivity. Both on a

---

* It is possible for a particular monopoly to shelter an individual whose productivity is so low that he would not be employable under competition. If such an individual is in the higher reaches of management, such a case does not invalidate the general argument since we have already recognized that monopoly may contain higher utility jobs for a few at the expense of others. For lower level jobs, large monopolies (in contrast to small Chamberlinian monopolistic-competitive firms such as small mom-and-pop shops) would appear to be the wrong social vehicle to provide for the needs of very low productivity individuals on a random basis.

priori grounds and on the basis of the empirical studies this appears unlikely.

If individuals receive satisfaction from a feeling of being productive, relation *II* is not apt to be the correct relation.

Case *III* is the most likely relation. Up to some point increased productivity is associated with increased utility, while beyond some point the curve marked III_m is of a similar shape as III_c—but at a lower level. It is possible that for every productivity level utility is lower under monopoly than under competition. This seems likely if for no other reason than that the lack of choice under monopoly means that people cannot move around and choose job contexts and peers that would yield the highest utility from aspects of the work environment external to the effort point chosen.

Compare the points x_1, x_2, and x_3. Because monopolies are less productive, x_1 may turn out to be the monopoly point and x_2 the point under competition. A question that arises is whether competitive pressures would not force firms to try to insist that their employees pick an effort position so highly productive requiring so much effort (or an effort position of such a nature)* that its utility is lower than under monopoly. There is no way of proving that this is not the case, but it is possible to argue that it is unlikely.

To start with there is apt to be an inverse relation between utility loss and resistance to movement to new effort points. There is no resistance to get people to move to x_2, or perhaps slightly to the right of x_2, but it is unlikely to go beyond that point. Resistance will take two forms: the direct refusal to move to a more onerous effort position; and the use of subtle types of industrial sabotage, such as reducing the quality component of the work and therefore productivity. The latter, in fact, is inconsistent with the idea that higher productivity points under competition can be associated with less effort.

Under competition it is possible for some firms to have high arbitrary constraining elements. However, if these arbitrary choices and constraints lead to high costs, the pressure of competition will cause such firms to reduce the arbitrary elements and lower costs—or force these firms out of the industry. As a result, under competition the functional constraining elements are likely to be greater than under monopoly. There is considerable evidence that high satisfaction is associated with the notion that achievement is felt if associated with a high contribution to the firm's objectives.[3] We therefore should expect that under competition the utility

---

* More than one effort point may be associated with a given effort level, that is, a given feeling of "effortfulness."

curve related to effort is above what that curve would be under monopoly.

How does the entry of new firms into the industry influence it? As a first approximation, assume a sequence of entering firms at constant intervals and compare the approaching end result with monopoly equilibrium. Suppose that the initial firm enters at a cost of c_1 (see Figure 30), the same cost as under monopoly. Obviously, there are incentives for new firms to enter at costs below c_1 since such firms will have a competitive advantage over the initial firms. We need not assume that every potential entering firm can organize fitself in such a way so that its costs will necessarily be below c_1, but at some point, probably fairly early in the sequence, we should expect some firm to organize itself successfully enough to enter at a cost below c_1—say, at the level c_2, which we assume to be halfway between c_1 and absolute minimum costs of c_3.

As more firms enter, the quantity of output increases and the price must fall. As this process continues, at some point output increases sufficiently so that the price falls below c_1. When this occurs two things take place. First, firms whose costs are above the new price ($p_1 < c_1$) face strong pressure to become more efficient. Members of such firms whose equilibrium positions involve relatively inefficient effort positions that manifest themselves in high unit costs feel the need to find and choose alternative effort positions (positions which contain lower cost $APQT$ bundles). These pressures will be difficult to resist since it is clear that the viability and survival of the firm is in danger unless change takes place. Second, firms whose members cannot reduce costs below c_1 will be forced out of the industry. Neither of these things is true under monopoly. Hence, we should expect that where, under monopoly, pressures to change from less efficient effort positions to more efficient ones could be successfully resisted, under competition there would be many instances under which the demands for such changes would appear to be reasonable under the circumstances, and would, in fact, occur. To put the matter another way, for inert areas of a given degree of tightness the pressure for change would be considerably greater under competition (compared to monopoly), especially for firms whose costs are above the sales price. At least some individuals in competitive firms would yield to such pressures. Hence, we would expect at least some of the higher-cost firms to be able to reduce their costs and compete successfully with the lower-cost firms.

At the same time, firms whose inert areas are too tight (inflexible), and which therefore cannot respond successfully to cost-reduction pressures, will not survive and will leave the industry. In the long run, because of the pressure to reduce costs as prices fall and because only the more efficient firms survive, we should expect the cost per unit of output of the average surviving firm to end up lower than under monopoly.

Competitive Equilibrium and Entropy

We should not presume on the basis of the foregoing that there will necessarily exist a competitive equilibrium at which the costs per unit of all firms are minimized. In fact, we should expect the contrary in almost all situations. As average costs get very low under competition, it becomes increasingly difficult for new firms to organize themselves in such a way so that they can enter at lower costs than existing firms. Also it is reasonable to expect that we do not obtain instantaneous responses to new cost conditions and that price is a lagged function of the costs of the various firms in the industry. Suppose that the price in a given period depends on the cost distribution of firms of the previous period. Now, the actual per-unit cost level, on the average, will depend on a balance of forces which determines the rates of change in unit costs in *both* directions.

It seems reasonable to assume that the lower the cost level, the greater the entropy effect. The greater the effort level everyone is trying to maintain, and the greater the constraints imposed by others or the environment under which everyone is working, the greater the likelihood that many firm members endeavor to obtain some relief from the pressure of trying to keep unit costs all that low. Accordingly it seems likely that the lower the cost level, the greater the reaction to any decline in the type of vigilance from any direction that helps to maintain costs that low. The greater the entropy effect that results, the greater the reaction *against* pressure, and the greater the movement toward less productive effort levels for a given decrease in pressure.

New firms enter, some at lower costs than the average for all firms, while at the same time existing relatively high-cost firms attempt to reduce unit-cost levels. The equilibrium unit-cost level will therefore be at the point at which there is a balance between the increases in unit costs resulting from the entropy effect in existing firms, and the decreases in costs resulting from the successful response to competitive pressure by some relatively high-cost firms to reduce their costs and the rate of entry of relatively low-cost new firms. Such a balance probably will be struck at a point where the costs of the various firms are not at a minimum. Nevertheless, we should expect the overall result to be one in which there is a lower cost level for the average firms under competition than under monopoly.*

* It is conceivable that an organizational "accident" could result so that a monopolistic firm starts out with a very low cost curve, but we should not expect such

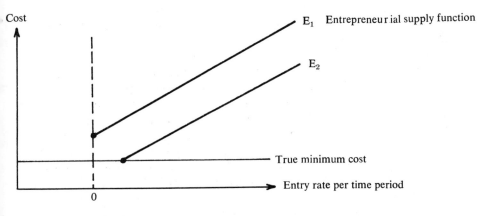

Cost

E_1 Entrepreneurial supply function

E_2

True minimum cost

Entry rate per time period

0

Figure 32

In the model elaborated in this chapter the supply of entrepreneurship is exogenous to the industry. The two elements that determine its flow are the willingness of entrepreneurs to enter at a given cost level, and the capacity for entrepreneurs to enter and to organize firms sufficiently well enough to achieve successively lower cost levels.

There is no reason internal to the system why the entrepreneurial supply level could not be zero above the true minimum cost level. (See curve E_1 in Figure 32.) Suppose that the entrepreneurial supply function at minimum cost is greater than zero. Nevertheless, the rate of entry and the size of new firms may be too small to affect the industry. Consider an industry of a thousand firms each producing 100 units. Each year one new firm enters which produces 100 units at true minimum costs. This will affect the supply price hardly at all. Entropy in the new firm may in some future year raise the costs of that particular firm, although another new firm may enter then at true minimum costs. As a result, it seems likely that the entropy rate and the entrepreneurial entry rate would result in a balance (an

---

low cost levels to persist. Eventually the effort levels of some individuals will slacken. It is more comfortable to operate under looser conditions (that is, the utility of the lesser effort levels is higher), and under monopoly there are no strong counter-disciplinary forces to remove the increase in X-inefficiency. Thus, we should expect entropylike forces to assert themselves so that the cost level rises to a point where the situation is relatively slack and the stress associated with high-effort levels is reduced. While the same entropylike forces exist for competitive firms, the pressure of competition does not allow the same degree of entropy to exist as does monopoly.

equilibrium) so that by and large firms are not producing at their true minimum costs. In principle such a balance may be struck considerably above true minimum unit costs.

There is no reason to suppose that new firms could in fact enter at true minimum costs. In the process of organizing the firm there is usually a "shakedown" and learning phase. In part this is a consequence of the fact that it is impossible to make a set of numerous and complex initial decisions which are consistent. As a result, changes are necessary so that the various organizational units can dovetail their activities. In addition, special knowledge has to be accumulated as to how newly organized units operate, carry out their tasks, and fit in with the overall presumed purposes of the organization. The critical question is whether the new firm can solve these problems so effectively that output is produced at true minimum unit cost. The main counterargument is that, while such problems are being solved the developing process of effort entropy is likely to assert itself; this in turn prevents or retards the movement toward much lower unit costs. Entropy must be viewed as an ubiquitous phenomenon applying not only to those usually viewed as employees of the new firm but also to management and the entrepreneurship itself.

A final aspect to be considered, referred to in Chapter 3 as the Horndahl Effect, is the observation that some firms will gradually increase productivity over time without any change in inputs whatsoever. Some scholars have attributed this to "learning by doing," but it is not clear that this captures all of the possibilities. Nevertheless, it is reasonable to suppose that for some firms under a fairly constant environment a learning phenomena takes place which increases productivity, while at the same time latent effort entropy is working in the opposite direction, though it may be held in check, in part, by a vigilant management aided by a competitive environment. The learning phenomena will probably slow down eventually and will have an upper asymptote, at which point what might be referred to as the Net Entropy Effect will emerge with larger values. On balance there may be a period for which the "learning by doing" is the dominant visible effect.

Price and Quantity Determination under Competitive Equilibrium

I have suggested that the geometrical representation of the long-run industry cost function would be a band rather than a line-curve. For any given quantity the width of the band would indicate the range of costs possible for a given firm that might supply that quantity, as well as reflect the random element as to which particular firms would supply which particular

Price or cost

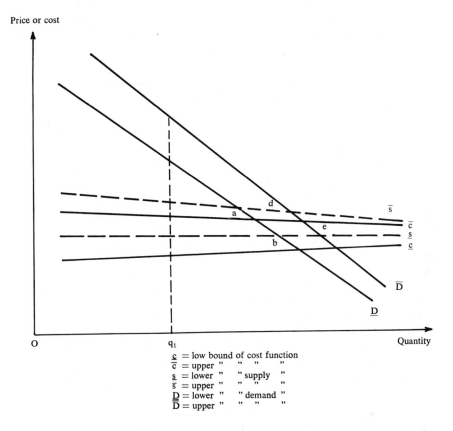

O q_1 Quantity

$\underline{c}$ = low bound of cost function
$\bar{c}$ = upper   "   "   "   "
$\underline{s}$ = lower   "   " supply   "
$\bar{s}$ = upper   "   "   "   "
$\underline{D}$ = lower   "   " demand "
$\bar{D}$ = upper   "   "   "   "

Figure 33

buyers. In Figure 33, the cost function (it is not a supply function) is drawn under the assumption that buyers randomly distribute their purchases approximately in proportion to the size of the sellers. For a given quantity of output q, four elements that contribute to the determination of costs can be distinguished. There are: a given number of firms for a given value of q; a distribution of sales among firms according to the tastes of consumers; a set of unit costs consistent with the inert areas and degrees of entropy in each firm; and a given set of assessments of demand conditions by the firms on which the inert areas and the entropy levels depend.

A significant element in this analysis which differs from the traditional analysis is a lack of independence between demand, cost, and supply. This is primarily the case on the cost and supply side. The reason is that effort levels, and consequent unit costs, depend in part on the expected price level that would rule for that quantity of output. The price level depends on which of a variety of price-setting procedures are used, but presumably if the expectations are realistic it would be somewhere between the price shown on the upper boundry of the demand function and the upper boundry of the cost function. In other words, for each value of q, and the resulting number of firms, there is an expectation by each firm as to the price that other firms would set and which would more or less rule in the industry. In accordance with our previous theory, the firms would set a "comfortable" price in terms of their capacity to survive, not a price which would maximize profits and hence not one which would necessarily be on the demand function. By the same token, it also would not be a price which would be equal to the costs of production, since at the quantity q there is no need to set prices that would result in keen competition.

We now consider a movement from smaller to larger quantities on the x-axis. Two forces are likely to be operative: on the one hand, in order to produce the larger quantity some less efficient firms are likely to enter the industry; but, on the other, the spread between demand and costs becomes progressively smaller, hence lower prices would be anticipated, resulting in somewhat lower cost levels than would otherwise be the case. There is no way to determine on an a priori basis which of these counteracting factors would be more important; as a consequence, we might presume that the lower bound of the long-run function would be either constant or slightly rising.

It is important to repeat that the cost function is not a supply function. In order to have a supply function we need some system of price-setting which can be arbitrary if there is great excess demand but must become less so as excess demand approaches zero. Once we have given up strict maximization as the firm's objective, the usual system of price-setting on the basis of comparing marginal costs and marginal revenues no longer holds. In Figure 33 let us assume that a "cost-plus" pricing system is utilized. Since costs differ for different firms, and since market prices are frequently much closer to each other than the cost differentials, we could not expect a truly constant markup. The broken lines in Figure 33 indicate the upper and lower bounds of the supply price for the firms in the industry. They are drawn so that, as we approach an equilibrium position, there is a closer approximation between price to cost than is the case when we are relatively far from equilibrium.

The demand function, also shown by a band in Figure 33, is a little more difficult to interpret. It reflects for any given quantity the inert areas among some buyers, so that for a given quantity they would be willing to absorb, within limits, a price increase. Thus, the inert areas for households are already reflected in the width of the band at each quantity point. Among the other elements reflected by the demand function are the following: for a given quantity q desired to be purchased we would expect that some maximum price exists for that q, which in turn determines the upper boundry of the demand function; and that some set of lower prices would reflect the inert areas existing in all households. There is the possibility that for some households the inert areas would reflect such sensitivity to price that the buyer would shift to a larger quantity if the price were lower. It is sufficient for our purposes that there be some households which have inert areas so that they absorb price changes without changing quantities purchased for the demand function to be a band rather than a line.

Thus far the demand and supply functions and the considerations that lie behind them are symmetrical. However, a complication which arises is the lack of complete independence between buyers and sellers in the theory developed in preceding chapters. Unlike conventional price theory, the firms in this model are not price takers. They do not necessarily have to accept the price on the market nor do they necessarily have to charge all customers the same price. This is a consequence of our weakening of the rationality assumptions. Buyers are not presumed to search for the lowest possible price, although for some given price differential they may be induced to do so. Nor need sellers search for buyers willing to pay the highest possible price. As a result, there is an area of fuzziness and indeterminacy in the domain of relations shown in Figure 33. But there is a determinate area which represents those prices (for the quantity involved) which are simultaneously acceptable to both buyers and sellers, that is, which are simultaneously in the inert areas of both groups. The actual exact price-quantity outcome is not determined, except to the extent that it will fall within the areas outlined by the intersection of the demand and supply functions abde. This theory allows us to predict the area in which the equilibrium price-quantity points will fall—but not the specific price-quantity outcome.

A change in expectations about the demand situation (an expected increase in demand) could lead to a movement of the upper bound of the cost function as well as the supply price function. If we start with a point b within the equilibrium rectangle, the shift in expected demand, whether based on fact or not, can lead to changes in inert areas and to an increase in price to the point d in the rectangle. This view of changes in the competitive situation allows for asymmetry between expected increases as against expected decreases in demand. For example, a small reduction in demand need not affect the inert areas, while an increase in demand would do so.

There is a sense in which if conditions of extreme price sensitivity by consumers (for example, the existence of extremely close substitutes) and extreme ease of entry (which overwhelms the entropy effect) were in effect, the equilibrium results in the conventional theory and the one presented here would approximate each other. However, even in this case, nonequilibrium circumstances would look very different. This chapter is based on the premise that extreme ease of entry and extreme price sensitivity are unlikely, but we cannot rule out circumstances under which the competitive equilibrium outcomes of the two theories approach each other asymtotically.

PART THREE

Applications and Implications

13 Duopoly and Monopolistic Competition

The ideas presented briefly in the pages that follow illustrate that the basic concepts of X-efficiency microtheory can be applied to a wide variety of market structures. The extension of the theory into these areas adds something to the picture that emerges from it over and above the conventional analysis. In some cases all that can be achieved is a greater sense of realism, but the conclusions in other cases have interesting applications for policy problems. For some readers, especially experts in the fields being considered, the treatment may suggest a more thorough consideration. My aim is to show that existing theoretical structures can be transformed in terms of such fundamental ideas as inert areas and effort entropy and be applied to almost every aspect of existing economic theory. Of course I do not claim that this will turn out to be a profitable exercise in all cases.

Once we leave the realm of pure competition, that which might be called the "personality" of the firm becomes a significant aspect of the analysis. This is especially true where the number of firms is relatively small or where a few large firms have a disproportionate influence on the industry.

Duopoly

Although there are special solutions for special sets of assumptions, traditional duopoly theory has no general solution. The critical literature is filled with articles attacking the lack of realism in some of the special assumptions. Some might argue that the more realistic model is that developed in terms of the Theory of Games, but here too this applies only to special cases. Because there is no general solution no attempt will be made to provide one. Rather, I shall limit myself to some simple models, containing some of the ideas developed in this book.

In theory duopoly is unstable. To maximize his gain each duopolist may want to do so at the expense of the other, but this can lead to a price war and involve great risks for survival. Once we introduce inert areas for each duopolist, we can obtain situations to which neither reacts. This results in the ability to describe duopoly markets with relatively high degrees of stability—a situation that reflects what is commonly observed in the real world. We now turn to illustrate these ideas with the aid of a graphical analysis, assuming a degree of product differentiation so that some price differences are consistent with the simultaneous survival of both firms.

Figure 34 is a variant of the "Reaction Curve" analysis of duopoly found in most intermediate texts. The variables considered are the prices set by firms A and B. For alternative prices of firm A we show a reaction curve R_b by firm B, and vice versa. The utility of profit rate $U(B)$ associated with each point on the reaction curve of firm B appears in quadrant II. Introducing in the conventional way the inert area for B, we obtain an area within which we should expect a stable solution to be found. The distance u_1u_2 is the cost of adjustment for firm B. The associated inert area is shown on R_b as an oval. The inert area denotes that for each price on R_b there is a range of prices that can be set by A that would be acceptable to B; that is, B would not react within that range. Thus, if R_a intersects the inert area of R_b, all points on the intersecting segment become potential equilibrium points.

In order to obtain stable duopoly "solutions," it may be enough to have an inert area for only one of the firms. Figure 34 includes only the inert area for firm B. On the reaction curve R_b the inert area is denoted by an oval. It can readily be seen that having an inert area on only one reaction curve through which another reaction curve passes is sufficient for an equilibrium to exist. If a is the price set by firm A and b is the price set by firm B, this turns out to be an equilibrium point. Firm A reacts to price b by maintaining price a or moving to it, but no further movement takes place. Thus, for every point on the segment of R_a that intersects the inert area of R_b there is a nonreaction point on R_b which halts any further reaction. It is interesting that the set of equilibrium positions consistent with the inert area on R_b need not be on the intersection between the two reaction curves. Hence in this case we do not have a unique equilibrium, but a set of equilibriums, any of which may be stable.

Let us consider how the inert area was established and whether it has any real meaning. Firm B may know its own reaction curve; it has a sense of its own intentions. However, there is no way necessarily for it to know the reaction curve of the opposing firm. After considerable experience it may be able to make some guesses about the opposing firm's reaction behavior. Nevertheless, it is sufficient that firm B not react to the revealed reaction of firm A for an equilibrium to exist. Thus, a great deal of

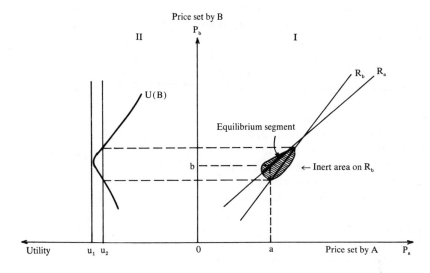

Figure 34

knowledge about the reaction curve of the other firm need not be presumed once we introduce the notion of inert areas. This contrasts somewhat with the situation where the only equilibrium point is the intersection of the two reaction curves. In this case the equilibrium is a single point if firm *B* is uncertain as to whether the other firm finds his price acceptable.*

In Figure 35 each reaction curve applies to the case where each firm either maintains its price or reacts to the other's price. The curves are drawn in the conventional way so that if we start from any point other than the intersection of the two curves, we obtain a series of reactions toward the intersection. This implies that there is an equilibrium position so that, if the reaction curves are stable, starting from any position below the equilibrium point we will reach the equilibrium. The main novelty in the

---

* A single-point equilibrium may not be a true equilibrium since firm B may experiment with other points in the absence of knowledge of whether the unique intersection point has any degree of stability or whether it is only a temporary position which forms part of a strategy of shifting positions. In other words, ignorance of the other firms' intentions is less significant in guaranteeing stability in the case in which there are inert areas as opposed to cases in which a hair-trigger equilibrium appears to exist as a consequence of the interaction of two reaction curves. With a segment equilibrium small movements on the part of one seller informs him that the other will not react, but no such information is conveyed in the case in which a single point equilibrium is involved.

figures as compared to the usual reaction curve analysis occurs when we examine quadrants II and IV. In quadrant II the curve marked $U(B)$ indicates the utility derived by the "firm," or, more accurately, derived by at least those members responsible for the price reactions associated with various points of the reaction curve for firm B. Similarly, quadrant IV contains a similar curve, $U(A)$, associated with the reaction curve for firm A. Surrounding the utility function we show an area determined by the two lines u_1 and u_2 which reflects the utility costs of moving from one position to another. This produces the usual inert areas which are then reflected on reaction curves R_a and R_b. As before the oval on R_b depicts the inert area for B, showing that within the oval for each associated price of B there is a range of prices that could be set by A, any of which would be acceptable to B. Similarly, the oval on R_a shows the inert area on A and denotes that for every price of A within the oval there is a range of prices that could be set by B that is acceptable to A. Note that all points in the intersection of the two ovals (the two inert areas of A and B) represent price combinations acceptable to both parties and are therefore equilibrium points. But note also that the extension of the segment on R_a that passes through B's inert area, but goes beyond the intersection of the two ovals (shaded area on Figure 35), is also part of the set of equilibrium points. The same holds for the similar segment on R_b.

By introducing the idea of inert areas we change the general conception of the solution. It is worthwhile considering whether by looking at the problem of inert areas we add some degree of realism. The initial single-point intersection of the two reaction curves is no longer the point necessarily arrived at through the process of mutual reactions. In fact, we can now ignore the exact process of mutual reaction to each other's moves and simply stipulate that there is some such approximate process which moves toward an equilibrium area when we start from below it. Once in the equilibrium area we make no assertion as to the exact point within it that the process of mutual adjustment leads.

Have we achieved anything more by substituting an area for a point, and adding a degree of fuzziness to the overall result? It seems unrealistic to presume that there should be a single, unique equilibrium position on which the two parties would implicitly agree. The essence of duopoly is that each firm has a very strong awareness of the other's behavior, as well as sensitivity to the potential gains and losses which are the consequences of overreacting to such behavior. It seems reasonable to assume that firms are extremely sensitive to starting an upward price spiral or a price war, finding themselves in a position where each follows the other, regardless of the consequences. As a result, in a number of situations they might deem it

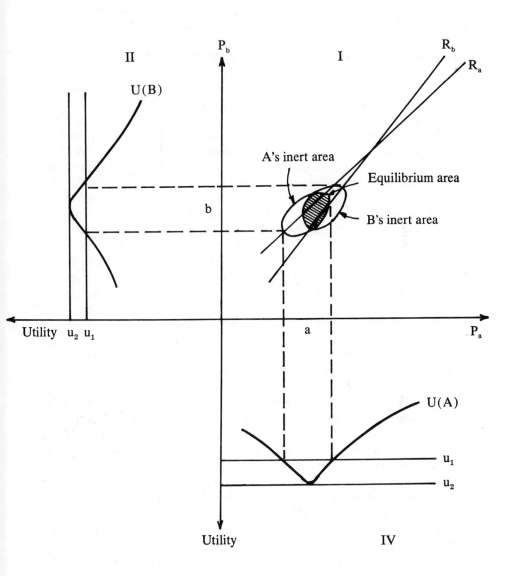

Figure 35

wise not to react. If the potential gain or loss of reaction to either party would be small, there would be a strong incentive not to react at all. It is also likely that under duopoly each duopolist has a degree of risk aversion. The reason for this is that the costs of risk in terms of a potential price war are so uncertain that the avoidance of risk would be a more reasonable component of a survival strategy under duopoly than under alternative market structures.

I have used prices as the variable that each firm could control. A similar analysis could be worked out with any other *control variable,* as long as one variable, or an index used to denote a variable, is employed. For some markets it might be more appropriate to substitute the quantities produced by firms *A* and *B* instead of the prices charged as the control variable. It is not necessary to go through the analysis of each control variable separately. The analytical structure that emerges should be approximately the same. Like the ideas expressed in the preceding paragraph, the utility functions shown in quadrants II and IV could also be altered to represent an index of any objective the firm might pursue.

A change in the utility of either firm would of course change the inert areas and might start a movement from what earlier appeared to be an equilibrium position. Thus, from this viewpoint, we have not only a system which indicates the nature of the equilibrium position but one that allows us to consider external changes and to trace the movements which result from such events. The main notion is that the external change affects the utility function of the individuals in the firm, which could in turn affect their inert area, which in turn could lead to shifts in the controlling variable. By a parallel type of reasoning, the approach illustrated in the two figures also allows us to consider changes which occur in the firm. Thus, a shift in personnel making different individuals responsible for price decisions (or any other control variable decision) may result in a shift in the utility function and operate as a destabilizing influence. We would then proceed with the analysis on the same basis as in the previous case where the destabilizing force came from outside the firm.

A question ignored so far is where the reaction curves come from. At least three elements are involved: the individuals in each firm who are in charge of or influence the setting of the control variable and the intrafirm influences on them; the economic considerations and objectives pursued by those individuals in the name of the firm; and the specific personalities of the individuals in the positions of influence to set the control variable. Consider the economic aspects. On the one hand, such elements as a desired profit level (without excluding profit maximization but without necessarily including it) or a desired growth level or economic considerations concerned with the survival of the firm, and, on the other hand, the strain or lack of strain of maintaining existing effort levels and productivity levels within the firm. Once again we do *not* separate the price-setting procedures and the cost-determining procedures as reflected in the pressures brought to bear on various individuals to maintain certain effort levels and certain productivity levels. If a relatively high price equilibrium results, we might expect fewer constraints on chosen effort positions, a lessening on the struggle against effort entropy, and somewhat higher costs. Unlike other duopoly theories, the prices chosen by the two firms do not determine by themselves the profit levels that result. We must also take into account the effort-level reactions to such prices.

The personalities of those in charge and the constraints under which they operate can be described in terms of attitudes toward reactions. Such attitudes are reflected by the size of their inert areas. The inert areas of relatively risk-averse individuals would be rather large. They avoid fights. For those who enjoy risk, the inert areas might be considerably smaller. An asymmetry would probably exist. The risk-averse would more likely follow prices upward rather than downward, and vice versa for the risk-enjoyers. Thus, duopolies in which risk-averse individuals are in control are likely to feed an inflationary process.

Theory of Monopolistic Competition

In the last three decades the theory of monopolistic competition has gradually receded in importance, if judged on the basis of the discussion of the theory in intermediate theory textbooks. In fact, in some books it has disappeared entirely. Yet at the time of its initial presentation and in later years both admirers and opponents recognized that in many respects it is more realistic than the theories of pure competition and monopoly it was supposed to replace.

I intend to reconsider the theory of monopolistic competition in terms of the X-efficiency theory and especially in the light of the criticism it has been subjected to. The main criticisms that have been presented against Chamberlin's monopolistic competition theory are: (1) the concept of the "group" is ambiguous; (2) the assumption that each firm faces identical demand and cost curves ignores interfirm effects; (3) the implication that excess capacity necessarily results has been questioned; and (4) its assumptions are too stringent to apply to situations in the real world. By applying some X-inefficiency ideas, we will see that much of the sense of the original theory can be retained; in this process we can meet to a considerable degree at least some of the objections that have been made.

A major difficulty according to some critics is the concept of the "group." The group is the set of firms, each of whose products is differentiated from every other, and yet the "cost curves for all the 'products' are uniform throughout the group."[1] There is little doubt that as Chamberlin used the concept certain logical difficulties exist. The group becomes a difficult concept to handle consistently and yet retain the realism which is one of the desirable attributes of the theory. However, to my mind the criticism of the group concept involves logic chopping. It is not a fatal aspect of the theory. But another of Stigler's criticisms is especially pertinent. He emphasizes that, "although Chamberlin could throw off the shackles of Marshall's view of economic life, he could not throw off the shackles of Marshall's view of economic analysis. Marshall's technique was appropriate to the problem set to it: it deals informatively and with tolerable logic with the world of competitive industries and monopolies."[2]

Another way of looking at the matter is that Chamberlin seeks a long-run solution which is in many respects similar to the Marshallian equilibrium in which prices equal the cost of production except for two elements: product differentiation costs, and the excess capacity outcome. I believe the basic defect arises from the fact that the theory misconstrues the firm's motivation in seeking a partial monopoly position through product differentiation. In other words, the theory is overburdened with the cost-minimization assumption.

Let us return to the pure monopoly case. I argued that a critical error of neoclassical theory is the assumption that monopolists seek to minimize costs. For any given output unit costs are the same under monopoly as under competition. I argued that under monopoly the degree of X-inefficiency would be higher and that this includes part of the social costs of having a monopolistic market structure as against a competitive one. A similar argument could be applied to monopolistic competition theory. Through product differentiation, selling costs, and advertising expenditures, and so on, the monopolistically competitive firm seeks a partial *safe haven* from the rigors of competition. It does so not only because short-run profits might be higher under these circumstances (long-run profits are the same, according to Chamberlin) but also because the firm need not put forth the effort to achieve as low a cost level as would be necessary under competition. Hence in reformulating the theory we should not assume that costs are the same for all firms. Instead we will adopt the notion that there are differential degrees of X-inefficiency in the effort positions of members of different firms.

One way of coping with effort entropy and effort inefficiency is by passing the higher costs along to consumers. And a way to insure that consumers accept the higher costs is by making the product appear sufficiently different from that of competitors at least to appear to be worth the increased cost. This is not to argue that profitability is not part of the motive of firms which attempt to differentiate their product, but it is to assert that a shelter from the strain of having to achieve very low costs is a matter greatly appreciated by firm members, especially those who belong to the higher levels of management. It makes a significant difference whether firms can achieve enough product differentiation so that they are price-*setters,* at least to some degree, as against the situation under perfect competition where they are forced to be price-*takers,* or at least approximate price-takers.

Let us now attempt very briefly to restate the theory for a given group by introducing step by step the various elements of the X-inefficiency theory. Suppose that a group of firms is producing an identical product and that each knows approximately the same methods of producing the product. Because of differences in organizational structure there are some differences in cost per unit for each firm. The demand curve that each firm faces is almost infinitely elastic. In other words, each firm sees itself as a price-taker and readily imagines the existence of potential new firms entering the industry in order to supply any excess demand that may exist. Almost all firms will find themselves in a position of constraining the effort positions of its members so that costs are kept low enough to assure the firm's survival. In other words, at least some members of some firms will feel that they must strain simply to survive. It would be natural under these circumstances for some firm to attempt to differentiate its product, if it could do so, in order to induce its customers to remain its customers even if the price of its product was slightly higher than that of competing firms.

The basic strategy any firm will seek to achieve is to change the elasticity of demand it faces from almost infinity to something sufficiently low so that it feels survival is assured even without straining to minimize costs. How it achieves this strategy is a detail that need not concern us; it is immaterial whether it does so by advertising expenditures, other types of selling costs, or any type of product differentiation which creates an actual or apparent quality difference. All that matters is that the firm now has the option of raising its price to some degree without losing most of its customers, and that the firm has become a partial monopolist. In some cases this will involve an increase in costs. *But it is not necessary to assume that this is so in all cases.*

If at all possible, that is, if the technology of the product allows it to happen, some degree of product differentiation will be achieved and a limited island of monopoly will be attained. It is conceivable that the degree of monopoly attainable through these means is not maximized. (There is no need to assume maximization here, just as there is no need to assume it anywhere else in our analysis.) In fact, our theory suggests that quite frequently this will be the case. All that is urgently desired is some sanctuary from the strains to keep costs as low as is necessary under perfect competition. New firms that enter would have similar incentives. While to some degree they would face competitors of close substitutes, they would nonetheless seek to avoid what they would consider "excessive competition."

Our theory of consumption suggests that the attainment of this sanctuary is feasible because of inert areas among consumers. In fact, it is the existence of inert areas among households that makes the theory much more plausible than would otherwise be the case, whereas it would be less so under circumstances where every buyer sought to spend his money in such a way as to avoid spending any more than necessary for any commodity. If the latter were true most buyers would scour markets thoroughly enough so that sellers could not count on what is frequently alluded to as "customer loyalty."

Given the partial "safe-haven" situation, firm members no longer have to strain to minimize costs, and effort entropy comes into force. The end result is that costs are higher not only because of the selling cost necessary to retain the quasi-monopolistic position but also because costs of production rise as the lack of the rigors of competition allows X-inefficiency to grow.

The solution for any firm within the group depends on the nature of the supply of entrepreneurs. It is reasonable to suppose that there is inertia among entrepreneurs as well as among any other individual or group, hence we will assume limits to entrepreneurial supply. In fact, we should expect that entrepreneurs would find it somewhat more difficult to enter an industry in which large selling costs are involved and in which brand names or their equivalents are well established. The outcome for each firm is illustrated in Figure 36a. The cost curve is, as usual in our type of analysis (a band rather than a line); in addition there is the likelihood that the demand function will intersect the cost function. Since, according to this theory, marginal costs do not determine price, we have to insert, as we did in the treatment of competition, a price area, given the costs and the demand function.

In the case in which there is an infinite supply of entrepreneurs we may obtain something that *roughly* approximates the Chamberlin tangency outcome. However, because we are dealing with bands rather than lines, there is an overlap between the cost and the demand functions, so even in this

Price

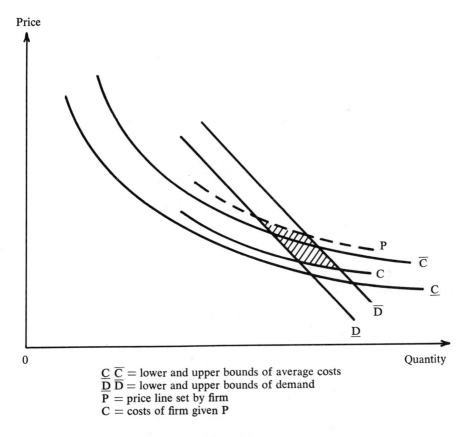

0   Quantity

<u>C</u> C = lower and upper bounds of average costs
<u>D</u> D = lower and upper bounds of demand
P = price line set by firm
C = costs of firm given P

Figure 36a

case, although profits are lower than would otherwise be the case, there is no reason to assume a zero profit outcome for all firms. There may be negative profits for some firms (see Figure 36b).

Figure 36b illustrates the case of extreme ease of entry of new firms into the industry. Almost all firms entering face demand and cost functions fairly similar to those already in the industry. The lower demand boundary is tangent to the lower cost boundary. However, in the case illustrated the upper demand boundary is below the upper cost boundary. The price-quantity equilibriums are shown in the shaded area. Firms which are sufficiently X-inefficient to achieve costs above the upper demand curve boundary $\bar{P}$ will suffer net losses. Thus, in the illustration, if the firm produces q_1 and C_2 it will fail and the firm will end up in bankruptcy. New

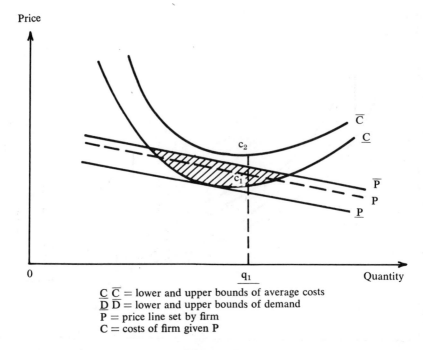

C $\overline{C}$ = lower and upper bounds of average costs
$\underline{D}$ $\overline{D}$ = lower and upper bounds of demand
P = price line set by firm
C = costs of firm given P

Figure 36b

entrants take the place of those that fail; some will also fail to achieve costs below the upper demand boundary, others will succeed. Ease of entry will keep the demand functions for the individual firms quite low, as indicated in the figure. This analysis provides us with at least part of a theory of bankruptcy—an ubiquitous normal real-life phenomenon that conventional theory fails to explain.

Let us return to criticisms of the original monopolistic competition theory. In the "group" concept our inert areas allow for degrees of independence. Will all firms in the economy be in the group? In a general equilibrium system they would. But in our system many firms would not see themselves as being in the same group because the action of, say, firm B would not cause any reaction by firm A because B's action would not get through A's inert area so to speak. Firms A and B are in the same group if a "reasonably large" change (of price, selling costs, or product) by A affects the demand function of B so that it gets through the inert areas of B's executives and vice versa. The term "reasonably large" is arbitrary and would have to be defined separately for each problem under analysis. The group notion may still appear fuzzy and imperfect, but it is not unusual for concepts to become fuzzy at the edges when applied to real situations.

Summary

According to the conventional theory, one would expect duopoly situations to be highly unstable, whereas in the real world duopolies exhibit a high degree of stability. However, in our considerations of duopoly, we saw that the introduction of the inert area concept increased the likelihood for stable solutions. Furthermore, since the likely outcome is a "solution area" rather than a unique situation, the introduction of inert areas increases the likelihood that a trial-and-error process of mutual reactions by duopolists to each others' moves would enable them to reach one of a number of potential stable duopoly outcomes.

Under monopolistic competition I argued that the usual motivation of firms is the search for a "safe haven" from the rigors of competition. This is relatively easy to achieve in many product areas if we presume that inert areas exist for consumers. As a consequence potential partial monopolists do not face the extreme likelihood of losing customers through experimental small increases in prices. In addition, what we have referred to as *present position preference* among consumers helps to explain that portion of buying behavior which is fairly habitual and which creates the possibility of loyalty to given sellers' products or brands, even if price differentials are involved. Finally, it was argued that in general the cost level depends on the overall price level and that costs are likely to be higher under monopolistic competition compared to competition as a result of a higher level of X-inefficiency.

14   More Implications of Inert Area Theory

An "Open" Theory

The set of interrelated ideas presented in this book should be viewed as an open system. There are several senses in which it is "open." One is that the set of interrelated concepts can be adapted, altered somewhat, and/or intertwined with other ideas employed in economics—and thereby adding something of value, I hope. The system is also open in the sense that the ideas can be broken down from their abstract level to subconcepts on a lower level of abstraction and be transformed into a more detailed and complex system of relations. In addition, the system is open in the sense that there are a great many areas of conventional economic analysis that can be examined and analytical apparatus reformulated from a new point of view. One possibility, not tackled in this book, is income distribution. I make no attempt to reconsider the marginal productivity theory of wages or other types of income distribution theories, though it is clear that reformulations are possible. Thus, the sense of openness exists in both "width" and "depth" in that many additional topics can be reconsidered from both types of extensions of X-efficiency microtheory. But the aim of this volume is not to produce a treatise complete in every way. Rather, the spirit is to present the basic ideas and to suggest something of their potential.

A theory is helpful if it adds to our understanding of behavior and/or if it has applications and implications that are both interesting and different from alternative theories. It is in this spirit that I have outlined some of the applications and implications of my theory. What follows is but a very small sample of possible applications.

Aspects of Innovational Diffusion

Many signals that might prompt changes end in inert areas. Most possibilities do not reach the point at which it will be to the interest of anyone to promote change, but once started there is a process of innovational diffusion, viewed in a very general sense, that is worth examining and to which some of our concepts are applicable.[1] In the traditional models an existing state of the arts is available to all firms and new techniques become equally available. The model suggested here departs from this extreme picture. A change in technical knowledge is transmitted to other firms in part by the force of example of successful adopters, but adoption is also resisted in terms of the considerations outlined above.

To illustrate the operation of an inert area "double threshold" model, we limit ourselves to the case of many firms of approximately equal size which produce an homogeneous product, where the pathway of diffusion is limited to a single industry and where the innovations reduce costs per unit. We should keep in mind the distinctions between the cost effects of an innovation under which costs per unit are reduced by the adopting firm but output remains the same, and a scale aspect under which output is increased to some degree, and which, other things equal, may force the price to fall.

In general we can think of three cost effects of innovations on noninnovating firms. First, given the uncertainty surrounding an innovation, the greater the number of adopters, the greater the decrease in the uncertainty and the lower the discount for risk. Second, information about the innovation increases with the number of adoptions. Third, as adoptions increase, the fixed costs of adoption (for example, the costs of search for more details about the innovation) and the costs of trial and error experimentation with adaptation possibilities are likely to decline to later adopters. (Let us call this last effect the "scale" effect.) All of these effects usually decrease costs per unit of output to later innovators.

Two scale elements can operate to lower profits per unit for later innovators. As adoptions take place, the total supply of output might rise and the price of the commodity might fall. Also, a firm that is already a successful innovator finds it easier to increase output with the new technique and thereby threaten the market share of nonadopters. In general, we might expect that for early adoptions the scale advantages—because there are many adopters—will be negligible and the cost effects will be dominant. As a result, profits per unit produced may rise for the earlier innovators as more adoptions take place. However, beyond some point the effects of the increase in output and growth of the innovating firms are likely to dominate.

The inert areas that surround the appropriate decisionmaker in each firm can be interpreted in terms of pull-push bounds. The vision of an opportunity that creates a marginal *gain* greater than the cost of shifting out of the inert area creates a "pull" to act, while a change in external circumstances that creates a potential marginal *loss* greater than the cost of shifting out of the inert area creates a "push" to act. The minimal marginal gains or losses to do so are the pull-push bounds. The wider the pull-push bounds and the wider the spread of these bounds between firms, the slower the initiation and spread of technological change. In the illustration that follows, the pull and push thresholds are in terms of profits per manager-owner. The basic idea is that in every firm there are individuals who are likely to be part of the ownership-managerial group that can gain or lose by innovation. The extent of the gain is likely to depend on the firm's profit rate and growth possibilities. To simplify matters, we will assume that profits per member of this group (manager-owner) are a monotone function of some index of the profit and growth possibilities inherent in the innovation. The essential parts of the analysis do not depend on the exact nature of this index. An adoption by a large firm is more important than that by a small firm; hence in calculating the adoption rate each adoption is weighted by some index of the size of the adopter.

In Figure 37 the curve marked *MIP* represents the minimum increase in profits (per manager-owner) that would induce firms to adopt the innovation. The curve is drawn in such a way that we start with the firms most eager to adopt. As we proceed along the X-axis to less sensitive firms the gap between different firms diminishes. For each firm's *MIP* there is associated an *MAP* point below the *MIP* level. *MAP* represents the minimum acceptable profits for different firms. Each point on curve *MAP* is the push bound associated with that firm's pull bound. The curve marked *IP* represents the innovational profit line as it changes with quantity of adoptions (that is, some weighted index of the quantity of firms). Initially *IP* rises as a consequence of the decreased risks and decreased costs of search and adaptation, but it falls as adoptions increase and output increases more than proportionately. The output increase is assumed to force down prices and profit levels.

The curve *NIP* represents the noninnovational profit locus. Each point indicates the profit level per manager for the noninnovating firms, assuming that all the previously more responsive firms had innovated. The effect of the innovation for at least some firms is in part to increase their output as well as the aggregate output of all firms. As a consequence, beyond some point the innovators reduce the profit level of the noninnovators.

Four possibilities appear. (1) In the diagram as drawn, the innovational profit level *IP* is above the minimum inducement profit level, and as a consequence the innovational process starts. (2) It would be possible for the innovational profit level to start below the *MIP* curve. In this case the innovational diffusion process would never get started. These two cases are

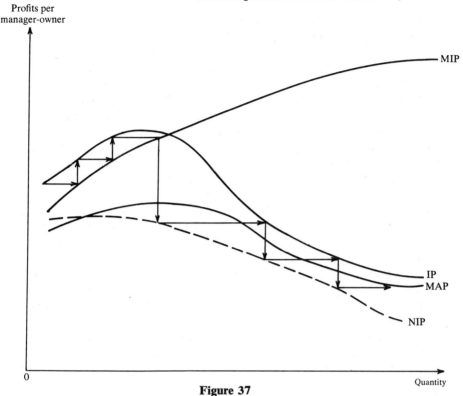

Figure 37

straightforward. (3) The next case is one in which the *NIP* curve falls below the *MAP* curve beyond some point and hence the push effect operates. This is illustrated in Figure 37.

(4) The final possibility is the case where the *NIP* curve remains above the *MAP* curve and the push effect does not operate. What is involved in the "nonpush" case is the possibility that the initial innovators reduce their costs but do not increase output to any great degree. As a consequence, their behavior has little effect on the profit levels of the noninnovating firms. Once the innovators who are motivated by the profit pull complete their innovations, the lack of an effect on the profits of noninnovators causes the innovating process to stop. The lesson of this example is that, for the noninnovational diffusion process to complete itself, it is not enough for the pull effect to be operative for some firms. The innovating firms must be sufficiently interested in growth that their activities reduce the profits of the noninnovators to a level below the noninnovator inert areas. Thus, innovation with little growth may stop the innovating process

or delay it until the current capital of the noninnovating firms is replaced by more productive capital that embodies the innovation.

There are a great many pathways of innovational diffusion. Obviously they need not all be through the interactions of similar firms producing the same commodity. The model can be expanded to include potential entrants who also possess pull-push thresholds. Potential entrants may be firms that do not produce the commodity in question but that use the improved process (the innovation) in another connection and may decide to apply it to the commodity in question; or firms producing a related commodity that may decide to adopt the innovation to produce the commodity in question; or a related innovation which may not be suitable to produce the commodity in question but which may work after the process has been refined in some way. It is clear that not only are the existing firms in the industry part of the diffusion path but firms doing something which potentially connects them to the commodity in question become possible adopters. Once these firms are included, the nature of the process continues as before: upper and lower push-pull bounds determine whether or not the adoption takes place. The point is that, whatever the innovational pathway considered, the size and nature of inert areas within firms determine in part the rate at which the innovation spreads.

In the interest of simplicity, we ignored the probability that there is a "time-impact" aspect to inert areas. It takes time for members of firms to realize that there is a sufficient "profit" gain in the innovation so that the gain (or loss prevention) goes beyond the inert area bounds. It takes time for information to be processed, assessed, and decisions taken. Thus, for each market signal there is a time period that it takes for the signal to penetrate, as it were, the inert area. A more realistic, more complex model of the innovational process can be developed if we attach a time-impact period to inert areas. For example, in Figure 37 we could associate with every point on *MIP* and *MAP* a time-impact period. On the basis of such impact periods, if we worked it out in detail, we could determine not only the sequence in which firms adopt but also the time path in which innovational adoptions are made. Of course the sequence could be different than that implied by the curves in Figure 37 if firms with a lower *MIP* value have a longer impact time than some firms with higher *MIP* values. Similar considerations held for *MAP* values. It should be apparent that, although the analysis becomes more complex, its general features would usually turn out to be quite similar if impact times are not exceptionally different for different firms (say, ten years for some firms and one month for others). A variety of possible complications to our postulates about inert areas can be invented, but at this juncture in the development of the theory it does not seem fruitful to pursue them. We must await empirical information before we can judge what type of complexities it would be useful to introduce.

Aspects of the Inflation-Fueling Process

What is the mechanism in the nongovernmental sector through which the gradually increasing demand for money increases is created? Let us make the extreme assumption that the economy operates under a perfectly permissive monetary authority. Firms or individuals who require an increase in liquidity are readily supplied. The relevance of the exercise lies in the notion that the more rapidly the demand for money is built up, the greater the difficulty that the monetary authorities will have in dampening potential or actual inflation. Essentially we are asking part of the question, What creates the pressure the monetary authorities face?

Popular treatments frequently define inflation as a process under which too much money is chasing too few goods. In order to avoid difficult questions inflation is usually treated on a purely macro basis. But specific firms raise prices or refrain from doing so, and specific households choose to buy at higher prices or refrain from doing so. Obviously these specific micro events must at least in part be explained on a micro basis.*

Consider a single firm. Some group or person in it is in charge of price-setting or price-setting policies. Such individuals make decisions within the framework of inert areas. But at some point, the environment in which they operate changes, which in turn dictates that they either lower or raise the prices in question. Nor is it necessary for a single environmental effect to be the sole cause of action. Frequently, *a cumulative process* becomes operative within the inert area so that, as the process proceeds in one direction, in some sense it "bursts the bounds" of the inert area and the individuals responsible are induced or forced to act. Another way of seeing this point, is to see various impacts as having the power to reduce the size of the inert area. Thus, at each stage in the cumulative process what is left is a "residual inert area" that gradually gets smaller and smaller and eventually leads to action.

A basic concept I will employ is "price-setting power" (to be referred to as P.S.P.). Different firms or individuals will be viewed as having different degrees of power to raise prices should they choose to do so. Though many examples are possible, the simplest is that of a monopoly which has not

---

* A few analysts have discussed some of these microeconomic policies, either under the title of discretionary pricing or under the concept of mark-up pricing, but their ideas have not become part of the mainline thinking in the profession.

previously changed its maximum price. Some P.S.P. can exist in markets that are close to perfect competition. The reason for this is that consumers are presumed to behave within inert areas and, as a consequence, do not immediately shift from one seller to another because the first has raised his price to some degree. Basically the following elements are involved in price-setting power: (1) degree of market imperfection; (2) size of inert areas on the part of the buyers; (3) degree of looseness inherent in the degree of selective rationality on the part of the buyers; (4) the general nonmaximizing behavior that takes place within the system; (5) the monetary and time costs of market information; and (6) the degree to which buyers have the power to express "voice," "exit," or both, or neither, in response to price changes.

A few remarks on the last point are in order. The relation between Hirschman's concepts of voice and exit and my notion of inert areas are worth exploring.[2] In industries in which there are relatively few sellers compared to buyers it may be very difficult for buyers to use voice in any effective sense. An individual voice usually seems useless, and it is too much trouble to organize a collective voice—it is too costly compared to the size of the buyers' inert areas. Similarly, an individual exit is likely to be ineffective as a signal to the seller, given the inert area. What is left frequently is no response in many cases of small price increases or a very limited response in terms of reducing the quantity purchased by a small amount. The outcome in many cases is that up to some point the situation may be such as to elicit almost no adverse signals to sellers.

Once we accept price-setting power as a genuine capacity on the part of sellers we can see a transmission mechanism which may be operative. It is very similar to the innovational diffusion mechanism just considered. This transmission mechanism works both within industries and between industries. Within industries some initiators raise the price; followers gradually see the opportunity to do likewise. The fact that some firms have raised prices reduces the risk of the followers. As a result, some follower firms also do so, which in turn reduces the risk for still more followers, and so on.

The inflation-fueling process will be treated as one that is analogous to the sequential diffusion of innovations. Just as an innovation gradually spreads throughout the system, *or fails to do so,* in accordance with the ideas presented in the preceding section, we shall consider price increases as a phenomenon that spreads in a similar manner. If some people have the power to raise prices, then it seems natural to view price increases as the introduction of *costless* innovations. They are costless only in the sense that no fixed cost is involved. Such innovations are by no means riskless. In general, the greater the price-setting power of a seller the likelier that such a seller will be a price-increase innovator.

The potential price-innovator faces a number of considerations before he makes his decision. One is the possibility that a higher price may result in a loss of sales. He may discount this in the belief that others will follow his example and also increase prices, but there is the risk that they may not do so. Finally, higher prices may induce an increase in X-inefficiency or increases in input costs.

On the other side, the potential innovator may take an optimistic view. He may feel that others will probably follow suit in raising prices, or little is lost if they do not do so since he can lower prices again, or the potential losses are likely to be small compared to the gains. Naturally, different potential innovators will assess these matters quite differently.

To examine the process on a slightly more formal basis, we assume a simple world of two industries, *A* and *B,* selling two commodities, both of which could be used either as consumers' goods or intermediate goods. Thus, each industry buys inputs from the other. We also assume that each industry is of a mildly monopolistic-competitive type. Within each, commodities are very close substitutes for each other (although some mild monopoly power exists), but between the two industries there is very little substitutability.

Let us turn to Figure 38, which in almost every way is similar to Figure 37. *MIP* is the minimum increase in profits that will induce the sellers to increase their prices; *IP* represents the profits expected to be achieved by the price-innovating firms. Since we have already examined the analysis of other types of innovations, we could jump to some of the conclusions of the earlier analysis. Some of the price increases may be so high that the innovation will never get started. The second possibility is for the price increase to be reasonably high so that the innovation does get started but the push effect is truncated. Completed diffusion does not occur. In this case we have to consider the possibility that the innovators may feel that the transfer of sales to noninnovating firms with lower prices is great enough to force them to retreat from the innovation and reduce prices.

Finally, we consider the case that we will emphasize: those sets of price increases which are neither too high nor too low, and which once tried as an innovation will induce followers to proceed, so that the entire diffusion process is completed. Part of the process is induced by the pull effect, and part by the push effect. The consequence of such a procedure is that at the end of the diffusion period, which takes place over a period of time, prices are higher than before but they need not be the same in industry *A* as in industry *B*. In this model labor has some degree of price-setting power. But

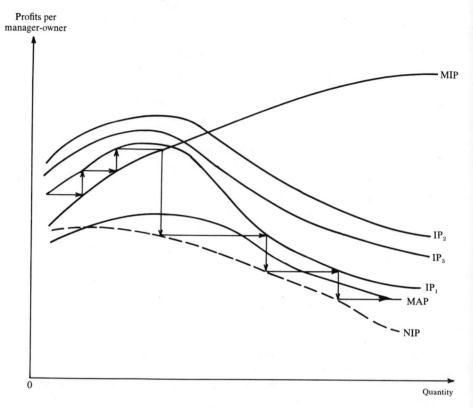

Figure 38

many segments may have very little of it so that at the end of the process some members of the work force have raised their price, so to speak, relatively little compared to others; as a result, their real income is lower than if the "price innovation" had never taken place.

The X-axis of Figure 38 includes all sellers. Employees as well as firms are included in the innovation process. Of course those employees who have very little price-setting power will find themselves near the tail end of each diffusion process during any round. The position of many segments of unorganized labor will be toward the extreme right in the diagram. Such employees make their decisions mostly on the basis of the push of higher consumer goods prices. (This would be less true of those with scarce skills.)

In my earlier discussion I started with an *assumed* price increase as the innovation by all sellers. A seller could try a variety of price increases. The

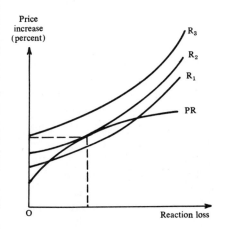

Figure 39a

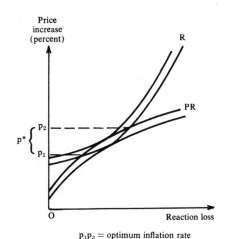

$p_1 p_2 =$ optimum inflation rate

Figure 39b

considerations determining the price increase chosen and the area in which
the outcome is likely to fall are considered with the aid of Figure 39. Figure
39a has price increases on the ordinate and the expected adverse reaction
to the increase on the abscissa. We have already discussd some of the
potential reactions that might make a seller worse off: others may not
follow the price increase, input costs might rise, the firm might become less
X-efficient, and so on.

The curves marked R_1, R_2, and R_3 represent iso-risk lines. A point on
R_1 associated with a greater anticipated reaction is paired with a higher
price to compensate for the greater reaction and leave the seller equally
well off. The curve marked PR represents the sellers' notions of the actual
relation between the price rise and the reaction the price rise is expected to
induce. The higher the price rise, the greater the marginal adverse reaction.
Hence, the curve is concave from below. The tangency point between the
iso-risk lines R_1, and the price-reaction line PR is the optimal price
increase.

Figure 39b contains the same ideas, but the curves have a certain
thickness to reflect degrees of indifference, a dislike for precision, and other
elements of selective rationality (see Chapter 5). The outcome is now a
segment of the price increase shown by the distance p_1, p_2. Thus, an

initiator will presumably choose a price rise within the segment and reflect what we view as an appropriate degree of indeterminancy in the system.

Additional considerations enter for followers. They risk less if they follow the initiators closely. In addition, they can anticipate reasonably known reactions because they can see how things have worked out for the initiators. Iso-risk curves and the price-reaction curve for the followers reflects this knowledge. Thus, there probably would be a tendency for followers to raise prices closer to that of initiators if initiators appear not to suffer unexpected reactions. Followers do not necessarily choose the same price increases as those who preceded them. Whether every seller raises his prices to the same degree is not especially important. If the choice made does not work out too well compared to that of earlier followers, they could make small price adjustments in either direction.

In addition, we assumed some degree of monopolistic competition and the persistance of inert areas for buyers. Hence, the process of diffusion is quite consistent with some differences in the price increases attempted by different sellers. However, in general we should expect that, after more experimentation, price increases of later followers would be no higher—and probably a little lower—than those of earlier followers, *other things equal.* This is because some late followers are late followers because their price-setting power is lower and they could impose it only because others in the industry had done so. In addition, their degree of monopolistic competition might be slightly less and, as a result, they have greater concern for reactions to higher prices compared to the nonadopters.

On the other hand, because this is a process that takes place over time, other things do not remain equal and later followers may have felt the impact of cost increases. In some cases they may allow such elements to enter their calculations and experiment with slightly higher increases than did their predecessors. In sum, if the cost-push elements are absent for the later adopters, we should expect that on the average they would choose equal or smaller increases in price than their predecessors during the diffusion process.

So far we have considered one round in the process. What happens in subsequent rounds depends on the relation between the actual IP curves and the expected IP rates. If the actual innovational profit levels are greater than expected, we would anticipate that they would try somewhat higher prices since this would reflect an increase in the IP curve. Thus, in Figure 38 IP_2 is above IP_1. But in the long run, when price increases get fairly high, we would expect a reversal. In other words, at very high price increases the reactions are somewhat more extreme and actual IP levels fall below the expected IP levels, with the result that the next round's expected

IP level is set at a lower level than before. If such adjustments take place round after round, then the whole process is likely to possess equilibrating elements, so through trial and error adjustments we eventually approximate an equilibrium rate of inflation under a passive monetary authority.

Figure 40a shows similar ideas on an aggregated level. The curve *PR* shows an index of price increases in relation to the adverse reactions expected. The curve marked *R* represents an index of reactions at given price increases. Note that all sellers contribute to the price-raising mechanism and, because they sell to each other, they contribute to the reaction mechanism as well. The intersection between the two curves yields the equilibrium rate of inflation for the system. Figure 40b illustrates the unlikely (but not impossible) situation in which the *PR* line and the reaction function *R* are almost parallel, so that the interaction of the two functions yields an explosive rate of inflation. Figure 40c includes the same information as 40a except that the curves are now bands for reasons similar to those stated before. The outcome is an equilibrium segment which represents a set of equilibrium inflation rates around which the economy is likely to wobble.

The exceedingly stylized ideas presented represent a greatly simplified picture of the inflation-fueling process. For the sake of simplicity and brevity a great many elements have been ignored. The possibility of "re-entries" into the process during any particular diffusion round has been ignored. Some firms might try to inject price increases twice or three times while others are still making their initial attempts. Reentries would complicate the picture, but in general we would expect that, the higher the proportion of sellers that reenter, the more rapid the rate of inflation diffusion.

On the basis of our partial model a few conclusions may be tentatively proffered. The larger the inert areas or, what is the same thing, the wider the push-pull bounds, the slower the rate of inflation. Detailed study of the conditions under which price innovational attempts fail can be especially useful, because the processes by which diffusion is stopped midstream are exceedingly important ones to try to understand fully if we are to find additional means of controlling inflation.

The question of time was left implicit. There is a time dimension to the period of complete diffusion. Also, if I had attempted to construct a more complicated model, a time element would have to be added to the inert areas. In other words, follower adopters do not respond immediately but within certain time boundaries after exposure to the opportunity. A slightly more complicated version of our model would use inert areas characterized by at least two dimensions, one of which would be the normal utility cost

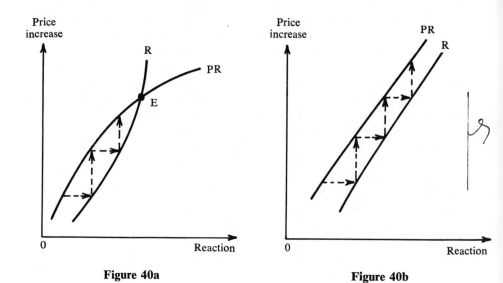

Figure 40a

Figure 40b

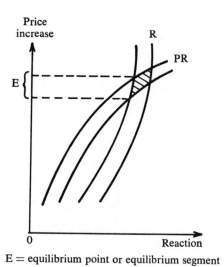

E = equilibrium point or equilibrium segment

Figure 40c

dimension, and the other a set of time boundaries within which the time lag of the action would fall—if action is dictated by the circumstances.

How time might enter during an *equilibrium* rate of inflation can be seen in the simple artificial illustration given in Table 11. The table illustrates the events for three groups of innovators. Assume that all in Group *I* raise prices simultaneously in the first period by 1 unit (for example, 1 *u*). Group *II* raises prices by 1 *u* in the second period, and Group *III* in the third period. Costs rise in the proportions they do because each group buys inputs from each other. Over the three periods (say, one cycle of three periods is one year), Group *I* gains 1½ units over two periods. Group *II* comes out even. Its members gain ½ in the second. Those in Group *III* are net losers of 1½ units. Once the three-period cycle ends, there is an incentive for those in Group *I* to raise prices again by one unit, given that it is within their price-setting power. And so the cycle repeats itself. This is one simple example of an infinitely repeating cycle with a constant equilibrium rate of inflation of one unit per year.

Nothing in the model is inconsistent with unemployment existing side by side with inflation. As prices rise, demand may fall off, production be cut back, employees be let go, and profit reductions avoided by raising prices still further. Nothing in the theory forces firms to hire unemployed workers and lower the overall wage rate. At least to some degree the inert areas would prevent that. Of course massive unemployment could work as a counterinflationary force, since at some point reduction in purchasing power resulting from unemployment leads firms to be cautious about price increases, and demand elasticities rise (for a given price increase) as

Table 11. The effect of time during an equilibrium rate of inflation.

Period	Changes in	Innovating group		
		I	II	III
1	Prices	+ 1 u	same	same
	Cost	same	+ ½ u	+ ½ u
	Profit	+ 1 u	− ½ u	− ½ u
2	Prices	+ 1 u	+ 1 u	same
	Cost	+ ½ u	+ ½ u	+ 1 u
	Profit	+ ½ u	+ ½ u	− 1 u
3	Prices	+ 1 u	+ 1 u	+ 1 u
	Cost	+ 1 u	+ 1 u	+ 1 u
	Profit	0	0	0

u = 1 unit of change

unemployment increases simultaneously. Eventually a growing reduction in buyers can put an end to price increases.

The attribution of price-setting power to sellers may appear arbitrary. However, one can show that there is likely to be a natural evolution of such power. In order to survive, firms have to have one of two capacities: either the ability to reduce the degree of X-inefficiency to the level of its competitors, or to pass on the increased costs to consumers or others. In other words, a firm with only one of these capacities may find it sufficient for survival, but its vulnerability will be higher than in cases where both capacities exist. The point to note is that each capacity is a substitute for the other.

Some firms may find that they cannot always counter increases in input costs by increasing efficiency, or always counter increases in X-inefficiency that may occur or increases in effort entropy. Consequently, the ability to establish at least a partial monopolistic arrangement, no matter how slight (or some equivalent arrangement), that yields an advantage in bargaining power is a great aid to survival. Hence, firms in competitive industries usually attempt through marketing arrangements, advertising, the use of brand names, or collusive agreements to establish some degree of monopoly power. Other examples are implicit collusive agreements and behavior not to compete on a price basis, as well as "cost plus" contracts with governments or other buyers. All of these means, which result in some degree of unequal bargaining power between firms and consumers yield some firms some degree of price-setting power.

It seems reasonable to expect in the competitive struggle to survive, and through the cycle of depression and prosperity, that firms with price-setting power have a survival advantage, since they can pass on all or some of the losses of temporary adversity to others in the economy. Of course, there are some counterinfluences, the main one being the supply of new entrepreneurs that can enter existing industries. The other is the existence of a steady stream of inventions leading to economic innovations. However, the supply of highly competitive entrepreneurs is usually limited, and innovations can be employed to set up (through patents, and so on) temporary monopolies as well as substitutes for existing products. Given these considerations, it should not be surprising that economies have evolved in such a way that many, perhaps most, surviving firms have emerged with a high degree of price-setting power.

Not too much should be concluded on the basis of this model of the inflation-fueling process. In the spirit of the methodological approach of Chapter 2, it is simply a sample of a type of analysis that might be useful—if it can be consolidated with other elements of the inflation process and become part of a reasonably realistic set of models that can be tested against real-world data.

One might assume that inflationary pressures would decline as per-capita income growth takes place over time since this tends to increase the rate of savings by households. (This was Keynes's view of the matter; Kuznets demonstrated statistically that it was not the case in the long run.) However, if we consider the arguments on consumption presented in Chapter 11, we find that elements on the consumers' demand side also feed the inflationary process.

Chapter 11 suggests that increases in income (whether money income or real income) set up very strong pressures for increases in consumption. Part of these pressures arise out of the shifting status targets already discussed, and part out of the claim drifts made by household members who are net receivers. Net receivers of household income can view their increase in claims as more or less free income. But in making expenditures they too are subject to interhousehold influences. Also there is a tendency for such individuals to maintain increased consumption expenditures at least equal to increased allowances; otherwise their claim to need such increases becomes suspect. Commitment claimants are under pressure to spend their receipts because otherwise the size of their claims are in jeopardy. As claims increase, so does the demand side of the inflationary pressure. Recipients of governmental allocations, even when they themselves are governmental bodies, are subject to similar pressures.

The Welfare Loss of Monopoly

A separate volume could easily be written on various applications of the X-efficiency–inert area theory. In Chapter 3 it was pointed out that the allocation efficiency loss resulting from misallocations is likely to be trivial under many circumstances. We now apply these ideas to a fairly standard welfare economics exercise: the determination of the welfare loss caused by monopoly. The results are likely to be considerably larger than those calculated in accordance with the conventional neoclassical apparatus.[3]

In Figure 41 the monopoly price is shown by A on the ordinate, the competitive price is shown by B, and the true minimum cost is shown by c; DD is the usual demand curve. The triangle abc reflects the loss to consumers of having a monopoly price and quantity Aa as against the competitive price and quantity Bc. Thus, the loss in consumer surplus is approximated by $ab \times bc$ divided by 2. Let us consider the following two cases. Suppose the cost difference between A and B is 5 percent of OB. Suppose also that the degree of X-inefficiency BC is also 5 percent of OB.

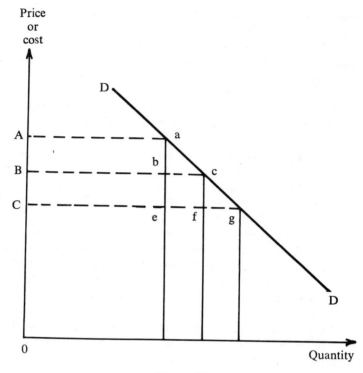

Figure 41

We now compare what might be viewed as the minimal welfare cost resulting from X-inefficiency compared to allocative inefficiency. We have already argued that allocative inefficiency is *abc*. X-inefficiency is at least the relatively large rectangle *BcfC*. Let us calculate the differences on a 5 percent basis. Allocative welfare loss is 5 percent of 5 percent divided by 2, which is approximately ⅛ of 1 percent. The X-efficiency loss is 5 percent of the value of the goods. The entire 5 percent is a loss to consumers. Hence there is something like a 40-fold difference to the X-inefficiency calculations compared to the allocative inefficiency measure. The X-inefficiency measure would also include the triangle *cfg*, which would make the difference all the larger. Different results would be achieved with different elasticities of course. Where an industry is inefficient in terms of costs, the entire cost differential is a loss to consumers. The allocative differential involves only the value to consumers between the consumption of the monopolistic good as against the counterpart expenditure on competitive goods.

Under monopoly the welfare loss may even be greater since the utility from work for the mass of workers may be lower. This may be counterbalanced by the somewhat higher utility of officials who use their less constrained monopoly positions in order to achieve satisfaction from arbitrary, unconstrained behavior that adversely affects some or many of those lower in the organizational hierarchy.

Consider the case in which two individuals interact. Individual A's role allows wider bounds (less initial constraint) in which to interpret his effort position than does that of B. Suppose B is a subordinate of A. The effect of A's choices on B can end in one of the following ways: both A's and B's utility are higher than otherwise (than, say, when both are more constrained by a third level of the hierarchy); both may be lower than otherwise; or one obtains a higher utility at the expense of the other.

Visualize an effort position as having arbitrary and functional components. The arbitrary components may be chosen as an expression of the personality of an individual or out of ignorance of what is genuinely functional. The less the constrained area, the greater the option possible for an individual to choose arbitrary components as part of his effort position. Some arbitrary components may adversely influence those over whom A has authority. Thus, A may use his authority position to choose arbitrary components; this imposes an onerous situation and may force the subordinate B to choose activities whose aim is in part to neutralize the arbitrary use of power by A.

Within this framework we can think of a host of examples in which effort points chosen by A may increase the utility of effort for A at the expense of the utility from effort B. Pressures on the firm to constrain effort areas also can be functional or arbitrary. Functional constraints should reduce the arbitrary elements in chosen effort positions. It seems reasonable to believe that monopoly need not impose functional constraints. There are costs involved in permitting arbitrary behavior on the part of some in the higher reaches of the organizational structure, just as there are costs involved in being rather loose about imposing functional constraints. But monopolists can pass on such costs to consumers, whereas under competition, whose ultimate *raison d'être* is to put pressure on cost, the competitive atmosphere pressures management to constrain nonfunctional effort positions. To this extent competition may be expected to operate in such a way as to reduce the arbitrary uses of power which would allow some in an organization to choose effort positions which would be arbitrary at the expense of the utility of others.

Governmental Regulation of Industry

A large literature exists on governmental regulation of industry through regulation of the rate of return. Ideally this type of regulation should apply to "natural monopolies," but other industries are sometimes regulated the same way. In recent years significant debate has developed on the question as to whether regulating the rate of return leads to "overcapitalization" by the industry. Whether or not this is true is an important issue. An important related issue is that such regulation is socially costly because of its X-inefficiency effects.

The point has already been noted by Baumol and Klevorick, who conclude:

> It has been suggested that it has sometimes been used by regulators as a means to keep inefficient firms in business, shoring them up by preventing their rivals from passing their lower costs on to the consumers. The regulator's apparent distaste for the demise of any business firm no matter how tenuous its economic justification may well contribute in no small measure to X-inefficiency.
>
> Moreover, a rate-of-return ceiling by its very nature tends to contribute another X-inefficient influence. By ruling out all profits in excess of some predetermined rate as potential fruits of monopoly, a rate-of-return constraint also precludes extraordinary rewards for extraordinary entrepreneurial accomplishment. Indeed, if such a constraint were applied with complete inflexibility it might well eliminate altogether any financial reward for efficiency and innovation. If the firm cannot hope to earn more than the ceiling, *even temporarily,* and if the demands for its products are inelastic so that it can reasonably count on that profit rate in any event, what can management hope to gain by working for increased efficiency in its operations?[4]

The policy implications hinted at in the quotation, which follows readily from the analytical apparatus presented in this book, is that the regulation of profits is socially a very costly means of regulating monopolies. Somehow the regulatory means must include elements that induce the monopoly to try to achieve approximately as low levels of X-inefficiency as are achieved, at least on the average, by competitive industries. This is not the place to consider the very complex problems of inventing regulatory systems that would meet this requirement in the regulation of "natural" monopolies.* This discussion was introduced simply to indicate that at the

* One possibility would be periodically to allow any company to take over the management of an existing monopoly if it guaranteed to provide the same goods

very least our analytical apparatus shows up the inadequate and socially wasteful means of the current mode of regulating some categories of monopolies.

Summary and Conclusions

This chapter has suggested some possible applications of X-efficiency microtheory. I attempted to show how my theory bears on the analysis of the diffusion of innovations and the diffusion aspects of the inflation process. The latter is especially interesting since this aspect of inflation is rarely considered a part of standard microeconomic theory. I suggested, albeit very briefly, that if we include impact times in association with my theory of inert areas, we can work out, at least in principle, both the time path of an innovation or the time path of what has been referred to as the inflation-fueling process. In the inflation case we would not expect actually to observe the time paths that the theory suggests, since the role of the banking system and governmental budgetary policies and processes have influences—in some cases strong influences—on the rate of inflation. Nevertheless, there is a significant microeconomic aspect to the inflation process, and my theory suggests ways of analyzing this process once we take into account the differential capacities of firms to set price increases and the nature of the inert areas of various firms under different market structures.

We also consider applications to the welfare economic aspects of monopoly and to the problem of regulating natural monopolies. While in neither of these cases did we go into great detail, the basic intent of this chapter was met in the sense that we indicated at the very least The possibility of some applications of specific problems of interest to economists was indicated. A wide variety of other applications are not mentioned in this chapter. Among those that come to mind readily are the following: In the field of public finance one could consider the effect of different tax systems on X-efficiency. For example, one can raise the question (and attempt to trace the consequences) as to whether or not the tax affects costs that cannot be transmitted to consumers, and the degree to which

---

at a lower cost. This could be done through sealed bids every so often. Needless to say, the details of such a procedure would have to be very carefully worked out. A suggestion along these lines is contained in an article by H. Demsetz, "Why Regulate Utilities?" *Journal of Law and Economics* (April 1968). It is not clear that Demsetz meant this to be a practical suggestion or simply a means of entering into a discussion of theoretical issues. In any event, the problem is far from solved, even intellectually, and the field is still wide open.

such a tax puts pressure on the inert areas of different firms. In the field of comparative systems it is clear that one of the main problems is that alternative modes of political and economic organization are likely to have very broad effects on the X-efficiency of the labor force as a whole. In the field of industrial organization the application of inert areas and X-efficiency ideas are quite natural since one would expect a clear relation between motivational aspects implied by some types of market structures and degrees of X-inefficiency. A more detailed analysis could have been presented on the application of these ideas to welfare economics. But rather than provide exhaustive list of possible applications, I simply want to suggest that a great many aspects of economic analysis, as well as a wide variety of economic problems, can be looked at from the viewpoint of at least some of the concepts presented in this book.

15 Applications to Management

All managers in all fields face one fundamental problem: they cannot fully control firm members. Nor would it be rational, economic, or humane for them to try to do so. All individuals have some scope for individual interpretations of their jobs. "Desirable" job interpretations, from management's viewpoint, depends on motivation—but motivation is not purchasable. Hence management's job is to provide motivational inputs to induce firm members to choose favorable job interpretations—*including* the jobs of management itself. This differs from the conventional view of management functions, which are designated by such shorthand terms as: planning, organizing, implementing, and measuring. Such activities are ineffectual without an appropriate motivational atmosphere. In a broad sense motivation may be seen as part of a firm's unique structure and "culture." But the structure and culture may be conducive to low performance levels. Thus, part of the management job is to assess the culture and determine whether it should be maintained or changed.

To demonstrate how the theory developed in this book could function as a diagnostic tool for certain kinds of managerial problems would probably require its application to a set of *real* management problems. This is beyond the scope of this volume but some possibilities are obvious. Since most of the book can be rewritten from the viewpoint of management, we will perforce have to be selective. But I will try to suggest how someone interested in management can translate some of the chapters so that it fits the area of applicability to managerial problems. For management students some of the materials may appear unusually abstract. However, the reader who perseveres to the end of this chapter will find a more specific mode of analysis suggested, one that might be helpful in solving a variety of management problems.

Although neither the mainstream microtheory nor this book is designed for managers, the interrelated complex of ideas presented here does have implications for the management of firms. Theories are not limited to any particular political system, but to simplify matters the discussion in this chapter will be confined to enterprises in the private property sector of an economy. With some variations, a not dissimilar analysis could be worked out for managers of firms in the nonprofit sector, or in nonprivate enterprise economies.

Managerial Considerations

Two broad aspects may be useful to management: considerations that would be useful to keep at the forefront of one's thoughts in the analysis of a firm's difficulties or problems; and the analysis of organizational structures in the interest of reducing X-inefficiency, increasing firm member satisfaction, or both.

Job Interpretations and Motivation. It is almost self-evident that if management is to decrease X-inefficiency it must at the very least be aware of certain elements that enter into the determination of X-efficiency. The first is the basic notion that all jobs have to be interpreted to a greater or lesser degree. Job interpretations made by employees and managers depend in part on the motivational system within the firm at large and also within the groups and subgroups within which work takes place. "Mechanical" changes, such as changes in formal job specifications, may have no impact or even a negative impact on X-efficiency. At this level the question that the manager has to ask is how changes within his control will affect an individual's motivation to choose a more efficient job interpretation.

An important aspect to keep in mind is the possibility of undesirable substitutions among the different dimensions that form the job interpretation. Chapter 6 characterized an effort level by choices with four components: activities, pace, quality, time magnitude and sequence. An effort level or effort point was referred to as an *APQT* bundle. Each of these components could be influenced or constrained to some degree by management. From a behavioral viewpoint an individual could adjust to a constraining influence on one component by changing others. For example, viewing a job interpretation as a set of closely related *APQT* bundles, management stress on pace may result in a reduction of the quality of the effort, as the individual interprets the job given a new higher pace constraint. Another possibility is that if pace is stressed it may influence the activities chosen by the firm member. A number of substitutions are possible. The main point is that, given the levels of constraint concern that characterize an individual or a group, management must be aware that attempts to constrain some aspects of the job interpretation will influence others, which in some instances may be inferior to the interpretations that would result without the imposition of the new constraint.

A major element to be kept in mind is that although productivity depends on motivation, motivation is not a purchasable input in the marketplace. Managers must regard motivation as an input in the production process. It is as important to production as steel or nails or raw materials or energy. For different degrees of motivation different outputs result for the same other inputs. Although what managers do is part of the motivation-creating process, it is only part of it. Managers must know not only how they influence motivation but how the activities that they do not normally associate with motivation *in fact* contribute to the motivational structure of the firm. In other words, problems may be created by management not only by the problems they recognize but by the problems they create but fail to recognize because they do not inquire about the consequences on motivation that results from their decisions, changes, and general behavior. Although these may be intrinsically difficult to handle, they certainly cannot be answered if they are not asked.

In discussing the psychological postulates that form the basis of my theory (Chapter 5) I suggested that in most work contexts individuals pursue their own motives as well as the interests of the firm. Usually, they try to work out a compromise between the two sets of interests. What was referred to as the degree of constraint concern can frequently be shifted toward greater identification with firm aims, provided the necessary positive motivations are introduced. The exact nature of such motivations is impossible to determine outside of specific contexts. Motivational stimuli that suggest approval or new challenges may be effective in some contexts. Perhaps of equal importance are stimuli introduced through supervisor-induced changes for nonmotivational reasons without recognizing their effects on motivation. At the same time, there may be individual efforts, apart from influences on specific individuals, since such changes may alter the "atmosphere" in which work takes place, which may in turn alter the motivational elements inherent in the general atmosphere.

Information and the Inverse Signal Law. Organizations are byproducts of their internal information mills. Without a constant flow of information human organization cannot function. The point I attempted to emphasize when we discussed the inverse signal postulate is that messages or signals contain more than informational context; they also contain *motivational* content.

Among the elements that make up the "signal flow" system of the firm are: (1) Is the scanning system which receives information from the outside world effective? (2) Is the "translation" of external to internal signals efficient, and consistent with aims of the firm? (3) Are the internal channels efficient or do signals get lost in inert areas? (4) And are intent signals in conformity with the implicit motivational content of the intent signals or are they inversely related to them?

Let us start with the last item. Two basic points about intent signals not usually considered by economic or organization theorists are involved. First, signals whose intent is to direct or generate performance also *have motivational content*. Second, although within some "scope range" the performance, intent, and motivational content may be consistent with each other, *beyond some point* in the "scope range" they are likely to be inversely related. If the intent signals as they proceed along the signal pathways suggest a narrower scope for many recipients than they believe is implicit in their choice of effort positions, this may be viewed as a sign of disapproval and may lower motivation and reduce initiative. Alternatively, if the scope allowed by the signals is greater than anticipated by the job interpretation, then we would expect that up to a point this would increase the individual's sense of being trusted and suggest approval by those at a higher level. Up to a point this should serve as a stimulus to initiative and lead to improved performance. But if the implicit scope is too large, in the absence of counterpart controls this may lead to a high level of effort entropy. This is an area where management can commit serious errors, and a situation in which errors may persist. Managers are not accustomed to think in terms of a close connection between intent signals and motivational signals. In some cases a dynamic sequence may develop which actually worsens the situation. One possible response to low productivity may be more specific intent signals which in turn may reduce motivation, lower productivity still further, and up to a point lead to counterproductive reactions to the observation of steadily falling productivity.

The problem is extremely complex. Its essential elements include not only the nature of the intent signals but also the pattern of signal flow through the system and the way similar signals may strike different individuals in the hierarchy. To some degree the outcome of the signal flow depends on the personalities of those who happen to be firm members and in the path of the signal flow. Although personalities undoubtedly make a difference, in general the inverse signal law applies to a wide variety of personality mixes.

Another important matter is the way in which signals are interpreted, reinterpreted, or reformulated as they flow through a hierarchial information channel. The same signals may be reworked in such a way that they imply larger scopes than anticipated at some junctures in the signal flow and lesser scopes than anticipated at other junctures. We cannot examine all the possible complexities that may exist in any specific organizational context. The main point is to alert managers to the importance of the motivational context inherent in the normal signal flow in the organization and the possibility of examining and assessing the motivational content as a source of possible productivity problems that may exist.

One of the firm's most important decision areas lies in recognizing signals from the environment. First the firm must distinguish between routine signals and those which indicate changes in the environmental situation, such as, changes in tastes, changes in competitive situations, or changes in potential technology. Second, problems may result from the evaluation and channeling of signals from those who receive them from the external world to those within the firm who can best evaluate them and make decisions on that basis. A large number of nonoptimal states persist in this area. Those who receive important signals may not be in a position to process them and send them through the appropriate channels. This is an area where a possible arbitrary use of power within the firm as well as arbitrary bureaucratic procedures may prevent or fail to motivate those who have useful information about the environment to channel such information to the appropriate decisionmakers. Here too the concept of inert areas can be a useful device for determining whether or not recipients of signals have the motivation and capacity to make the appropriate decisions or to channel them to those who possess the necessary responsibility and power.

Motivation and the Carte-Blanche Principle. In discussing the carte-blanche principle (Chapter 8), I indicated that there may be a great many instances in which unnecessary constraints are imposed simply because those who have the power to do so find that there is no disadvantage in imposing constraints, or that the constraints appear to remove some extremely small risks. As a result, excess bureaucratic procedures may be imposed on an organization. Such procedures reduce the motivation for individuals to take initiative. The problem involves not only the capacity of individuals to take initiative but the fact that the unnecessary constraints, and the bother and difficulty of overcoming bureaucratic rules, may be sufficient to dampen the enthusiasm of anyone who has an interest in taking initiative. Initiatives become exceedingly limited, and though the bureaucracy can handle routine problems it becomes excessively rigid and finds it difficult to cope with appropriate nonroutine situations. The carte-blanche principle encompasses the overall area of procedural rules, which requires continuing analysis to determine whether or not existing rules are necessary and whether or not they have a dampening effect on motivation. In other words, management has to consider whether it is currently burdened with an outdated unnecessary use of bureaucratic powers which impose dysfunctional procedures and constraints.

Motivation and the Theory of Games. In Chapter 9, which related motivational influences within the firm to games of strategy, I suggested that the hierarchy's upper levels, which impose rules on lower levels, may be faced with the "prisoner's dilemma" game. If they set up exceedingly cautious rules for the lower level, then it is likely that they may reduce the payoffs from effort to those at the lower level. Such constraints may also reduce the motivation to perform at high productivity levels. If accompanied by severe rules for nonproductivity at the lower level (such as being fired), this creates in a sense a "chicken" game for the peer group at the lower level. The outcome is likely to be a considerable narrowing of potential outputs at the lower level, though at the same time it may increase the likelihood of achieving some preset minimal output level.

On the other hand, more liberal rules for the lower level allow them greater choice and initiative. Such rules simultaneously permit a greater opportunity for high productivity as well as a greater possibility (through increased shirking) for lower productivity than may be the case if "chicken" type rules are imposed. A management faced with low productivity problems may find it useful to analyze and reconsider the type of rules it has imposed on those in lower levels in the organization. Are they tight "chicken" rules or much looser "prisoner's dilemma" rules?

The underlying viewpoint that is the basis for this discussion is the belief that management groups at one level of a hierarchy do not hold all the cards to determine behavior at lower levels. Management has a range of options that influence motivation—and its actions may change specific motivations or the motivational atmosphere—but these do not lead to *predetermined* consequences. Options that involve tight control are likely to narrow the productivity range; loose control is likely to widen it. If management chooses tight control there may be a greater chance that some minimum productivity level will result—but at the price of a smaller probability of stimulating high productivity levels. On the other hand, if managers choose a form of loose control there is an increased risk of a lower minimum output than under tight control but also a higher probability of a higher level of productivity or performance. The critical idea to remember is that there is no determinate relation between managerial actions and the consequent performance levels of those who are managed. Hence, the possible connection between management actions and games of strategy. This is a highly stylized way of looking at the complex problem of motivation and the options open to individuals at various levels of the hierarchy. I believe it is a useful and realistic one.

Similar considerations determine working group sizes. An organization with a given manpower can be divided into relatively few groups, each of which is relatively large, or a great many groups, each of which is relatively small, or something in between. Once again it seems likely that relatively small size units involve a larger range of productivity possibilities as well as a greater range of payoffs. If in small groups things go well, morale is high and there is the *possibility* of relatively high outputs. However, if in small groups people are largely mismatched in terms of group membership and there is little scope for transfer from one group to another, then overall morale may be lower than in a larger group. Peer group influences are likely to be much more intense in smaller than in larger groups; as a result, the possibilities of high morale and high output are likely to be associated with smaller groups. Thus, the determination of group size depends on overall management strategy in determining organization structure as well as on the risks it is willing to take with respect to variations in output.

Impactee-Structure Analysis

Earlier in this chapter we discussed a number of considerations that management might take into account in analyzing problems, especially those that involve lower levels of productivity than management desires. Now, still concerned with the same problem areas, a specific analytical procedure will be outlined. We start with the question of how the basic structure of the organization is related to the analysis of X-inefficiency.

Figure 42 shows a simple organizational plan composed of four layers. The lowest layer, T, includes a variety of groups (effort teams) whose team efforts contribute to the output of the organization. The next layer, S, is the first supervisor layer; IM represents intermediate management; and TM represents top management. The "supervisor groups" may be a single individual or they may be sets of individuals.

Let us consider some of the questions management might wish to ask if it wishes to increase productivity through changes in organizational structure. We start with the implicit assumption that the productivity level is low enough so that increases are possible if management could ask the right questions, obtain the right answers, and introduce the necessary changes. We still assume, as in the previous chapters, that management has only limited control of the effort of others. But although effort cannot be controlled completely, various elements can be changed—especially those which influence the motivational structure—making increases in the productivity level possible.

TM

IM

S

T

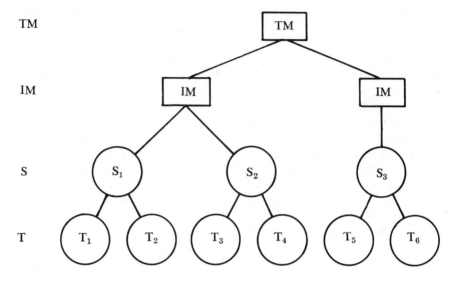

Figure 42

We have already raised the question whether the lowest level production groups are of optimal size. An additional question concerns their motivational structure, especially peer group influences within the group. But our concern here is not in asking interesting questions. Rather, an analysis of the nature of certain aspects of the structure, especially of the bonds that exist among various units of the organization, can lead to an understanding of the reasons of X-inefficiency. This depends essentially on relations among groups and on the *location* and *nature* of what has been referred to elsewhere as "impactees." Consider the relation between T_1, T_2, and S_1. A critical question is whether S_1 is an impactee with respect to T_1 and T_2—whether the outcome of the activities of T_1 and T_2 in any way influences the utility derived by S_1 for his job, that is, his effort position. Consider an extreme case in which S_1 is supposed to supervise T_1 and T_2, but S_1, either has no way of discovering the results of his efforts or does not have to take note of the outcome of the activities of T_1 and T_2. In this case S_1 may be a supervisor but he is not an impactee. Nothing that goes on at the T level affects the activities of S_1. Despite the fact that there is an organizational relation between groups at the T level and individuals on the S level, it may have no effect on productivity.

The other extreme is that under which the output of T_1 and T_2 is reported to S_1 and checked by S_1; furthermore, the career of S_1 depends on the degree of efficiency demonstrated by T_1 and T_2. In other words, S_1 has to pass on the results of T_1 and T_2 or he has to inform someone at a higher level of the results, who has an impact on both the short-run utilities derived by S_1 and perhaps on the long-run career progress of S_1. Assume that top management are also the owners, so that they feel that their income is lower if efficiency is lower, and vice-versa. If such a scheme exists all along the line, through the four levels of the hierarchy, and if efficiency information flows both ways, then we have very close relations between interdependent teams, intermediate impactees such as S and *IM,* and the residual impactees, which in this case are the top managers and owners.

The idealized structure just pictured need not exist in reality. In reality, firms may be composed of a variety of groups with various degrees of involvement in impactee relationships. Some portions of the firm may operate within streams of impactee relations that flow to residual impactees, but other portions may have gaps in this relation so that the performance of these parts of the firm are not monitored within significant bounds. We may view the idealized picture in the previous paragraph as a *well-monitored* organizational structure. Clearly, one type of analysis which management can carry out is to determine to what extent the actual structure is a well-monitored structure and to determine where there are "impactee gaps" in the organization. For instance, it may be possible that the results of output from one level land in the inert areas of the impactees at some point, and as a result the consequences are not sufficiently great for the impactee to pass on the information to still higher levels in a position to make changes. Enough has been said about the nature of the structure and about the potential analysis in terms of intermediate impactees and residual impactees so that the extent to which the structure is well-monitored or not can be worked out in analyzing specific problems.

An important distinction exists between a well-monitored structure and a well-motivated structure (one responsive to low levels of efficiency). Even if the structure is well-monitored, the environment may be highly permissive. For example, if the firm is a monopoly in which impactees are in a position to raise prices whenever its costs increase, the impact of various degrees of X-inefficiency is simply passed on to consumers. This may be the case if it is a regulated monopoly, limited to a given profit rate, which in turn depends on the relation between costs and price to consumers rather than on the level of absolute costs. If the environment creates pressures for the firm to be more efficient, it is important that the inert areas of various impactees be relatively narrow, that the impactees have reasonable effects on the utilities of various supervisory personnel at different levels, and that there is an information channeling path as well as a decisionmaking process which could correct the conditions responsible for low levels of X-efficiency.

Managers can undertake two major types of activities to increase productivity. The first is to improve the monitoring capability of the organization. Is the structure as well-monitored as it could be? If this is not the case, it is necessary to fill gaps where impactees may be absent, or to change or influence the job interpretations of individuals who should be impactees but who are not, or to rearrange a hierarchial position and its rewards and punishments so that at optimal junctures in the hierarchy such individuals become intermediate impactees.

But introducing changes to create a well-monitored structure may not be sufficient to increase productivity. A second group of activities that have to be considered are those that influence the motivational relations between individuals. Are these such that the structure, though well-monitored, is responsive to reports of low levels of performance? Attempts may be made to assess the width of inert areas of various individuals and to alter the rules and rewards so as to narrow the inert areas. If such changes are possible, this should increase the responsiveness to deviations from desired performance. At the same time, entirely apart from the inert areas, attempts may be made to alter the utilities received by various individuals from their effort positions through interpersonal relationships. Attempts could be made so that relations between individuals result in various degrees of approval and disapproval, in accordance with degrees of productivity or the desirability or undesirability of their performance, rather than in accordance with other elements of the organizational behavior.

Information and its channeling is a paramount feature of a well-monitored structure. But attempts should be made to assess the *motivational* elements involved in the collection and channeling of useful information that may directly or indirectly influence productivity. At the same time, consideration should be given to the notions already discussed as the "carte-blanche" principle. Information collection, and its channeling, which is not useful but which happens to be part of bureaucratic procedure, should be pruned or eliminated.

Finally, enough decisionmaking capability should be provided at various junctures, and positioned close enough to the impactees in the structure, so that they are in a position to see that decisions which influence the productivity of those within their sphere are made and implemented. In addition, this should reflect on the careers of the impactees, and on the utilities they derive from their effort positions.

Changes are normally introduced one at a time. In considering all of the elements that management may possibly try to change, there is an *overall* consideration which may at times be inconsistent with one-at-a-time changes. One-at-a-time changes unquestionably affect the motivational atmosphere. They affect the overall feeling of trust or distrust, the sense of approval or disapproval, which individuals may take into account. If individual changes inadvertently narrow the scope range of various individuals or appear to result in closer supervision than desired in order to stimulate initiative, then these changes may contain counterproductive elements. It is not only desirable to consider changes which improve motivation; when we introduce changes one at a time, we should *not* assume that the rest of the motivation system stays constant.

One of the problems the "impactee-structure-" analyst must face is determining whether the organization of teams within the firm is so arranged that performance can be measured in some way. Without measurement it would be very difficult to assess performance and to work out a well-monitored structure. This is not to imply that the performance of all portions of an organization need be of a measurable type. It is simply that measurable possibilities should be considered and organized wherever practicable.*

These ideas may appear rather general to the management-oriented reader. During a seminar in which they were presented, a graduate student of business administration asked, "What specifically would a manager do if he agreed with the general points covered?" The answer, it seems to me, is that any top management official who attempted to trace the structure of the organization—to locate all its impactees; to locate their positions in the structure; to assess whether or not the structure was well-monitored; to attempt to assess whether each impactee or his group was well-motivated to make decisions in the face of performance deficiencies—would learn a great deal about his firm. Furthermore, it seems likely that the process of seriously carrying out such an exercise would by itself suggest or reveal a number of possibilities for improvement.†

---

* To proceed with the analysis of the type discussed above, arbitrary ordinal measures may have to be invented; in assessing the results the degree of arbitrariness of the measures used must be taken into account.

† The type of "impactee-structure-" analysis suggested is also useful for nonprofit organizations, such as school systems, eleemosynary firms, and local, state, or national governmental agencies. Were such attempts made the results often might turn out to be of considerable interest.

16 Beyond Economic Man

Economic man as a basic postulate for economic theories has been with us at least since 1776. It is time to consider the formulation of alternative modes of analysis. To what extent the economic-man postulate was adequate for 1776, or even 1876, it is difficult to say, but it is certainly less adequate today than it was then. There is a need for new approaches that go beyond economic man, even though we need not displace economic-man-based analysis for all purposes. To help meet this need has been the aim of this book.*

The theory whose basic outlines we have developed differs from conventional microeconomics in a number of fundamental ways. It differs in the following: (1) its psychological underpinnings; (2) it is based primarily on individual behavior rather than on firms and households; (3) it is applicable to the behavior of agents as well as of principals; (4) under it, effort is a fundamental economic variable; (5) in the fact that it takes into account a new type of inefficiency ignored by conventional economics that I have called X-inefficiency; and (6) the theory implies that typically firms neither minimize costs nor maximize profits.

---

* Parenthetically I might add that the need for new modes of analysis exists even in the face of the conservative pressures of the economics profession to retain existing modes of analysis. "Conservative" is used in a nonpolitical sense. The economics profession is no more conservative than any other well-organized scientific group. Almost all well-established sciences resist new approaches. This has advantages as well as defects. In nonlaboratory, nonclinical sciences it is probably easier to ignore the deficiencies of existing approaches or the virtues of new ones, since it is more difficult in a lab science to ignore replicable laboratory evidence. On the conservative nature of organized science see Thomas S. Kuhn, *The Structure of Scientific Revolutions* (Cambridge, Mass., Harvard University Press, 1962), esp. p. 151. Also see Thomas S. Kuhn, "Reflections on My Critics," in Imre Lakatos and Alan Musgrave, eds., *Criticism and the Growth of Knowledge* (London, Cambridge University Press, 1970), pp. 235–249.

Economic Man versus S.R. Man

For want of a better term I refer to the psychological assumptions developed in Chapter 5 as belonging to "S.R." man—S.R. for selective rationality. Although the theory developed here does not exclude the economic-man-assumption, in general it is quite different. It includes economic man as a very special case, likely to exist under extreme conditions. A simple way of indicating the relation between selective rationality and the economic-man postulate is suggested by a variant of the basic diagram used in Chapter 5. There constraint concern was used as a *portmanteau* term for the variety of psychological traits an individual brings to the work context. We measured it along the x-axis on a scale from zero to one. These

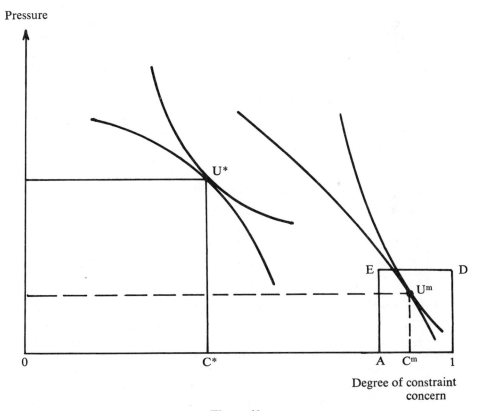

Figure 43

traits—perseverance in the pursuit of goals, degree of concern for the constraints of the environment, and so on—are equal to one under the economic-man assumption. But in the general case they are less than one; in most cases they are significantly less than one.

I argued that individuals compromise between behaving the way they would like to behave if constraints were absent and behaving the way they feel they *ought* to behave. This compromise normally is well to the left of "complete constraint concern" (the point at which constraint concern is equal to one). However, cases are possible where the optimal point of tangency is in the neighborhood of a degree of constraint concern equal to one. (In the figure the area bounded by *AED*.) The economic-man assumption is an abstraction, and should not be interpreted as a claim that people behave entirely and completely as economic men. Nevertheless, it obviously makes a difference whether behavior is "in the neighborhood" of the economic-man assumption or significantly to the left of it. Thus, the S.R. postulate employed and the arguments on which it is based result in (point U^* and C^*) the choice of a comfortable level of constraint concern for the individual, rather than something which approximates the maximal level of constraint concern (U^m and C^m). For most instances of economic behavior in the real world U^* and C^* represent a better fit than U^m and C^m. This does not cancel out the possibility that there may be applications for which an economic-man type of theory may be adequate. But there are innumerable other instances under which the selective rationality theory leads to a more realistic analysis—and sometimes to quite different results.

Micro-Micro Theory and Agent-Agent Trade

The theory developed in this volume is especially applicable in a world in which agents carry out the basic transactions for others. I have alluded to the fact that we live in a world in which a large proportion of transactions are carried out by some in the name of others, by agents; we live in a world of agent-agent trade.

A curious silent transformation of the economic-man theory has occurred in the course of its development. The psychological postulate behind economic man presumably applies to individuals and refers to individual behavior. Gradually it became clear that the basic economic actors are households and firms. But households and firms are primarily, especially in a modern economy, collections of individuals. Conventional microtheory gradually slipped into the practice of ascribing economic-man psychology to organized groups, although it seems a questionable procedure to ascribe to groups the psychological characteristics of an individual. Hence I have attempted to formulate a *micro-micro* theory, and to reformulate micro-theory in terms of individuals who are members of groups, and to consider intragroup interactions before household or firm behavior.

One of the results shows that there is little reason to believe that firms composed of many individuals normally minimize costs of production. This result, and a number of others, was bolstered by the fact that individuals who are members of production (or consumption) groups, and act in part as agents for their groups, have split loyalties (or split motivations)—loyalties to their own ends as well as loyalties to what they see as the group's objectives. In going beyond economic man and in developing the theory of selective rationality I stressed this aspect and applied this distinction to a variety of problems.

Some Fundamental Differences in Results

The conclusions reached based on postulates which go beyond "economic man" differ fundamentally for a number of significant problem areas from those based on mainstream economics. Consider four areas of application: the regulation of monopolies, the generation of inflation, intercountry productivity differences, and applications to business management.

Under the X-Efficiency theory firms generally do not minimize costs nor do they maximize profits. Therefore, the regulation of natural monopolies must be based on different principles than they currently are—if they are to be in the interest of the consumer. If it were true, as mainstream economics argues, that firms minimize costs, then it would make sense to regulate prices in terms of a "fair profit rate." According to this view, X-efficiency is assumed axiomatically. Firms are X-efficient because we assume that they minimize costs. However, if firms do not minimize costs, then regulating prices in accordance with normal profit rate criteria does not guarantee efficiency. If the costs are twice as high, the regulated price will be increased accordingly and the consequences of the high degree of inefficiency will be forced upon consumers. Indeed one expects that this is frequently the case.

Conventional microtheory says almost nothing about inflation. Microtheory is designed as a theory of relative prices rather than a theory of absolute prices. It can say something about price ratios of tons of steel versus tons of potatoes, but it can say nothing about the absolute monetary prices of these commodities. If firms minimize costs and maximize profits there is no reason for them to change prices unless something external to the system changes. The conventional theory implies that firms do not play a critical role in determining inflationary pressures or in the generation of inflation. But in the theory developed here, since firms neither minimize costs nor maximize profits, there is a clear-cut area in the decision process under which firms play a distinct role in generating inflationary pressure. This works out especially well if we assume that the inert areas have a time dimension before price changes take place. Any condition which results in the prospects of utility gains to those in the firms who raise prices greater than the utility cost of doing so results in a decision to increase prices after the time period necessary to penetrate the inert areas. This follows especially since we do not hold strictly to the independence postulate of microtheory. Firms react directly or indirectly to the behavior of other firms.

Inert area theory also suggests strong reasons why firms would in fact under various circumstances raise prices. Since the inert areas also apply to consumers there are some price increases to which consumers will not react. Certain price increases fall within the consumers' inert areas; as a result, the amount consumed of some commodities does not change as the price rises. As some prices rise and the general price level rises, the laggards in the process (those who have the power to raise prices but have not yet done so) gradually get to feel sufficiently worse off and they too raise prices as the generated pressures penetrate their inert areas. Earlier chapters have shown that we may view inflation as a process similar to innovational diffusion processes. Furthermore, I have suggested that the inert areas theory explains something about the speed of the inflationary process, including why inflations are neither zero nor, at the other extreme, why they do not accelerate indefinitely to become runaway inflations.

An equally significant area in which X-efficiency theory is applicable is the analysis of intercountry productive differences, although I have not examined this application in this volume. It is striking that at some points in time countries with similar knowledge and the same capacities to save and invest, as well as the same industries and roughly similar ratios of capital and labor, have significantly large differences in productivity per man. Productivity studies after World War II established that differences in physical capital explain very little of the differences in productivity. I suggest that the main differences can be explained by the motivations of firm's members during their work, by the motivational atmosphere they find on the job, and on the type of interactions and influences toward work and production that people have on each other as well as the attitudes they bring to the work context. These factors are probably the most significant ones in explaining differences in productivity in the same industry and between countries at roughly similar stages of development.

In addition, in Chapter 15 I suggested a specific mode of analysis for firms that would enable them to analyze production performance within a firm, and by extending the process to carry out the analysis of productivity differences between firms and industries.

General Significance—An "Open" Theory

Some psychological postulates implied functional relations, illustrated in figures as bands rather than lines. This refers to the idea that individuals do not necessarily care to make small distinctions. As a result, the price-quantity equilibrium for an industry is not determinate; there is an area within which price-quantity equilibriums exist. Although it can be argued that such fuzziness fits reality better than a unique equilibrium, this is not really a very important point. The basic points go much deeper and are fundamentally different from the fact that demand and supply functions could be looked upon as bands rather than straight lines.

To see the nature of the fundamental differences between my analysis and the conventional one recall that for the most part we live in a world in which decisions are made by agents rather than by principals. Motivations of agents differ from those of principals. Inefficiencies are usually seen in terms of the interests of the principals, rather than those of the agents. My psychological postulates are especially suitable for the analysis of agent behavior. The combination of these postulates and the fact that we are dealing with agents who make decisions for others frequently lead to results different from conventional ones. Choices made by agents may result in much lower orders of efficiency than would be the case if all agents acted only as extentions of their principals' personalities and interests.

For instance, the high degree of price discrimination that one should expect in this world is not only a consequence of a lack of information by consumers but also a consequence of living in a world in which agents may wish to make specific purchases in terms of quantity rather than price. In other words, the signals given by principals and the signals interpreted by agents lead to different results than had the principals carried out these activities.

The approach developed may be used to examine the productivity of services provided by governments to their citizens. Signals from consumers (citizens) go through very complex political processes in which they are transformed and translated by political rules so that the bureaucracy decides on services on the basis of very different criteria than the citizen would, although it is the citizen who in fact pays for them. A case in point is legislation which requires various governmental entities to provide services of various types without counterpart legislation which raises funds to pay for these services. School boards and their powers in various communities are a good example. In fact, we could go one step farther and question whether the services produced are in any way connected with the prices citizens are willing to pay for them. Needless to say, there is usually no mechanism for establishing such implications between services and prices in terms of willingness to pay special taxes or subsidies for specific services. Something similar occurs in regulated private industries which have large bureaucratic layers between the consumers and the industry. Even in industries which may not be regulated but in which strong monopolistic elements exist, similar bureaucratic features and a lack of concern for consumers' sovereignty may lead to results that are highly X-inefficient. The considerations of decisionmaking processes, which include the inert areas of various agents and which take into account the transmission and transformation of signals into something other than those initially introduced, leads to a vision of the decisionmaking process that is fundamentally different from the one considered in conventional microtheory analysis.

One final point deserves repetition. The theory developed in this volume is an *"open"* theory. It can be expanded, amplified, and applied in many more directions than have been suggested or alluded to. Applications to management problems, inflation, analysis of public services, intercountry productivity differentials, and so on can be expanded and worked out to a degree of detail much beyond our brief forays into and allusions to these problems.

Appendix

Toward a Mathematical Formalization
of X-Efficiency Theory

by Harvey Leibenstein and Peter J. Kalman

This appendix is limited in scope by necessity and intent.* It represents little more than a stab at formalizing a few of the basic ideas (in Chapters 5, 6, 7, and 10) and indicating some of their implications. Our intent is exceedingly modest: to suggest the possibility of formalizing a few of the essential aspects of the "Beyond Economic Man" theory. For the most part, the basic concepts contrast sharply with those employed in conventional microtheory. For example, psychological spaces and inert areas have no exact counterparts in standard theory. Because the concepts employed are treated extensively in the text, they are defined with considerable brevity here. No attempt is made to have an identical translation from the words used in the text to a mathematical statement. Nevertheless, we feel that the essence and spirit of the ideas in the text is retained.

We intend to show that (given our psychological assumptions, and especially our specific interpretation of limited knowledge) neither individuals nor firms optimize. In particular, firms do not maximize outputs for given inputs. This is equivalent to showing the existence of X-inefficiency.

Psychological Space

We first define two concepts: *pressure,* which is some degree of "feeling" of nonperformed obligation represented by an ordinal scale from 0 to 1, and

---

* The necessity aspect was determined by the severe time constraints under which it was written. It was written jointly over a brief period during which both authors were extensively engaged in other duties. We thank our students Lee Edlefsen and Kuan Pin Lin for helpful comments on this appendix.

denoted by p, $0 \leq p \leq 1$; and *constraint concern,* which represents the degree to which a person is willing to use his capacities to meet obligations and to abide by constraints, which is also represented by an ordinal scale such that $0 \leq c \leq 1$. This is denoted by the Cartesian product

$$P \times C = \{(p, c) : 0 \leq p \leq 1, 0 \leq c \leq 1\}.$$

We now define two mappings from $P \times C$ to the real line: the *id* mapping denoted by $i : P \times C \rightarrow R$; and the *superego* mapping denoted $s : P \times C \rightarrow R$, where we assume that i is continuous and convex on $P \times C$ and s is strictly concave and continuous on $P \times C$. A particular pair of these two mappings represents attitudes toward behavior which we usually view as a personality and which manifest themselves in specific situations considered below.

We now briefly define an ordering on $P \times C$ which we assume is a complete preordering denoted by α where α denotes "at least as preferred as" so any two points (p_1, c_1) and (p_2, c_2) can be compared by α. We assume that if $(p_1, c_1) \; \alpha \; (p_2, c_2)$, then $i(p_1, c_1) \leq i(p_2, c_2)$ and $s(p_1, c_1) \geq s(p_2, c_2)$. Also if $(p_1, c_1) \geq (p_2, c_2)$, then $s(p_1, c_1) \geq s(p_2, c_2)$ and $i(p_1, c_1) \leq i(p_2, c_2)$. Hence we obtain (locally) a saddle point.

Because we will have many individuals in the model we will index $i(p, c)$ and $s(p, c)$ by $i^z(p, c)$ and $s^z(p, c)$ to indicate the z-th individual, $z = 1, 2, \ldots Z$.

Let the functions $i^z(p, c)$ and $s^z(p, c)$ belong to the function spaces I and S.

In general we presume that individuals attempt to strike a compromise between the demands of their id and those of their superego. We assume that most individuals are not extreme personalities, that their behavior is not dominated by their superegos in such a way that they are completely committed to fulfilling obligations to others; nor are their personalities so dominated by their id that their behavior completely ignores obligations to themselves and to others. We assume we have a normal distribution of personality types so that the comfortable level of behavior for most individuals is characterized by the neighborhood of a saddle point in the $I \times S$ space rather than any extremum value in the $I \times S$ space.

The Effort Space

We now introduce the concept of an *effort point* e. Let A be the set of feasible activity vectors in the world, and $a = (a_1, \ldots a_k) \in A$ an *activity vector* where the k-th component a_k is called the k-th *activity.* An effort point e is completely specified by a four tuple composed of a (real) activity vector $a = (a_1, \ldots a_k)$; a *pace level* $p = (p_1, \ldots p_k)$ for each a; the *quality* by which each activity in A is performed denoted $q = (q_1, \ldots q_k)$; and the *clock time* $t = (t_1, \ldots t_k)$ of performance of each activity in a. So we can represent an effort point e by (a, p, q, t) which is assumed to be an element of the non-negative orthant R_+^{4k} of Euclidean space R^{4k}. We call R_+^{4k} the *effort space* for every individual. Clearly, each individual may have his unique effort space.

We define a conditional ordering β read "at least as preferred as" on R_+^{4k}, which we assume to be a complete preordering. For each economic context, let u^z be a mapping from R_+^{4k} to R_+ which preserves the ordering β on R_+^{4k}. We assume that u^z is continuous and locally strictly concave on R_+^{4k}, that is, u^z is strictly concave in some neighborhood of at least one point in R_+^{4k}. For each point in R_+^{4k} there is a compact neighborhood, since R_+^{4k} is locally compact and Hausdorff. Hence, u^z attains a local maximum and it is unique in the neighborhood by strict concavity.

Effort position E is a nonempty set of effort points, that is, a nonempty subset of the effort space R_+^{4k}. The space of effort positions is a collection of nonempty subsets of R_+^{4k}, denoted by E. We also want to define a *direct utility* function on the space of effort positions E. This space E is a subset of the power set of R_+^{4k}. In particular,

$$E = 2^{R_+^{4k}} \mid \{\emptyset\}.$$

For every effort position $E \in E$, we let $U^z : E \to R_+$ defined by $U^z(E) = g[u^z(e) \in R_+ : e \in E] \in R_+$. We assume that U^z has the same properties as u^z (continuity and local strict concavity on E).

Parameterized Effort Space

We now introduce some parameters into the model which will influence the shape of u^z (and hence U^z). These parameters are the income y associated with the economic context and the position personalities that the individual can potentially interact with in the context. Hence, for any individual z his utility u^z now is a mapping from the Cartesian product of

$$R_+^{4k} \times R_+ \times I \times S \to R_+$$

where $R_+ \times I \times S$ is the parameter space. Similarly, $U^z(E)$ is now a mapping from the set of utility values of a set of effort points contained in an effort position E together with the Cartesian product of $I \times S$ to the reals.

The Cost of Shifting Effort Positions

We now introduce a concept of the cost for individual z as he becomes established in an effort position E when all other individuals in the context have already chosen their positions. The effort position will normally contain effort points some of whose components are activities involving interactions between z and other individuals which, in turn, determines the degree of acceptance by other individuals of z's performance. Thus, the cost of becoming established in an effort position depends on the signals received from the other individuals in the context (assume there are Z individuals) which are composed of two types—informational, and signals of positive and negative approval. The signals are a consequence of the effort points in E^z which influence the effort points in the positions of the other individuals. Let

$$C^z_e = C^z(E^1, \ldots E^Z, i^1(\cdot), s^1(\cdot), \ldots i^Z(\cdot), s^Z(\cdot))$$

be the *cost of entry*. We will consider only the cases when $C^z_e > 0$.

Similarly we have a cost of leaving denoted C^z_l We consider only the cases when $C^z_l > 0$. The utility cost of moving is $C^z_e + C^z_l$ denoted U^z_{Cel}. We will assume that these cost functions are continuous.

Any individual z facing an economic context in which performance is involved has to "interpret" his job. A job interpretation is characterized by the choice of a specific effort position by individual z.

We now discuss the basis for choice of an effort position E. Because full information is not available, initially individual z must choose an effort position which at the same time will yield additional information about the parameters, which in turn may induce shifts to different effort positions.

Inert Areas

We now introduce the concept of an inert area that plays a critical role in determining the final point of the choice process. For simplicity we assume that there are two periods in which the effort position choice options for all individuals in the context reappear in the second period. A shift from an effort position for individual z in period t_1 to an effort position for z in period t_2—that is, *a change in effort positions*—will be denoted $E^z_{t_1} \neq E^z_{t_2}$. An *inert area* A^z for individual z is a set of options $O \subset E$ which we assume is bounded and contains effort positions such that if $E^z_{t_1} \in A^z$ is chosen in period t_1 then $E^z_{t_1}$ will be chosen again in period 2 if choice is restricted to A^z.

A *local optimal effort position* E^* is an effort position satisfying $U^z(E^*) \geqq U^z(E)$ for all E in the context for z in a neighborhood of E^*. An *optimal inert area* A^{*z} is an inert area containing at least one local optimal effort position E^*. In general, we assume that z will choose a preferred effort position if there is no cost associated with the choice.

THEOREM 1.   Under the foregoing assumptions, an optimal inert area A^{*z} exists. Further, A^{*z} contains at least two effort positions, E_j and E_k, such that if E_j is an optimal effort position then E_k would not be optimal.

Proof.   The existence of an local optimal effort position E^* follows from the continuity and strict concavity of the utility function on a compact neighborhood of E^* in R^{4k}_+ using the Weierstrass theorem. Hence we have an optimal inert area A^{*z}. Let E_k be an effort position in the neighborhood of E^*_j. We now look at the utility cost of moving from E_k to E^*_j. This is $C^z_e + C^z_l = U^z_{Cel}$. Since we choose E_k arbitrarily, we can choose it so that

$$U^z(E^*_j) - U^z(E_k) = \Delta U > 0.$$

This Δ U can be as small as we please since the utility function is continuous. We choose $\Delta U < U^z_{Cel}$. Hence, if E_k is chosen in the first period it will also be chosen in the second period, since the utility cost of moving U^z_{Cel} is greater than the utility gain of moving to E^*_j (that is, Δ U) and hence $E_k \in A^{*z}$ (by definition of A^{*z}). By strict concavity locally, E_k is not a local optimal.   Q.E.D.

We like to remark that the bounds of the local optimal inert area A^* is determined by the inequality between utility and utility costs.

THEOREM 2.   Under the conditions of Theorem 1, if $\hat{U}^z_{Cel}$ has an associated inert area $\hat{A}^z$ and $\tilde{U}_{Cel}$ has an associated optimal inert area $\bar{A}^z$, and if $\hat{A}^z$ and $\bar{A}^z$ are comparable—that is, if either $\hat{A}^z \subseteq \bar{A}^z$, or $\hat{A}^z \supseteq \bar{A}^z$, then if $\hat{U}^z_{Cel} > \tilde{U}^z_{Cel} \rightarrow \hat{A}^z \supset \bar{A}^z$.

Proof.   Let $\hat{U}^z_{Cel}$ and $\hat{U}^z_{Cel}$ be the utility costs of moving between two arbitrary positions in $\bar{A}^z$ and $\hat{A}^z$, respectively.

$E^*_k \in \bar{A}^z$ is the local optimum effort position.

Now we define $\Delta U = U^z(E^*_k) - U^z(E_j)$ for $E_j \in \hat{A}^z$

We choose E_j so that $\tilde{U}^z_{Cel} < \Delta U < \tilde{U}^z_{Cel}$.

Hence, E_j is not a member of $\check{A}^z$ since if $\tilde{U}_{Cel} < \Delta U$, then E_j cannot be in an inert area in which the utility cost of moving < utility gain.

Since $\hat{A}^z$ and $\check{A}^z$ are comparable, and since E_j is not a member of $\check{A}^z$ but $E_j \in \hat{A}^z \therefore \hat{A}^z \supset \check{A}^z$.   Q.E.D.

Remark. In general this implies that for comparable inert areas the greater the utility cost the "greater" the inert area. We suggest informally that if we view an individual or a group of individuals as being in equilibrium if they are in their inert areas, this suggests that the larger the inert area the more stable the equilibrium involved, other things remaining equal.

The Weakest Link Information Theorem

For the purposes of this appendix we limit our characterization of information as follows. Information is transmitted through language and experience. Language normally contains redundancy. We employ the concept of a kernel sentence K_{ij} which denotes the i-th kernel sentence[1] applicable to the j-th component in R^{4k}_+. A kernel sentence is a processed piece of information stripped of all redundancy which provides knowledge about some characteristic of the component. If a kernel sentence applies to $l > 1$ components then we view the kernel sentence as being applied to each of the l components. For each component we assume there is a *minimal* number of specific kernel sentences which yields just enough knowledge to determine the utility of that particular component given the utilities of the other components in R^{4k}_+.

Remark. If we view information as being composed of a number of independent components and we define incomplete information as zero knowledge of one or more of its components, then incomplete information in this sense is equivalent to having no information. Suppose we have to choose an optimal point $E^* = (x^*_1, \ldots x^*_{4k})$; one would have to know each of the 4k components. Suppose there is no information about one of these components, say, the j-th. The probability of choosing E^* is the joint probability of choosing each of the components of E^*. If the probability of choosing the ith component is σ_i, then this joint probability is $\pi^{4k}_{i=1} \sigma_i$. Since $\sigma_j = 0$, $\pi^{4k}_{i=1} \sigma_i = 0$.

We assume that if one has to make a choice on the basis of no information it is equivalent to choosing randomly.

THEOREM 3.   If there is a nondegenerate probability measure defined on the set of effort positions, E, the probability of choosing an optimal effort position is zero.

Proof.   First note that incomplete information is equivalent to no information and, by assumption, choice with no information is equivalent to choosing randomly. The theorem now follows from the fact that we are choosing randomly a point from the set

$$2^{R_+^{4k}} \mid \{\emptyset\} = E. \qquad \text{Q.E.D.}$$

Hence, the probability of choosing an optimal point is not improved if we add information which remains incomplete in the sense indicated above. In other words, this type of incomplete information is equivalent to choosing with no information. One of the components of every context is the reliability of information obtained through interaction with other individuals in the context: a message that may appear to be favorable may turn out to be a false message.

COROLLARY 1.   Under incomplete information of the type above and the assumptions of this appendix, if individual z selects effort position E $\in A^{*z}$ then E is a locally nonoptimal effort position.†

Proof.   This follows from Theorem 3 and our definition of incomplete information.

† It would be of interest to determine the probability of choosing a point in a neighborhood "N" of radius r that contains the global optimal point $\bar{U}^*$. We can only discuss this matter informally here. Recall that for many contexts the set of effort positions is very large since E is the power set of the effort space. Some effort positions in E could be eliminated immediately since they contain too many effort points to be feasible. Therefore, consider $\bar{E} \subset E$ out of which the choice of a neighborhood is to be made. Suppose the space $\bar{E}$ is covered by a net of n disjoint subsets of approximately radius r, and that $\bar{U}^*$ is in one and only one of these subsets. With incomplete information the probability of picking N* (which contains $\bar{U}^*$) is 1/n. The smaller the size of r the larger the value of n. Now suppose that there are m subsets which on a priori probabilistic grounds are eliminated because it seems improbable (but with a probability of less than one) that any of these contain $\bar{U}^*$. Thus, the probability of choosing a neighborhood containing the global optimum is at most 1/n-m. (It may of course be smaller than that since there is a lack of certainty about the m neighborhoods which have been eliminated.) Clearly, for those effort position spaces which are large, and for a reasonably small radius, the probability of choosing a point in the neighborhood which contains the global optimum will be relatively small. The above arguments apply equally well to local optima.

Production

We will view a firm as a set of integrated economic contexts and assume that a variety of psychological types are members of it. In general, the combination of id and superego influences lie along a continuum. We assume that there are some individuals (probably most) who are among the Z members of the firm who are not of the extreme psychological types whose superegos so dominate their ids that their utility is derived only from behavior according with the constraints implicit in maximizing their contribution of output to the firm.

We associate with each effort position and the psychological state of each of the individuals a contribution to output of the firm for a given capital stock and its distribution to contexts within the firm. Formally, we define a mapping for the z-th individual which represents his contribution to output of the firm for a given capital, that is,

$$E \times I \times S \xrightarrow{\gamma^z} R^+,$$

where we recall E is the space of effort positions and $I \times S$ is the space of psychological states. Hence, the contribution of the Z individuals to output of the firm for a given capital stock is γ which is the map

$$E \times I \times S \xrightarrow{\gamma} \prod_1^z R^+$$

where γ is given as $\gamma(\cdot) = (\gamma^1(\cdot), \ldots \gamma^z(\cdot))$.

Next the firm transforms the contributions of the Z individuals to the output of the firm. This is represented by the map f defined by

$$\prod_1^z R^+ \xrightarrow{f} R^+.$$

It is understood that if we were to consider many firms we would have (in general) a different transformation for each firm.

It follows from the above transformations that the firm's output $f(\cdot)$ is uniquely determined by the effort positions chosen by the Z firm members and their psychological states. This can formally be seen by the composition

$$f \circ \gamma(E, i, s) = f(\gamma(E, i, s)).$$

Let $r = f(\gamma(E, i, s))$ for a given set of effort positions chosen by the Z individuals and for a given set of psychological states. We assume $r \in$

$[0, J] \equiv \pi$. Note that π is completely ordered. We assume that all the above maps are continuous. Clearly, there exists a nondenumerable set of effort positions in E as well as a nondenumerable set of r's in π.

We assume that each individual z will also take into account the utility he derives from his contribution to output given by $\gamma^z(E, i, s)$. This means that his total utility will now be a function of his direct utility $U^z(E, i, s)$ and his contribution to output gives by $\gamma^z(E, i, s)$. We assume that his total utility $U^z_T (E, i, s)$ has the form

$$U^z_T (E, i, s) = U^z(E, i, s) + h(\gamma^z(E, i, s))$$

where $h : R_+ \to R_+$. Also we assume that $\gamma^z(E, i, s)$ has the same properties as U^z (local strict convexity and continuity).

The contribution to output given by γ^z where z is a nonextreme individual is bounded from below and above, that is, $\hat{a}^z \leq \gamma^z \leq \hat{b}^z$, because we assume in the text that each individual will be pressured by peers to have an output below some level and will be influenced by supervisors to satisfy some minimal output level. In view of this, we restrict h as follows:

$$h = \begin{cases} \bar{h} & \text{when } \hat{a}^z \leq \gamma^z \leq \hat{b}^z. \\ h(\gamma^z) & \text{otherwise} \end{cases}$$

THEOREM 4. Assume that there is a given psychological environment and a given capital endowment for the firm. Also assume that individual z is not of the extreme type. Further assume $\exists \, \hat{E} \in E \ni U^z(\hat{E}, i(\cdot), s(\cdot))$ is a local maximum. Then the probability that $\hat{E}$ will maximize $\gamma^z(E, i(\cdot), s(\cdot))$ is zero.

Proof. First there exists a nondenumerable set of effort positions in E. Next the set $\hat{E} \subset E$ which yields local maxima of U^z is at most denumerable infinite (by our assumptions above).

Further the functions $\gamma^z(E, i, s)$ and $U^z(E, i, s)$ are independent: neither γ^z nor U^z are functions of each other. Let the set of effort positions which yield local maxima for γ be $\tilde{E} \subset E$. This again is at most a denumerable infinite set (by our assumptions). We now want to see what the probability is that $\hat{E} \in \tilde{E}$ under our conditions. Since the functions U^z and γ^z are independent and since the choice space E is nondenumerable it follows that this probability is 0.   Q.E.D.

Under the conditions of Theorem 4, if $\hat{E}$ maximizes (globally) U^z the probability that it will maximize γ^z is zero. By definition of total utility U^z_T we have the probability of maximizing U^z_T is zero for every z.

We will now briefly look at the total output of the firm given above by

$f : \Pi_1^z R_+ \to R_+$. We will define the firm's total output as being maximized if each $\gamma^z(E, i, s)$ is maximized given other outputs, $z = 1, 2, \ldots Z$.

THEOREM 5.   Assume the conditions of Theorem 4. Then the probability that a firm will maximize total output is zero.

Proof.   The proof follows as in Theorem 4 where the probability of a nonextreme individual maximizes his output contribution is zero and from the definition of total output.   Q.E.D.

We have established that firms composed of individuals of the type as in Theorem 4 have a zero probability of maximizing output.

NOTES

INDEX

Notes

2 Romance and Realism in the Theory of Theories

p. 12   1. Milton Friedman, "The Methodology of Positive Economics," in *Essays in Positive Economics* (Chicago, University of Chicago Press, 1953), pp. 3–43.

p. 27   2. See Spiro J. Latsis, "Situational Determinism in Economics," *British Journal of Philosophy of Science*, 23:207–245 (1972); and Imre Lakatos, "Falsification and the Methodology of Scientific Research Programmes," In Imre Lakatos and A. E. Musgrave, eds., *Criticism and the Growth of Knowledge* (London, Cambridge University Press, 1970), pp. 91–195.

3 X-Efficiency versus Allocative Efficiency

p. 29   1. See A. C. Harberger, "Using the Resources at Hand More Effectively," *American Economic Review,* 59:134–147 (May 1954); and David Schwartzman, "The Burden of Monopoly," *Journal of Political Economy,* 68:727–729 (December 1960).

p. 29   2. See H. G. Johnson, "The Gains from Freer Trade with Europe: An Estimate," *Journal, Manchester School of Economic and Social Studies,* 26: 247–255 (September 1958); Tibor Scitovsky, *Economic Theory and Western European Integration* (Stanford, Stanford University Press, 1958); Jozias Wemelsfelder, "The Short-Term Effect of Lowering Import Duties in Germany," *Economic Journal,* 60:94–104 (March 1960); and L. H. Janssen, *Free Trade, Protection and Customs Union* (Leiden, Kroese, 1961), p. 132.

p. 30   3. Scitovsky, *Economic Theory and Western European Integration,* p. 64.

p. 30   4. Wemelsfelder, "Short-Term Effect of Lowering Import Duties," p. 100.

p. 30   5. H. Johnson, "Gains from Freer Trade with Europe," pp. 247–255.

p. 31   6. Janssen, *Free Trade, Protection and Customs Union,* p. 132.

p. 31   7. Based on data found in A. A. Faraq, "Economic Integration: A

Theoretical Empirical Study," unpublished diss., University of Michigan, 1963.

p. 31   8. Harberger, "Using the Resources at Hand More Effectively."

p. 35   9. Ohlin review of Eric Lundberg, *Productivity and Profitability: Studies of the Role of Capital in the Swedish Economy,* in *American Economic Review,* 52:827–829 (September 1962).

p. 35   10. F. H. Harbison, "Entrepreneurial Organization as a Factor in Economic Development," *Quarterly Journal of Economics,* 70:373 (August 1965).

p. 35   11. N. W. Chamberlain, *The Firm: Micro-Economic Planning and Action* (New York, McGraw-Hill, 1962), p. 341.

p. 37   12. Peter Kilby, "Organization and Productivity in Backward Economies," *Quarterly Journal of Economics,* 76:303–310 (May 1962).

p. 37   13. Laszlo Rostas, *Comparative Productivity in British and American Industry,* Research Paper 13 (Cambridge, National Institute of Economic Sociology, 1964), p. 64.

p. 38   14. J. P. Davison, P. S. Florence, B. Gray, and N. Ross, *Productivity and Economic Incentives* (London, Allen and Unwin, 1958), p. 203.

p. 38   15. International Labor Organization, *Payment by Results,* ILO Studies and Reports, n.s. no. 27 (Geneva, 1951), pp. 54–75.

p. 38   16. R. T. Roethlisberger and W. J. Dickson, *Management and the Worker* (Cambridge, Mass., Harvard University Press, 1939).

p. 38   17. H. A. Landsberger, *Hawthorne Revisited* Cornell Studies in Industrial and Labor Relations, vol. 9 (Ithaca, N.Y., Cornell, 1958), pp. 13 ff.

p. 38   18. International Labor Organization, "ILO Productivity Missions to Underdeveloped Countries, Part I," *International Labor Review,* 76:1–29 (July 1957); and International Labor Organization, "ILO Productivity Missions to Underdeveloped Countries, Part II," *International Labor Review,* 76:139–166 (August 1957).

p. 38   19. E. E. Ghiselli and C. W. Brown, *Personnel and Industrial Psychology* (New York: McGraw-Hill, 1948), p. 147.

p. 38   20. Michael Argyle, Godfrey Gardner, and Frank Cioffi, "Supervisory Methods Related to Productivity, Absenteeism, and Labor Turnover," *Human Relations,* 11:23–40 (1958).

p. 39   21. Tomislav Tomekovic, "Levels of Knowledge of Requirements as a Motivational Factor in the Work Situation," *Human Relations,* 15:197–216 (1962).

p. 39   22. The empirical findings and experimental literature are reviewed in a number of places. For a brief review of the literature see, "ILO Productivity Missions to Underdeveloped Countries, Part I." See p. 5 for bibliography of major works in the area.

p. 39   23. C. F. Carter and B. R. Williams, *Investment in Innovations* (London, Oxford University Press, 1958), pp. 57 ff.

p. 39   24. See the table in J. L. Enos, "Invention and Innovation in the Petroleum Refining Industry," in National Bureau of Economic Research, *The Rate and Direction of Inventive Activity: Economic and Social Factors* (Princeton, Princeton University Press, 1962), pp. 305–306.

p. 39   25. W. E. G. Salter, *Productivity and Technical Change* (Cambridge, Cambridge University Press, 1960), p. 98. See also appendix to ch. 7, "Evidence Relating to the Delay in the Utilization of New Techniques." It seems to me that Salter did not quite draw the only possible conclusion from his table 11. Plants with no significant changes in equipment, method, and plant layout had quite startling changes in output per man-hour, especially if we consider the fact demonstrated in the table that output per man-hour frequently falls under such circumstances. The range of variation in the changes (24 percent) is larger for plants without significant changes in equipment, and so on, than for those with significant improvements. This is not to argue against the thesis that changes in techniques are important, but to suggest that significant variations in production can and do occur without such changes.

p. 39   26. Yale Brozen, "Research, Technology, and Productivity," in Industrial Relations Research Association, *Industrial Productivity* (Madison, Wisc., 1951), p. 30.

p. 40   27. John Johnston, "The Productivity of Management Consultants," *Journal of the Royal Statistical Society,* series A, 126:248, 273 (1963).

p. 40   28. Odd Aukrust, "Investment and Economic Growth," *Productivity Measures Review,* 16:35–53 (February 1959); Solomon Fabricant, *Basic Facts on Productivity* (New York, National Bureau of Economic Research, 1959); Olavi Niitamo, "Development of Productivity in Finnish Industry, 1925–1952," *Productivity Measure Review,* 15:30–41 (November 1958); R. M. Solow, "Technical Progress and the Aggregate Production Function," *Review of Economics and Statistics,* 39:312–320 (August 1957); and R. M. Solow, "Investment and Economic Growth," *Productivity Measure Review,* 16:62–68.

p. 41   29. J. J. Friedman, "Top Management Faces the Cost Challenge," *Dun's Review and Modern Industry,* 77:34–36 (January 1961).

p. 41   30. "ILO Productivity Missions to Underdeveloped Countries, Part II," p. 157.

p. 42   31. Johnston, "Productivity of Management Consultants," p. 237.

p. 43   32. J. P. Shelton, "Allocative Efficiency vs. X-Efficiency—Comment," *American Economic Review,* 57:1252–1258 (1967).

p. 43   33. W. J. Primeaux, Jr., "An Assessment of X-Efficiency Gained through Competition," unpublished ms., University of Illinois, 1973.

p. 43   34. T. Y. Shen, "Technology Diffusion, Substitution, and X-Efficiency," *Econometrica*, 41:263–284 (1973).

p. 44   35. W. G. Shepherd, "The Elements of Market Structure," *Review of Economics and Statistics*, 54:35–37.

p. 44   36. Joel Bergsman, "Commercial Policy, Allocative Efficiency, and 'X-Efficiency,' " *Quarterly Journal of Economics*' 88:409–433 (August 1974).

p. 44   37. R. J. Monsen, J. S. Chiu, and D. E. Cooley, "The Effect of Separation of Ownership and Control on the Performance of the Large Firm," *Quarterly Journal of Economics*, 82:435–451 (August 1968); Brian Hindly, "Separation of Ownership and Control in the Modern Corporation," *Journal of Law and Economics*, 13:185–222 (April 1970); R. T. Masson, "Executive Motivations, Earnings and Consequent Equity Performance," *Journal of Political Economy*, 79:1278–1292 (November/December 1971); H. K. Radide, "Control Type, Profitability and Growth in Large Firms," *Economic Journal*, 81:547–562 (September 1971); John Palmer, "The Profit-Performance Effects of the Separation of Ownership from Control in Large U.S. Industrial Corporations," *The Bell Journal of Economics and Management Science*, 4:293–303 (1973); and Steve Nyman, "Directors' Shareholding and Company Performance—Empirical Evidence," unpublished manuscript, Nuffield College, Oxford, 1974.

p. 44   38. *New York Times*, February 25, 1974, p. 2.

p. 46   39. R. M. Cyert and J. G. March, *A Behavioral Theory of the Firm* (Englewood Cliffs, N.J., Prentice-Hall, 1963), pp. 37, 38, 242.

4 Bandwagon, Snob, and Veblen Effects in the Theory of Consumers' Demand

p. 49   1. John Rae, *The Sociological Theory of Capital* (London, Macmillan, 1905), esp. ch. 13, "Of Economic Stratification," and appendix 1, "Of Luxury," pp. 218–276, 249, 253.

p. 49   2. *Economic Journal*, 3:457–474 (1893).

p. 49   3. *Studies in the Theory of Welfare Economics* (New York, Columbia University Press, 1947), p. 64; italics mine.

p. 49   4. Meade, "Mr. Lerner on the Economics of Control," *Economic Journal*, 55:51–56 (1945); A. C. Pigou, *The Economics of Welfare* (London, Macmillan, 1929), pp. 190–192, 225–226, 808; Cunynghame, "Some Improvements in Simple Geometrical Methods for Treating Exchange Value, Monopoly, and Rent," *Economic Journal*, 2:35–39 (1892); Rae, *Sociological Theory of Capital*, pp. 277–296.

p. 49   5. M. W. Reder, *Studies in the Theory of Welfare Economics* (New York, Columbia University Press, 1947); Rae, *Sociological Theory of Capital*, pp. 282–288.

p. 49   6. A. C. Pigou, *Memorials of Alfred Marshall* (London, Macmillan,

1925), pp. 433, 450. These are Marshall's letters to Pigou and Cunynghame which indicate that Marshall had read the articles (in the *Economic Journal* of 1892 and 1903) where Pigou and Cunynghame consider the matter.

p. 49   7. Reder, *Studies in the Theory of Welfare Economics,* p. 67. "We shall assume, throughout its remainder, that the satisfaction of one individual does not depend on the consumption of another." Paul Anthony Samuelson, *Foundations of Economic Analysis* (Cambridge, Mass., Harvard University Press, 1947), p. 224.

p. 50   8. James S. Duesenberry in his book, *Income, Saving, and the Theory of Consumer Behavior* (Cambridge, Mass., Harvard University Press, 1949), considers problems of a somewhat similar nature but handles them in quite a different manner. Ch. VI on interdependent preferences and the "new" welfare analysis is especially worthy of mention.

p. 50   9. A. C. Pigou, "The Interdependence of Different Sources of Demand and Supply in a Market," *Economic Journal,* 23:18–24 (1913).

p. 50   10. On this point see Oscar Morgenstern, "Professor Hicks on Value and Capital," *Journal of Political Economy,* 49:361–393 (June 1941). See also part of an article by Don Patinkin, "The Indeterminacy of Absolute Prices in Classical Economic Theory," *Econometrica,* 17:310–311 (January 1949), which sets out the conditions under which systems of homogeneous equations will possess no solution.

p. 51   11. An excellent discussion of this problem, the relation between the notions of time in economics and various definitions of statics and dynamics, can be found in W. C. Hood, "Some Aspects of the Treatment of Time in Economic Theory," *The Canadian Journal of Economics and Political Science,* 14:453–468 (November 1948).

p. 51   12. *Value and Capital,* p. 115.

5   The Theory of Selective Rationality

p. 92   1. See Anatol Rapoport and Albert M. Chammah, *Prisoner's Dilemma* (Ann Arbor, University of Michigan Press, 1966) for a description of these "games." See also Thomas C. Schelling, *The Strategy of Conflict* (New York, Oxford University Press, 1963), pp. 83–120, and esp. pp. 214–215.

8   The "Carte-Blanche" Preference Principle

p. 142   1. See A. O. Hirschman, *Exit, Voice, and Loyalty: Responses to Decline in Firms, Organizations, and States* (Cambridge, Mass., Harvard University Press, 1970).

p. 144   2. For fuller treatments of this idea see William J. Baumol, *Welfare Economics and the Theory of the State,* 2nd ed., (Cambridge, Mass., Harvard University Press, 1965); A. K. Sen, "Isolation, Assurance, and the Social Rate of Discount," *Quarterly Journal of Economics,* 81:112–124 (February 1967); and Steven Marglin, "The Social Rate of Discount and the Optimal Rate of Investment," *Quarterly Journal of Economics,* 77:95–111 (February 1963).

p. 144   3. See Anatol Rapoport, *Two Person Game Theory* (Ann Arbor, University of Michigan Press, 1965).

9   Effort Games: "Chicken" versus "Prisoner's Dilemma"

p. 148   1. For a very interesting but somewhat different discussion of the relation between game theory and motivation see Amartya Sen, *On Economic Inequality* (London, Clarendon, 1973), pp. 96–106. For standard descriptions of the games of Chicken and Prisoner's Dilemma see Anatol Rapoport and Albert M. Chammah, *Prisoner's Dilemma* (Ann Arbor, University of Michigan Press, 1966). The other standard works in this area are Duncan R. Luce and Howard Raiffa, *Games and Decisions* (New York, Wiley, 1957); John von Neumann and Oskar Morgenstern, *The Theory of Games and Economic Behavior,* 2nd ed. (Princeton, Princeton University Press, 1947).

12   Competition and Monopoly

p. 201   1. F. A. Hayek, "The Use of Knowledge in Society," *American Economic Review,* 55:523 (September 1945).

p. 205   2. R. L. Opsahl and M. D. Dunett, "The Role of Financial Compensation in Industrial Motivation," in V. H. Vroom and E. L. Deci, eds., *Management and Motivation* (New York, Penguin, 1970), pp. 149–153; E. E. Lawler, "Job Design and Employee Motivation," in Vroom and Deci, *Management and Motivation,* pp. 160–169.

p. 210   3. Opsahl and Dunett, "Role of Financial Compensation."

13   Duopoly and Monopolistic Competition

p. 228   1. George Stigler, *Five Lectures on Economic Problems* (New York, Macmillan, 1949), p. 16.

p. 228   2. Ibid., p. 22.

14   More Implications of Inert Area Theory

p. 235   1. This model is a slight variation of one which appeared in Harvey Leibenstein, "Organizational or Frictional Equilibria, X-Efficiency, and the Rate of Innovation," *Quarterly Journal of Economics,* 83:600–623 (November 1969).

p. 240   2. Hirschman, *Exit, Voice and Loyalty,* p. 12.

p. 249   3. For a more elaborate treatment of this view see William S. Comanor and Harvey Leibenstein, "Allocative Efficiency, X-Efficiency and the Measurement of Welfare Loss," *Economica,* 36:304–309 1969).

p. 252   4. See William J. Baumol and Alvin K. Klevorick, "Input Choices and Rate-of-Return Regulation: An Overview of the Discussion," *Bell Journal of Economics and Management Science*, 1:162–190 (Autumn 1970).

Appendix

p. 278   1. Although our usage differs somewhat from that employed in transformational linguistics, the concept of a kernel sentence should be credited to Zellig Harris. See Zellig S. Harris, "Linguistic Transformations for Information Retrieval," *Papers in Structural and Transformational Linguistics* (Dordrecht, Holland, Reidel, 1970), pp. 458–471.

Index